The Case for the

CRUISING TRIMARAN

The Case for the
CRUISING
TRIMARAN

By JIM BROWN

INTERNATIONAL MARINE PUBLISHING COMPANY

CAMDEN, MAINE

Copyright© 1979
by International Marine Publishing Company

Library of Congress Catalog Card Number 78-64789
International Standard Book Number 0-87742-100-5

Typeset by A & B Typesetters, Inc.,
Concord, New Hampshire
Printed and bound by the Alpine Press,
South Braintree, Massachusetts

The cartoons in this book were drawn by Jo Hudson.

Published by International Marine Publishing Company
21 Elm Street
Camden, Maine 04843

To Jo

Yes, both of you:

Jo Anna—wife, navigatrix, typist, and most cohesive critic, with your
    implorement, "You can't put in *everything.*"

and

Jo Hudson—confidant, shipmate, and co-communicative cartoonist, with
    your entreaty, "You can't leave out the *sea stories.*"

Contents

Acknowledgments

Much critical assistance was necessary for me to write this book; the best of it came from my monohull mentors Griff and Iris Andersen, Michael O'Brien, and Sean and Pid Rafter.

Besides taking many of the photos, Tom Crabb commented on the manuscript from the unique vantage point of being undecided about which type of craft to build for himself, monohull or multihull, while having offshore experience in both.

Dale Nouse made me face squarely a long-avoided personal conflict, and resolve it in this book, when he said, "Don't tell me you don't know what happened to Arthur Piver. . . ."

Kathleen Brandes is the editor at International Marine who turned the book around from a dour safety manual to the positive multihull message, "I want to run right out and buy one."

Many multihull enthusiasts also helped with constructive criticism of the manuscript. And it is the multihull *sailors* who provided the real stuff of the book. This is their story of survival, by them, and for them.

Jim Brown
North, Virginia
March 1979

Foreword

The book you are about to read will definitely augment your sea knowledge, and it may well change your entire outlook. For years I made my daily bread in the search and rescue business with the U. S. Coast Guard and thus have an inordinate familiarity with disaster and calamity. If there is one lesson to be learned, it must be *safety first:* safety in design, in construction, and in operation—whether cruising or racing. Any trip, no matter how rough or unpleasant, is successful if it is safe. The most important step toward safety is preparation. After all, good luck is the coincidence of preparation and opportunity. To be lucky, we must prepare. This book tells about preparation for safety in multihulls.

I have lived aboard *Kajak*, a monohull sailboat, for over six years now. She's my home and also my livelihood. I am fond of *Kajak* and have great confidence in her traditional ballasted stability, especially when contemplating the ultimate wave or that insane maximum blow. But there is no room for complacency. There is little reason to believe that lead is the ultimate and only safe answer. Might there be a new, better design approach? Mother Nature herself specializes in diverse and multiple solutions.

All of our experience shows that change is the only constant and that progress moves along in waves. So read on, and ride a great new wave in safe seafaring concepts.

Sean Rafter
Kajak

1

How Do You Justify
The Multihull Concept?

We had met just that morning on the dock, John and I. We agreed about a lot of things as we talked. Both of us had done some distance cruising, neither of us had a bent toward racing, and we each enjoyed boats . . . if not all boats.

When I pointed across the harbor to my little trimaran cutter, the *Scrimshaw*, and explained that my family and I had come from California in the boat, John seemed to stiffen a bit. "We'll have to talk about multihulls sometime," he remarked.

Now it was evening of the same day and my newfound friend and I were standing toe-to-toe in a very crowded harborfront lounge. It was July 1976 in Newport, Rhode Island. We were trying to talk above the noise of a celebration in honor of the singlehanded racers. John leaned closer to make himself heard and, speaking over his glass, he asked me this question:

"I don't know how to broach this except to just come out with it. We all know that multihulls are capable of such wonderful things, but we also know that they can capsize. Now, you must tell me, how can you justify this concept? How can you rationally go to sea, with your wife and family aboard, in a craft that is just as stable upside-down as otherwise? What's the point of cruising in a boat that has the potential to put you in such a helpless position?"

I never had the chance to answer him. First of all, I was unprepared for his directness. Having made my life around multihulls for about 20 years, I've become accustomed to the controversy that they cause. On the West Coast, particularly, I enjoy bouncing back the good-natured razz that comes from conventional sailors. But there I was in Newport—the very seat of traditional yachting—and suddenly this friendly traditionalist had put it to me point blank!

Stalling for time with a laugh, I started to say (as though to clear the air of

Now how can you justify this concept?

any animosity), "It's okay, John, it's okay with me . . . you can sail *any kind* of boat you like . . . it's all right with me. . . ." But as I spoke there was someone tugging on his sleeve. It was time for the ceremony and John was to present a trophy. I never had a chance to finish that conversation.

Maybe we should leave it there, with a point-blank, honest question and an unheard, honest answer. He's got his kind of boat and I've got mine. We are both secure in our preferences; who could ask for more? And who would wish to take away, from any sailor, the kind of boat he likes?

Nevertheless, ever since John Letcher asked me to defend multihulls, I've often thought about how I would answer him, if given another opportunity. It was a good question, and many contemporary boatmen, upon noticing the emergence of multihull craft on the sailing scene, have doubtless asked themselves the same. It deserves a complete answer.

We could have talked all night in that bar about practical considerations such as light versus heavy, wide versus deep, fast versus fast enough, and self-righting versus nonsinking. Weighing all that logic can be quite an intellectual exercise, one that often deteriorates into an emotional disagreement, and there lies the key. A man's choice of boat is an emotional choice. He looks at her, and they speak to each other, not with words but instantaneously, as when eyes meet in a crowd. A faint thunder in the distance warns, "Thou shalt not covet," but he does covet. And slowly he realizes that it's all right because she's only a boat.

So it seems to me that the intellectual exercise of selecting a boat is largely a self-deluding justification for an emotional decision. I like multihulls because they speak to my emotions. Therefore, throughout the rest of this book it will be up to the reader to decide whether my practical words about multihulls are simply self-delusions or real truth.

2

The Case for Cruising Multihulls

Not too long ago it was sometimes said that, "The best racing boat makes the best cruising boat." This opinion was held by many sailors who had experience in both.

Today that situation has changed, and there is real need for a distinct separation to be made between ocean racing and ocean cruising. Competition on the high seas has progressed to such zealous extremes that boats designed for winning distance races bear only faint resemblance to those designed for ocean travel.

This divergence can be seen in both monohulls and multihulls, but the contrast is surely more apparent in the multis. The no-compromise multihull raceboat, with its extremely wide stance on extremely narrow hulls, and with its powerful sailplan standing straight on a super-lightweight vehicle, is such a dramatic sailing machine that it belongs alone. It will go *so* fast, and in such *rough* conditions, that nothing else its size can hold a candle to its flaming speed. But this is not the safe, comfortable, and economical craft that people want for cruising.

When investigating multihull design, the newcomer is immediately impressed by the bewildering variety of configurations and the often conflicting design philosophies that now characterize the type. If one's interest prevails through this confusion, the usual result is a voracious appetite for information. Hopes of satiating this appetite, this willingness to learn, appear to rest in sorting out the wheat from the chaff, and reaching some conclusions. But as with most developmental disciplines, multihull conclusions are illusory, and the learning itself becomes the only satiation.

In time, one is able to reach certain *personal* conclusions, but the route is crowded with controversies: lightness vs. strength, catamaran vs. trimaran, cruising vs. racing, accommodations vs. performance, one designer vs. another, and cost vs. almost everything.

To begin at the beginning, we should realize that the utter simplicity and economy of the early Arthur Piver trimarans and James Wharram catamarans are still with us; they incorporate a design philosophy that has prevailed through 20 years of evolution. It has been *by far* the most popular numerically and successful financially. And these multis are safe. Relatively few of the early, basic boats that were built to plan have come to grief, either from massive structural failure or from capsize.

Beginning around the same period, the late 1950s, the catamarans produced under the direction of Rudy Choy were much more sophisticated. They were not inexpensive and not simple. They were built much like wooden aircraft and demonstrated a very high degree of technical achievement in design. They had high strength for low weight, and as such exemplified at an early date the central quest in multihull construction. Just about the only marks against their safety record have occurred when they were being raced hard in close competition, whereas the cruising boats (produced by C/S/K) have achieved an enviable record of safety and performance in long-range voyages.

The next phase of design development is represented by the cruising trimarans initially conceived in the 1960s by such designers as Brown, Cross, Harris, Horstman, Kantola, Macouillard, Nicol, Piver, and Rodriguez; and by the cruising catamarans of Macalpine-Downie and Prout. These vessels were somewhat more sophisticated than the original Pivers and Wharrams. Most

are owner-built, many have traveled the world, and in the main their safety record is remarkably good. They still represent the mainstay of the movement, and their basic design and construction have stood the test of time.

Appearing concurrently with these conservative designs were the early racing multihulls, extending through into the 1970s with the emergence of spectacular speed machines by designers such as Allegre, Crowther, Kelsall, Macalpine-Downie, Myers, Newick, and Simpson. It is in this group that contrasting design features are most apparent. Wide sterns vs. fine exits, submersible amas vs. full-buoyancy floats, various wing configurations, hull forms, sail/rigging arrangements, drop keels, rudders, etc.—all attest to an almost frantic search for improvement of the multihull anatomy. This design phase amounts to a program of research, privately financed, with the racecourse as its proving ground. Such a program must accept failure as a normal concomitant of success, and participants assume a fair degree of risk.

The attention attracted by racing has perhaps caused undue emphasis on these risks and failures without due coverage of success. Meanwhile, the public's overblown impression of risk and failure has unrightfully permeated the cruising sector, and cruising boats produced to poor designs, or hideously modified by nonsailors and/or nonbuilders, have cast a pall of ugliness over the entire movement. Inexperienced sailors, proceeding on the advertised assumption that experience is not necessary, have contributed a large share of lubberliness, and some have even been lured into heated competition by the racing hoopla. Despite stormy beginnings, the modern oceangoing multihull lives because its basic design is sound and its potential enormous.

A variety of materials is used in multihull construction. These have progressed from Piver's "sheet plywood over a simple frame" through various molded wood and fiberglass composites. Fiberglass-foam sandwich laminates, aircraft-type match molded fiberglass-and-honeycomb laminates, Kevlar and carbon fiber reinforcements, and even welded aluminum all have been used. But good old wood (when treated with the Epoxy Saturation Technique developed by the Gougeon Brothers in Bay City, Michigan) still produces the nicest looking and perhaps the highest strength-to-weight multihull structures. Piver's oft-repeated axiom still rings true: "It's hard to beat good-old-plywood-and-glue," especially when it is given this modern epoxy treatment. If anything comes close, it is fiberglass-foam sandwich construction. The experts disagree on which material is best for modern multihulls, so they are all used, sometimes in the same boat.

Wood, incidentally, is no longer inexpensive. It retains its widespread familiarity, and a degree of availability, but good wood in any form is getting to be precious stuff. It is still cheaper than the plastics, true enough, but wooden boats are rather labor-intensive and best suit the meticulous owner-builder, or the man willing to spend freely for a racer, whether it is to be the latest far-out experiment or an embodiment of the best-trusted results from previous experiments. In either case, cost is certainly a prime factor. It would seem impossible to build a modern multihull without adequate funding.

"We see them stopping off and moving on. . . ." Multihulls from far and wide assemble in the author's Virginia anchorage for a conflab. (Photo by Tom Crabb)

Designer Dick Newick includes two other factors with cost in his penetrating analysis of the multihull design challenge. Dick says, "Beware of anyone who promises a fast, cheap, roomy boat. You cannot have all three. You can have two, any two of the three—high performance, low cost, and large accommodations—and choose whichever two you want. But you cannot have all three together."

This dilemma is most easily resolved if money is available. Then you can forget economy and build a boat with a reasonable accommodation and a high degree of performance. Unhappily, it is usually size that is compromised, resulting in cramped accommodations or disappointing performance.

Now, the enlightened trend is toward longer boats with quality construction, but of simpler design in order to reduce cost. Owners appear to be less interested in a fancy interior, and more demanding of safety and performance—a healthy sign indeed. The contemporary multihull sailor is far more sophisticated than he used to be; he has been to sea in multihulls, he knows what he wants, and he requires that the boat be well designed and well built. This shift in demand is the most significant evidence of progress in multihull development.

The cruising designs that best meet cruising requirements are not exactly cheap, and the racing boats that win aren't cheap either, except when compared to the racing monohulls. As yet, there is not a whole lot of organized competition for multihulls, which is intriguing, since undertaking high-level competition in a multihull requires substantially less investment than in monohull ocean racing.

7

In the quest for large accommodations, or high performance, or low cost, one multihull design factor is still too often overlooked: safety. It emerges now as the single most important lag in multihull development.

"Spinoff" from racing is said to improve the cruiser's lot. Something is always learned from the racers who win, and from those who do not finish, but safety on the big-time racecourse has just one meaning: "You've got to finish to win!" A more sophisticated concept is needed to make racing anything more than stunt sailing. Alone around the world nonstop! Four thousand miles in 20 days! One hundred singlehanders beating across the North Atlantic all at once! What kind of spinoff do we get from such unreal racing criteria? It is also said that wars improve the quality of peacetime—but that method of improvement is damned expensive.

Pushing on for more speed is counterproductive to multihull development at this time. What we need is more safety. In this area, ocean racing has the opportunity to foster very positive spinoff. Every offshore multihull can now be designed or modified to offer long-term capsize habitation for the crew. At the very least, the life raft can be equipped with duplicate tethers, and features for "spiderwebbing" the raft between the hulls so that a capsize crew does not become separated from the mothership. There may be nothing to enforce this logic on the individual cruiser—except common sense—but no boat should be allowed to race offshore without it.

Would that take the fun out of modern ocean racing? Surely not. Sailing at a breakneck speed, under the influence of heavy competition, it will always be a challenge for the crew to carry aggression to the limits of survival. Perhaps the essence of all breakneck pursuits is the drawing of that limit.

Another very practical aspect of multihulls is the matter of "reserve." If one drives a fine and able vehicle, capable of high speeds, at half throttle, that vehicle is relatively safe. It is being driven with reserve.

If one takes a racing multihull, "capable of wonderful things," and intentionally sails the open sea on the very brink of boatcrash (no reserve), then that multihull is perhaps more dangerous than a similar monohull in the same race. But as mentioned earlier, safety has never been the name of the racing game. For sure, the multihull sailboat eggs on a mortal sailor with promises of very lofty thrills. In the press of competition, such thrills can make it difficult for the sailor to choose between aggression and survival.

But cruising, now, is something very different. So different that the multihull's speed, when combined with several other attributes, seems to make it inherently better for cruising than for racing . . . and inherently safer, as I see it, than its keelboat counterparts.

Raw speed is in short supply for most cruising boats. In light airs, multihulls can certainly make good use of their speed potential without holding any in reserve: in *Scrimshaw* we don't motor much. When the wind comes up, we start slowing down. We can keep pace with monohulls, even to windward, and watch them driving hard, flat-out, bottoming on every bump, while our little trimaran lopes along as if she were half asleep.

If it is fair to define big-time ocean racing as the skill of taking aggression to the edge of survival, then what is a fair definition of ocean cruising?

Like racing, the word "cruising" means different things to different sailors. A dash around the buoys is different from the Round Britain Race in the same sense that a weekend on the Waterway differs from a year in the Caribbean. Big-time, competitive ocean racing is perhaps comparable in degree to the brand of cruising for which multihulls are particularly well-suited—"total cruising," a type of voyaging that demands a complete commitment by the participant. Such sailing may involve a study of survival, but it has nothing to do with aggression. Rather, the travel-sailor's challenge is to distinguish between fantasy and reality.

In the preparatory phases of acquiring the boat and planning the route and stocking the ship—preparations that often take years of one's life—the aspiring voyager continuously conjures up images of what the cruise, or the cruiser's world, is going to be like. More often than not, these preconceptions are pathetically bland when compared with the real thing. One's fondest hopes and greatest fears simply go unrealized, and are replaced by a shockingly intense bombardment of all the senses. To be strafed continually by strange and penetrating stimuli, often very beautiful and sometimes rather ugly, interspersed with protracted periods of boredom, and punctuated by a few colossal bombs of super-good and super-bad experience—this is ocean cruising in reality.

Among those who decide cruising is not for them, casualties from maritime hazards such as capsize and sinking and shipwreck constitute only a trifle. A higher rate of defection occurs when uninitiated sailors refuse to accept reality as recompense for fantasy. To make this acceptance can be very enlightening, but holding out for fantasy often leads to devastation: "I wanna go home!" If each would-be voyager could confront this dichotomy beforehand, it would not necessarily increase the numbers of those who go, but it would certainly increase their chances of pulling off a successful trip. What a paradox it is that racing is the less demanding of one's flexibility.

Racing Cat

This cerebral comparison between racing and cruising reveals another interesting contrast: The racer is specialized, the cruiser generalized. Tom Follett, an illustrious multihull racer, has said, "In a multihull, if you ain't got speed, you ain't got nothin'." Any specialist would agree. Of what use is a slow raceboat? But a fast cruiser, now, has another purpose. The generalist would say, "In any boat, if you ain't got something *besides* speed, you ain't got enough." The all-out racing multihull has brought speed to sail as with no other kind of boat, but it serves not as a sailor's citadel. Except in the very largest sizes, it is extremely limited in its usefulness for anything but going fast. It is highly specialized, and its potential for safety is often wagered in the race.

On the other hand, good cruising catamarans and trimarans now come on the scene displaying speed, comfort, utility, *and safety* in a broad combination that is also unlike any other kind of boat. They represent a real alternative to fantasy.

Therefore, if we separate racing from cruising, and aim for positive results in each, we can make a faster racer and a better cruiser . . . but *not* with the same boat.

On this point I'd like to lay the cornerstone of my case for the cruising multihull. If it is safety that you want, a feeling of security, a justifiable concept, then try cruising in a boat capable of over 20 knots, and when the wind is up, just keep her down to something less than 10. When things get tough, just throttle back for comfort, and gain safety.

What, honestly, is the threat of capsize when compared with the threat of going down? Which seems more menacing when the rigging screams and the

cruising cat

The author's Searunner 31 Scrimshaw, *loaded for family cruising, is closehauled at seven knots in trade-wind conditions off the Darien coast, Panama. (Photo by Nelly Bly)*

greenies curl and the boat complains about the pounding? Or when you find yourself tiptoeing through a pod of whales, or flirting with a jagged reef offshore? Let's say you're fighting fire in the galley, or searching for a propane leak. Or bailing with a bucket after running down a log. Have you ever counted the rivets on a freighter's hull with a flashlight on a foggy night and thought about the consequences of collision? Have you ever had a through-hull fitting break off in your hand? Have you ever seen a boat with big holes all around the waterline, at the ends of the chainplates, blown by lightning? These are the *common* accidents, the kind that are responsible for most boat disasters and casualties at sea.

If we sail enough, we're going to be faced with one or more of these hazards. I'd prefer to face any one of them in a multihull. Why? Because no matter what the hell happens out there, I know that my vehicle, my domicile, my citadel, my sanctuary, my life-support system—the very bucket in which I am afloat—*is not going to sink.*

Even if, someday, I find myself floating upside down, squirming in my hammock after several insufferable days (or weeks or even months) waiting for rescue; even if I find myself half-starved, my body covered with seawater boils, my mind hallucinating on the virtues of the ballast keel (like wishing I was sunk); even then I'll know there is still a chance.

At least that's the way I feel about it now. Maybe now's the time to tell you how I feel about it, because so far I've been lucky. While I hesitate to draw solely on personal experience, I nonetheless believe that my experience with multihulls justifies the concept. My wife and I were the first to go to sea in a modern trimaran, in 1959. Starting in the early 1960s, with no formal training in design and zero capital investment, we developed a series of plans for cruising multihulls known today as Searunner Trimarans. At present we estimate that there are about 300 of these craft in service and about 700 under construction, most having been built by individual backyard builders. With these same builders at the helm, Searunners have made many significant voyages, including a family world cruise and a record trans-Pacific race, both feats accomplished by sisterships.

So, we're talking about just one designer's work, but there are several hundred boats in this sampling, each actively involved in ocean cruising. They sailed for hundreds of thousands of sea miles, with a large and varied crew of mostly neophytes, and they did this for over 15 years before one capsized.

Some of that had to be luck. During those years, when I knew that friends of mine were on passage, I did a fair amount of walking the beach. It seemed inevitable that one day we would get the news that somebody's Searunner had capsized. It finally happened during the final phase of writing this book, and is described in Chapter 7.

Actually, my greater fears have always been for the more likely accidents such as collision and falling overboard, and they still are. But the odds were against our no-capsize record continuing indefinitely. Now that a capsize has occurred, I get the feeling that 15 years without a capsize still means that multihulls can be very safe boats. If all Searunners were designed with ballast, I suspect that at least one of them would be resting somewhere on the bottom.

If anyone should take the trouble to examine the entire multihull phenomenon (with the other eye on boating in general), and if he considers all aspects of safety without prejudice, I think he'll see that multihulls have a remarkably good safety record. Fifteen or 20 years is a short time to have come as far as we have. Look at the challenge to the designers, a bunch of individual experimenters who started from scratch with a classic case of re-invention. We haven't had a whole lot of wherewithal, and many of our sailors have been beginners. Then look at the ambitious nature of the passages we've made, and the races we've won . . . and the fun we've had. All things considered, I think we've pulled it off rather well.

And we've learned a lot. In the future, multihulls can and will be made even safer than those early designs.

... can be beached between tides

Any multihull proponent who contends that his boats "combine the best of everything" had better qualify his statements. All this business about ultimate safety and great spaciousness and high speed and easy motion and cheap to build and easy to maintain . . . well, yes and no.

Take maintenance, for instance. It is true that multihulls can be beached between tides or hauled out with rudimentary equipment for bottom maintenance. And, because most of these boats are built by their owners, when things go wrong they can usually be fixed by their owners. But those same owner-builders are all too familiar with the inordinately vast surface area of a multihull. They know what it's like to paint all the way around two or three hulls, plus underwings and decks. More joints, ports, hatches: more boat(s) to maintain. Any real advantage seems to go to the serious cruiser, the real "seasteader," the person who uses his boat as the vehicle of a full-time self-sufficient sailing life. "Total-cruising" sailors find that multihulls offer almost complete independence from shipyard facilities (and attendant costs) for normal maintenance of their boats. But maintaining a racing multihull, or a recreational multihull *yacht* in true yacht condition, is surely no cheaper or easier than maintaining a similar monohull. If you consider berthing and winter storage, then most multihull yachtsmen face greater costs.

Berthing and storage . . . now there's a rub. The outside dimensions of these boats demand more real estate, whether in the water or hauled out. In marinas, multihulls usually occupy the end ties, so their beam does not consume two slips, but instead they may restrict the fairway. One-sided tie-ups require good fenders on the inboard side to contend with channel slop, and traffic damage to the outboard hulls is not uncommon.

Haulouts are sometimes hard to arrange. Marine railways and TraveLifts are designed for deep, narrow, heavy boats. Multihulls are shallow, wide, and light. Some have such sensitive underbodies that the weight of the vessel, however slight, cannot be rested safely on the usual railway's chocks. Winter storage and yard space are sometimes charged at a higher rate than the multihull's length would justify.

THE CASE FOR CRUISING MULTIHULLS

But the multihull's bulk has another dimension. Often a multihull can use a berth that is too shallow for other boats. Bottom maintenance can be performed between tides, and hauling for dry winter storage can be accomplished without need of a marine railway or even a formal boatyard. In this area, the multihull concept is very forward-looking, because the yachtmakers are stamping out boats far faster than marinas can possibly be built, and yard rates are skyrocketing.

Again, it is the committed cruising sailor who benefits most. He has the time and inclination to arrange for a shallow backwater mooring. He prefers to row ashore rather than live with the high cost and hubbub of the dockside ghetto. His craft is self-contained (or he is satisfied with its sometimes primitive containments), so that when he's on the move, he is almost never forced to seek the modern inconvenience of an overnight tie-up. For him, sitting on the mud doesn't mean lying on his side, and he may even select a wintering location that puts him on the bottom at every low tide—thus breaking up the ice around the boat. There may even be a nearby grassy riverbank where he can be hauled out by a highway wrecker. So, the

Jentami, owner-built by Jan Amble, lying at Jenner, Oslofjord, Norway. (Photo by Jan Amble)

multihull gives more trouble on the sides than a monohull, but a whole lot less from underneath.

Cheap to build? Well, it's like anything else: you get what you pay for, and when you build it yourself, you're paying just the same. It all depends on what you put in it. We've seen that backyard builders can produce fine cruising multihulls at roughly the cost of similar cruising monohulls. But the front-yard builder can't.

The production yachtmaker sees the multihull phenomenon percolating all through the yachting world. From the bottom, it is boiling up in the important youth market, with something like 250,000 Hobie-type catamarans. (How can the boating moguls ignore the most popular class boat of all time?) From the top, it is filtering down from impressive multihull achievements in big-time ocean racing. In the backyard, individual builders are banging out their own boats and wafting off across the oceans as if to say that Columbus didn't need Queen Isabella—he just had the wrong sort of cruising boat. And up front, the manufacturers don't have much of anything to sell! Not in inexpensive cruising multihulls they don't, and cruising is what's happening in the yacht market.

Yes, there are those who, like myself, have tried commercial multihull production, and found that as a commercial product—given today's designs, today's technology, and today's market—cruising multihulls are just too darned expensive. They can't compete in price with what the public considers to be good-quality, mass-produced cruising monohulls. Multihulls are like aircraft; they've got to be well built. Their high-strength, low-weight structures are labor-intensive, and labor is expensive. One reason that the boating industry is anti-multihull, then, is that it hasn't figured out a way to build them cheaply.

Enter the owner-builder! I contend that the only way to get a good cruising multihull, at a reasonable price, is to build it yourself. Many fine aircraft are built the same way. But they do require good plans.

Judging from my experience with the backyard builder, he is an absolutely beautiful guy to deal with, if he is given enough information to ensure success with his project. If he feels that he has received real value for the money he has spent on plans, and if he can get follow-up service, then he will gladly use those plans. And it shows in his boat; many owner-built multihulls are among the finest to be seen. Usually such an owner could never afford to buy a good cruising boat; instead he builds his own distinctive craft. That's all I have to say about the cost of multihulls.

Except for a word about the relationship of cost to safety. I've heard it said that multihulls should be outlawed because of the expense of searching for those that capsize. I've looked into this cost, and found that it is not really the *number* of searches that runs it up (relative to the percentage of monohulls that the Coast Guard has to look for) but instead the *duration* of a few, widely publicized searches. The Coast Guard cannot simply say, "We can't find it, so it must be sunk," because the relatives ashore keep answering, "But you can't just quit looking . . . They've *got* to be out there!" Does that sound like a good reason to outlaw multihulls?

Now about motion. In some conditions, like a deep, rolling seaway or an open anchorage invaded by the swell, certainly the multihull rides more smoothly than the keelboat. These sprawling craft must conform to the shape of the surface, but they cannot roll. There is a smaller residual component in their motion, no pendulum effect.

But in a nasty chop, with the wind against the current, or in a harbor cut up by motorboats and commercial traffic, there's no denying that a multihull can really knock you around, especially if you insist on going fast.

Let's consider the old, much-touted multihull attribute of "level ride." That always sounds like an advertisement for the wide-trackers, but it's true that multihulls really do sail flat . . . in flat water. Yet no matter how light the pressure of the wind, she is going to heel according to the contour of the wave she's on. Remember, she must conform to the surface. While we don't spend days "walking on the walls," there are some of us who've briefly seen the mast close to horizontal, with the lee deck dry. Conforming to the wave, that's all.

Motion and heeling, of course, relate to speed. Most multihull sailors don't enjoy the full benefits of comfort that they could. They're always trying to go so fast! I happen to prefer a nice, comfortable ride . . . that's fast enough for a long haul. How fast is that? Well, let's say that your monohull is about the same size as my multihull, and that we are cruising the same route together. Assuming a full variety of sailing conditions, I would guess that for me to ride along with slightly smoother motion than you, I might have to hold her back to about half-again your speed.

The very concept of outrigger stability is easier for some of us to understand than that business of ballast. Instead of pondering the sub-surface, invisible mystery of gravity, we can *see* that leeward hull out there, performing. Just the sight of it makes us feel comfortable.

But what about the feeling, the sensation of sailing a multihull at sea? Even more than other types, multihulls differ greatly one from another, ranging from good seaboats to blundering slushbuckets. The good ones give a truly marvelous ride.

Once in a while we have the chance to hear a qualified opinion from an experienced monohull sailor who has made a long passage in a multihull for the first time. Following is a report given us by a friend and longtime monohull sailorman named Tom Crabb on his return from a 1,500-mile run from Morehead City, North Carolina, to St. Thomas aboard Robert Puffer's 31-foot trimaran cutter *Misumbo:*

After the first few days out, we caught a little norther and went surfing off downwind with long bursts of speed in the 15-knot range. The ride was fantastic . . . we weren't sailing through the water, we were skating *over* it. Then the wind went into the southeast and blew in the forties. The seas were very high and quite confused. We shortened down and drove right through the crests, only to get slammed beam-on by cross seas which were rolling down the troughs. It was rough as hell, like driving too fast on a bumpy road, and very noisy down below. . . .

But the boat really felt secure. It's been said, you know, that for every action there is an equal and opposite reaction—well, that boat would drive into a sea and react faster than the initial action. She would pop up, or jump sideways, always away from any solid water. Just like the proverbial golf ball that's been teed-off inside a tile bathroom. There was no way to get that baby underwater. Once, the main hull bow drove into a wave top and the boat reacted upwards so fast that it threw the water on the foredeck clean over the cockpit! We kept on sailing close-hauled when we probably should have stopped . . . really punished the boat. But we didn't have to steer her much. That self-steering is great stuff . . . the two of us stood watches six-on and six-off. It takes quite a boat to allow that. We finished the trip with a fabulous two-day spinnaker run . . . I was pretty impressed.

It takes a passage like that to get the full feeling of a multihull. The sensations can't be described; you have to go and do it like Tom did. The downwind "skating" and the upwind "bumpy road" are each more extreme than with an equivalent monohull (with the absence of rolling and the presence of occasional severe accelerations) on all axes. The best acceleration is the one that takes you straight ahead, for even if you sail a rather burdensome multihull cruiser, you'll still sometimes find yourself ripping down a wave at 15 or 20 knots. And *that's* a sensation.

Spaciousness is another multihull attribute that needs qualifying. Any domicile with a larger floorplan or more floor levels is a bigger house, right? I'm sure you are aware that there are lots of old multihulls around that look like houses, and that's why many of them never go anywhere. All of the vehicular aspects of multihulls, especially safety, can be largely nullified by the old-time conflict between mobility and spaciousness. Take any vehicle, of any given size, and try to do too much with the accommodation and you'll end up with a house. Never was this design axiom truer than with multihulls, where the floorplan and the levels are terribly tempting.

Nonetheless, the separated compartments of a multihull can make for a private, seamanlike accommodation, and for plenty of well-organized

Private, seamanlike accommodation with well-organized cruising stowage. (Photo by Tom Crabb)

"...The old conflict between
mobility and spaciousness"

cruising storage. The full-time cruiser must beware of overloading, but he surely has a place to stow the myriad appurtenances of his self-sufficient lifestyle, and the means to separate the crew for live-aboard privacy. This is the kind of space that a multihull affords best.

There's one more multihull attribute that I haven't mentioned yet, and this one needs more touting than it gets. In sailor talk it is called "shoal draft," but that doesn't really say it for multihulls. "Forgiving draft" maybe says it better. In the statistical sense, this feature of the multihull is far more meaningful than any comparison of self-righting with nonsinking, because most accidents involve some contact with the land: stranding. And a stranded multihull is far more forgiving than its monohull equivalent.

Thirty inches ···Twenty-nine inches ···Twenty eight 'n a half....

Sailing in a shoal boat does not necessarily reduce the frequency of running aground. In fact, shallow craft are often asked to sneak around in thin water, so they run aground a lot. When we run *Scrimshaw* aground, even hard aground, my sons and I just jump out and push off. We get our shirt tails wet, but we can push her out through quite a nasty chop. Still, sneaking around in shallows is usually limited to selected circumstances, nothing really threatening.

But what about unselected circumstances? This is another case where the multihull disaster lacks finality, relieving the sailor of some part of the threat. A stranding has reduced consequences. Some examples follow.

Jo Anna and I were on our first voyage together in 1959, off the tip of Baja California, when we encountered pre-*chubasco* conditions and realized we were trapped. Out of range of any safe harbors, we chose to shoot the surf at Cabo San Lucas and run up on the beach. The villagers knew that we were coming, so our little 24-foot Nugget trimaran was caught by a hundred hands, dragged ashore, and pushed 200 feet inland. That night the waves almost reached the boat, which was lashed down to deadmen buried deep in the sand, to keep her from blowing away. The wind force was 115 m.p.h. in nearby La Paz, and it sandblasted the bark off the trees at San Lucas. The beach was our salvation, instead of our destruction.

In the winter of 1966, Mark and Bonnie Hassall were anchored in their 38-footer, *Lono Kai,* in a tight cove at Anacapa Island, California, hiding from a storm. The front passed, the wind shifted, and the boat, with two anchors holding, was backed up against the rocks by seas boarding all three bows. In the crew's attempt to extricate the boat with sails and engine, one of the anchor lines was cut too late. This anchor caused the boat to tack itself and sail full-steam up on the frothing boulders. Successive waves threw

Mark Hassall.

19

Bonnie's first cruise

the boat higher and higher, bashing in the bottoms of all three hulls, but the platform was preserved. After the storm, the boat rested well above high water, so Mark and Bonnie stepped off onto a rock unharmed. A keelboat would have dumped the crew onto the frothing boulders. With equipment scavenged from the wreck (this was Bonnie's first cruise), they outfitted a similar craft in which they later cruised the world.

Way out in the middle of the South Pacific is a dreaded place called Argo Reef. Bob and Anne Steg were on passage to Australia in 1968, aboard their 38-foot trimaran, *Vacilador.* On the day they crossed the International Date Line, Bob made a simple, common mistake. When reducing his celestial observations for the day, he entered the tables with the wrong date. The position lines he came up with put them in the clear, so they settled down to sailing for another day. A while later, they were bouncing over coral, really bouncing. Gentle swells would lift their boat and drop her down again in a new position; listing, squatting, rooting, depending on how she came down on the "treetops" of the coral jungle underneath. From the spreaders, Anne could see no way out, for the multicolored reef stretched as far as she could see against the glare. At times the bows would dip down into a deep coral canyon while the stern, caught by the rudder, was hanging high and dry. So it went for hours, hundreds of miles from land. Just as darkness fell, they found themselves in open water, not really knowing why or where.

Yes, there are many monohull designs that take the bottom well and are able offshore vessels, too. When one thinks of good, shoal-draft cruisers, some famous designers come to mind: Alden, Bolger, Crocker, Dunbar, L. F. Herreshoff, Munroe, etc.

Nor do monohulls *have* to sink when holed. Ample flotation could keep some of them from sinking out of sight. But a fair distinction can be drawn between floating just barely awash and floating high enough for habitation.

20

This five-foot model has scale weight and scale buoyancy, even when flooded. Shown here with the central hull completely open to the sea, it is held up by the buoyancy of the outboard hulls. (Photo by Tom Crabb)

So also can we distinguish between simply running aground and really stacking up. Consider the consequences of such common predicaments as these if they had occurred in ballasted boats:

The 37-foot trimaran *Calafia* was anchored in Hawaii in 1969 while Frank Wurz and crew visited ashore. Coral cut the anchor rode and the boat drifted onto a nearby reef. The main hull was holed and the boat scuttled herself firmly on the reeftop. A great length of hawser was assembled (using every piece locally available) to reach land behind the reef. With this hawser the boat was dragged across the reef into the lagoon behind. Because the outer hulls were still intact, the main hull was held up high enough for the crew to use the bunks that night. The next day she was *sailed* to a nearby beach, where she was hauled out with makeshift equipment and her bottom rebuilt.

Wintertime swells make the harbor mouth at Santa Cruz, California, a surf-rider's paradise. Greg Johnson, owner-builder of the 31-footer *Do Raku*, was sailing out with his family—through the surfers—on a day when it was imprudent to go in an engineless boat. A combination of commercial traffic and a set of swells nailed the trimaran to the jetty. A spectator crowd was already assembled (watching Sunday surfers), so a human chain was formed to pass the Johnson youngsters above the surf to safety. The boat sustained several sets of swells, but the jetty rock eventually broke its way in and subsequent waves drove through the gaping holes to burst the hulls from inside. Finally, the *Do Raku* was towed free and into the harbor, where she floated, loosely hung together, with the mast still standing and the decks still above the surface. Greg repaired the craft completely and she sails today.

Looking up through the bottom and out the hatches of Do-Raku.

Rebuilding Do-Raku; *she sails today.*

In the spring of 1973, my family and I were off the Pacific coast of Guatemala in fair weather but bad trouble. I was sick with hepatitis, washed-out, and barely able to command our 31-footer. We had to go in, but that meant running the river bar at Ixtapa, a terrible place for a boat. Fair weather or foul, that coast is always pounded by the swell. We chose our timing with care, and made it past the break line with luck. But once inside the wash zone, we were instantly broached. Listing sharply on the face of a broad white hillock, we were borne along sideways for a great distance and a serious fright. We regained control but were again broached in the shallows by a lesser wave. Finally, we were deposited, aground, close to the beach. We had missed the mouth by a few yards, but a strong flood tide dragged us laterally, parallel with the beach. We were bouncing on the bottom, but the current sucked us safely into the river. A deep, heavy vessel would still be on that bar.

Our brief multihull heritage is full of these examples, but let's face it, contemporary cruising has grown so fast that it must be populated largely with newcomers to seafaring. No amount of academic preparation will make up for the fact that real seamanship is learned by hard experience. This alone seems sufficient reason to get the lead out. When I'm bouncing on the bottom in "unselected circumstances," the last thing I want is ballast.

What I'd like to have is shoal draft, so that I can wade around the boat, or wade ashore. And light weight, so that I can push with my back against the bow, or pull with my arms on anchors—anchors that are light enough for me to carry through the surf, out into water deep enough to float my boat. And compartments galore, so that if one hull takes water, maybe the other(s) can take over. And most of all, stability! I'm not talking about self-righting now; I'm talking about a craft that keeps its feet . . . real wide-track, stand-up stability. If I'm out on the deep sea with a bad leak, or perhaps a broken mast or rudder, I want to be able to be up-and-at-'em, not lying down to simply take what comes. In most emergency situations, and during most normal cruises, self-righting ability is not nearly as blessed as initial stability. The former comes at too great a cost. In the very worst of any situation, I want a boat that cannot sink. And in all the lesser, common predicaments, I want my boat to *stand up.*

The best example of forgiving draft arrived in the mail while this was being written. A letter from Chris White provides the perfect illustration:

I'm sitting in the sterncastle of *Shadowfax* in a beautiful anchorage (Exuma Cays, Bahamas), sort of thinking about the last few days. It's really nice here, and all the more so because I came very close to destroying my boat a few days ago.

Since I saw you last I've sailed the Antilles, Venezuela, Haiti, Dominican Republic, and now the Bahamas. There are about eight thousand miles on the boat since I built her in New York, all engineless, and she's had lots of dings, scratches, and near-misses. But what I did the other night beats all. . . .

I was catnapping in the cockpit while sailing along under self-steering. A loud "clunk" from the centerboard woke me up, for it was a *loud* clunk. So I jumped up

Chris White of Shadowfax *navigating with a miniature sextant built by his grandfather.*

and saw just what I've always dreaded—my boat surfing down the breakers onto a reef! Everything plainly visible in bright moonlight.

It was too late to turn around. I was caught sleeping on the job and there was no time for me to do anything. We hit. Several times. Loud scrapings and bangings and the sound of splintering wood and I knew the jig was up.

But somehow we got through the breakers! I, my girlfriend Donna, and her friend Sissy—we all jumped out and somehow managed to push her off some coral heads into a clear spot in the reef, and get all the anchors out. This at 3 A.M.

When I had time to thank Neptune for still being afloat, I checked the bilges and found water only in the port float. It was not till morning that I could get a better look at the bottom with mask and snorkel. Total damage: small holes in the port float at the waterline, some dings in the main hull, some big chunks taken out of the minikeel, and a completely shattered rudder skeg—*but the rudder is intact.*

Amazing!!

The surf wasn't wild but it was at least average. Maybe we were lucky and found the only hole to pass through, but I think shallow draft and light weight had a lot to do with it. I can't imagine a keelboat getting through that at all.

Anyway, I patched the float with a shelf taken from the galley and lots of mastic. Just temporary, but it only leaks about one bucketful per day. Then with Donna on the spreaders we managed to sail out through a pass in the reef, and make the 30 miles to this protected anchorage. Tomorrow we go up on the beach at high tide and epoxy-up the holes and amputate the rudder skeg. . . .

Well, just thought you'd like to know what one of these boats has pulled off. I can't believe I've been given another chance, and believe me, I've learned my lesson. That self-steering can really get you into trouble, but this boat must have 19 lives.

Chris White
Shadowfax
April 5 or 6 or 7, 1977

For sailors like Chris White, the multihull makes a lot of safe sense. He had learned his seamanship the hard way—from experience—but the reason he chose a multihull in the first place can be seen as a sign of our times.

Most tradition-minded sailors have been conditioned to fear the sea, but today's new water-people have not. They are the splashing progeny of Rachel Carson and Jacques Cousteau. They have grown up with swimfins, wetsuits, and surfboards, and they have been conditioned since childhood with sea-life coloring books and underwater TV specials. These enticing seascapes no longer show a world unknown and feared, but instead a world waiting to be experienced.

Many of these youths have cut their teeth in the new dinghy classes and the little catamarans. When they progress to seafaring, they bring a completely new approach; they perceive the marine environment in a different way. To them, water is to be gotten into as well as on. A big wave is something to be enjoyed.

Boats are designed to fit a particular environment. The marine environment is largely unchanged—we hope—but our perception of that environment is changing fast, and so our boats are changing, too. We are seeing an evolutionary adaptation of the sailor, and his boat, to work with and not against the sea.

3

The Searunner 34

This chapter is a detailed examination of one cruising multihull specimen. Instead of undertaking a broad survey of designs, or a catalog to illustrate variety, let's see how the many factors of design, including the safety factor, are employed in a particular boat, the 34-foot Searunner. This boat is not a state-of-the-art multihull but is one statement of the multihull art.

The 34 is the most recent model in the Searunner series. I worked alone on all the earlier designs, which range in size from 25 to 40 feet in length; the new 34, however, benefits from the talents of John Marples, who was co-designer. The two of us have enjoyed a long sailing and business friendship, and we have both lived aboard and cruised widely in boats that are near-sisterships to the 34. Because ocean cruising requirements are distinct from weekend and vacation-sailing requirements, it is often said among travel-sailors that if you want a serious cruising boat, you'd better go to a serious cruising designer. John Marples and I believe that we are qualified in this respect by being among those rare cruising designers who have subjected themselves to their own treatment, beginning with the piece-by-piece construction of our own craft and continuing through years of operation and maintenance in foreign waters. As this is being written, Marples is on his second tour of the Tuamotu Archipelago in French Polynesia aboard his 37-footer, *Bacchanal*, and I am hunched up to the lamp in *Scrimshaw*'s sterncastle, feeling very envious, and a little guilty for allowing my boat to become stuck solid in six inches of Chesapeake ice. Both boats were built in California; we've sailed them far enough to know what's wrong with them and what's right about them; and we drew the 34 to take advantage of that knowledge.

When preparing the new design we also were able to draw upon information collected while operating a consulting service for our clients—10

SEARUNNER 34

SPECIFICATIONS

LOA	34'0"
LWL	31'1"
Beam	20'9"
Draft, centerboard up	2'9½"
centerboard down	6'5"
Headroom	6'5"
Displacement	7,950 lbs.
Sail Area	505 sq. ft.
Power	Any 300 lb. engine
Construction	Ply-glass composite
Displacement/Length Ratio	113.8
Sail Area/Displacement Ratio	21
Bruce Number	1.14
Extreme Beam/Length Ratio	1.63

MAIN HULL

Prismatic Coefficient	.57
CB Position	55%
CLR Position	47%
CE Position	49%
Fineness Ratio	7.4

AMA HULLS

Full displacement	7,800 lbs. (plus wing)
CB Position	47%
Half-Depressed Displacement	4,400 lbs.
Half-Depressed Fineness Ratio	14.3
Half-Depressed Prismatic Coefficient	.66

Co-Designers: Jim Brown
John Marples

SEARUNNER TRIMARANS
P.O. Box 14
North, VA 23128

years of boatbuilding and seafaring experience by hundreds of sailors. This background made the designing of the 34 a very satisfying project.

Of course, it is a great opportunity for us to be able to present the new design in this book, but I would like to add a disclaimer. We are proud of the boat, and especially anxious to explain her safety features, but we do not wish to imply that the Searunner 34 is the best of all multihulls. There are many ways in which cruising requirements can be satisfied, and lots of safe, capable cruising craft that meet those requirements.

The field of multihull design seems beleaguered at times by its own speedy evolution. We believe this example is worthy of scrutiny not for its innovation, but for its maturity. It is one answer to a well-defined problem: to design a real "cruising machine."

Here are the salient features:

- Central cockpit combined with cutter rig, which locates the mast in the cockpit. This allows easy access to the mast for sail reduction, gives the crew best protection from boarding seas, and minimizes risk of falling overboard.

- Deep pivot-centerboard combined with a minikeel and a skeg-type rudder. This combination gives fine upwind ability in open ocean, good maneuverability in close quarters, and firm steering at high speed downwind, while still allowing "forgiving draft," ability to take the ground, and the freedom to slide sideways (centerboard retracted) when hit abeam by heavy water.

- Divided cabin layout, for privacy and crew rejuvenation underway. The social center is in the sterncastle, as remote from the sea bunks as possible.

- Extremely deep and centralized location of machinery, tankage, equipment, and stores. This gives easy riding motion and inherent stability, even at great angles of heel.

- Very rugged construction.

The 34 is built of sheet plywood to scantlings common in 40-footers. She is fiberglass-covered outside for low maintenance and epoxy-saturated inside for longevity. This selection of materials is believed to give the amateur builder his best chance for success in terms of cost for service rendered, availability of materials, skills required, and backyard working conditions. The platform design combines full-width sandwich bulkheads with solid wing decks, a method known to eliminate structural dismemberment. The thick bottom planking is protected by a massive minikeel, and the rudder is shielded by a fixed skeg of the same draft as the minikeel. This combination of protective features gives super-strong and sacrificial shielding to the propeller and to the hull itself, allowing routine haulouts with makeshift equipment, and accidental groundings with minimal consequences.

As we go now through the vessel, notice that the interior is a sequence of special-purpose modular compartments, each overlapping the others as little as possible, and considerations of safety pervade the entire vehicle.

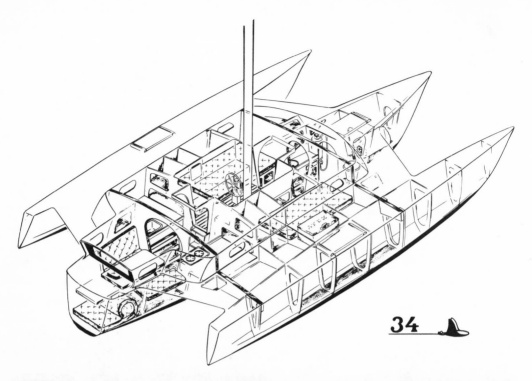

Rugged multihull scantlings are evident in this model by Dick Crockett of the Searunner 31. (Photo by Dudley, Hardin and Yang, Seattle)

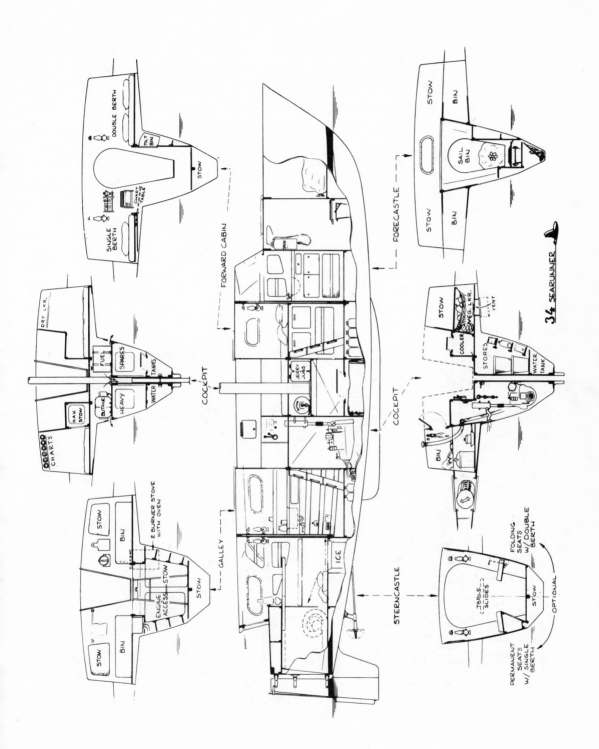

DOUBLE BERTH

TILT BIN

STOW

CHART TABLE

SINGLE BERTH

FORWARD CABIN

STOW

BIN

SAIL BIN

STOW

BIN

FORECASTLE

34 SEARUNNER

DRY LKR.

FUEL

SPARES

WATER TANKS

NAV. STOW

BUTANE

HEAVY

WATER

CHARTS

COCKPIT

JERRY JUGS

STOW

COOLER

VEG. LKR.

VENT

STORES

WATER TANK

BIN

COCKPIT

STOW

BIN

2 BURNER STOVE WITH OVEN

STOW

ENGINE ACCESS

STOW

STOW

BIN

GALLEY

ICE

STERNCASTLE

TABLE SLIDES

FOLDING SEATS W/DOUBLE BERTH

STOW

OPTIONAL

PERMANENT SEATS W/ SINGLE BERTH

From bow to stern, here is an overview of the habitat:

- The forecastle includes a sailbin, a "wet room" with the head and shower, and a separate lavatory-dressing room.

- The forward sleeping cabin has sea bunks, the navigation area, and gives access to the forward stowage holds.

- Amidships, the stowage holds are separated by the centerboard trunk, with the mast and the cockpit above.

- The galley is aft of the cockpit, arranged on both sides of the main hull with the cooking area to starboard and food preparation and washup to port.

- The sterncastle lounge seats four persons at a large "sliding breadboard" table. With the table slid away aft, the lounge converts to a generous bunk.

- Each compartment is served by easy-access storage bins.

In going now to the particulars, it will be helpful to refer frequently to the drawings.

FORECASTLE

There are no bunks in the bow. This area is unsuitable for rest in any small vessel when the craft is beating to windward, and so it is devoted entirely to utility.

There is a sailbin in the forepeak: no wet sails need ever come close to bunks, charts, carpets, or clothing.

Wetness in the cabins is the greatest source of discomfort on passages. Most sailors can withstand cold and wet on deck as long as they've got a dry bunk below. For this reason, a head compartment is isolated from the rest of the accommodation by a door or shower curtain, and is directly available from the foredeck through a large hatch. This provides a wet room for stuffing wet sails and line below in clutch situations. Bathers may come below directly into the shower for rinsing off, and this is the place for the crew to crawl out of wet boots and clothing, dry off, and change, without dripping water through the rest of the accommodation.

The foredeck hatch may be left ajar for ventilation. During heavy tropic rains, when a breath of fresh air in a small boat becomes a precious thing, spatter entering through this hatch is confined to the wet room, but the air circulates aft.

By virtue of complete protection with epoxy, the wet room also serves as the shower stall, thus keeping steam and condensation out of dry areas. No pressure water system is prescribed, but instead a garden sprayer is used for bathing. Because of its adjustable nozzle—from straight squirt to fine spray—this device rinses with the very least possible consumption of fresh water. Hot water from the galley's kettle can be added to the sprayer tank,

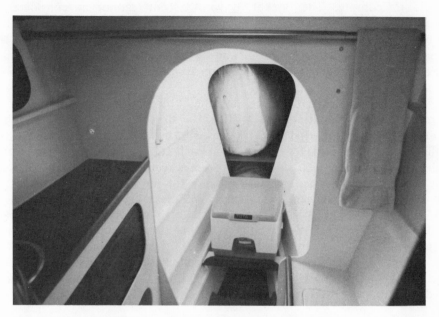

The "wet room." This new boat has a portable head—which won't survive regular service—and no shower curtains on the wet room . . . yet. (Photo by Dave Reis)

or the tank itself may be heated on the stove. Portability makes the device ready for many other jobs around the boat, such as cleaning machinery parts and rinsing away salt before the bottom is repainted.

The wet room bilge is fiberglass-sealed to form a sump, covered with a grate, and evacuated with a manual diaphragm pump. This same pump may be connected by plumbing to the deepest bilge, and also to the ama hulls, to serve as the main bilge pump. However, note that any pumping system leading to the amas must be fitted with valves, which are normally kept closed. In case of capsize, airlock in the amas could otherwise escape through the plumbing and the pump.

The bucket head is specified as a simple solution to a complex problem. This alternative is usually rejected by fastidious persons as unacceptably crude, but the good old bucket is regarded highly by some experienced sailors who have lived with its simplicity for long-term cruises. In this installation the bucket itself is well constrained beneath a household-size seat, and is easily emptied through the forward hatch without the user climbing out all the way on deck; the hull is narrow enough to allow reaching overside to dump starboard, rinse port, and replace the bucket with about two inches of clean water. The bucket is made of lightweight plastic, is cheap, quiet in operation, and easy to clean or replace. It has no plumbing to stink, obstruct in cleaning, or to leak—experienced cruising sailors don't call the pump-type head a "torpedo" without reason. Sewage discharge regulations are in such a scramble as to make it practically impossible for the public to comply. The bucket, it would seem, cannot be considered a "flow-through device," and may in fact represent a holding tank. With a shot of bleach added to its contents to control odor, and a bit of discretion at the time and place of emptying (even waiting for a pumpout station), it appears that the bucket head is as good a solution as any to the overall problem. Best of all—the bucket won't plug!

An even simpler alternative to the "torpedo" head is the Peter Spronk-designed "multipurpose orifice," a simple hole in the underwing panel of any multihull that discharges straight down into the sea between the hulls. One of these may be installed in each cabin of the 34, but a strong, tight-fitting lid must be included to prevent wavetops from entering. Because the hull side dictates an awkward posture for the males, the Spronk heads should bear the instruction, "Gentlemen will please be seated."

Adjacent to the 34's head compartment is the dressing room. This space has six-foot five-inch headroom, a small seat, and a countertop with handbasin for washing up, brushing teeth, etc. There are drawers and lockers for personal effects. Contiguous to the dressing room are several large bins in the wings for dry stowage of such things as linens, off-season clothing, ship's medicines, paper products, and books.

The "dressing room," with bins for storage. (Photo by Dave Reis)

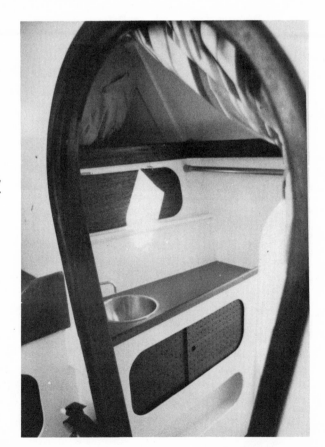

The largest anchor is stowed beneath the sole in this compartment. With its chain and rode flaked down in readiness, it can be quickly gotten out the foredeck hatch. When the vessel goes to sea, the weight of this large chain and anchor is positioned to advantage deep within the bilge. For passage-making, at least one of the two working anchors can be stowed here also.

Since synthetics comprise the bulk of today's cruising wardrobe, traditional hanging lockers make inefficient use of space and so do not appear in this interior. Rough-and-ready clothing is best for the most part, and that can be kept in bins. Good permanent-press shore clothes can be folded neatly and kept sealed in plastic bags. Short-length garment bags may be hung in the dressing room for convenient access, but fancy clothes don't deserve to be hung loosely in shippy little closets—if chafe doesn't eat them up, then probably vermin will. Wet oilskins can be hung in the wet room until dry, then kept in the sailbin.

The foregoing description of this forecastle is detailed to show contrast with the usual arrangement of big bunks in the bow, tiny commodes near the main cabin, and profuse domestic gadgetry like pressure water and pump toilets, which are always breaking down. Designed for weekend use, those features ill fit the realities of full-time cruising, and are in fact a major reason why people quit cruising: the layout of their vessels does not give the crew a floating chance of keeping clean and dry.

FORWARD CABIN

Sea bunks are located in the forward cabin. Their position is well back from the bow, near the centerline, and high up in the wings for the smoothest motion, the least water noise, the most dryness, and the greatest privacy. These bunks do not double as seats, and are remote from the ruckus in the galley, but are very handy to the cockpit. They have three-foot sitting headroom for reading, and good ventilation from a natural draft between the foredeck hatch and the nearby companionway. Each of these openings is large and easily screened. Note that there are no opening ports or ventilators over bunks: they inevitably lead to sleeping in the wet.

The port bunk is a standard double (4'6" x 6'6") for use by a couple, and the starboard bunk is a generous single (2'9" x 6'6") for use by the navigator. A large sliding chart table emerges from beneath this bunk. Stowage for clothing, books, and personal paraphernalia is arranged around and beneath the bunks. Pullman curtains add privacy.

The lower portions of these sea bunks extend aft behind the cockpit seats. Over the foot of each bunk is a shallow locker, up against the deckhead, for charts, documents, and perhaps musical instruments. The sun's heat on deck will tend to keep the contents of these lockers dry. Note also that beneath the portside cockpit seat there is a large locker, accessible from the front and the side, for stowage of radios, instruments, and other navigation gear, all adjoining the navigator's bunk.

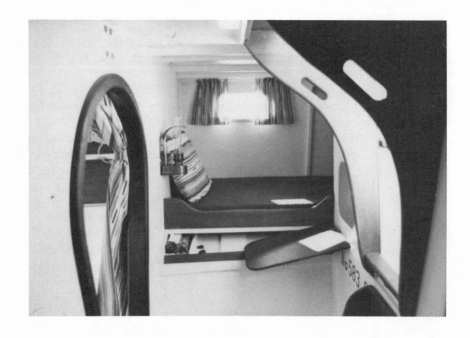

Sea bunks in the forward cabin, a single to starboard (above) and a double to port (below). (Photos by Dave Reis)

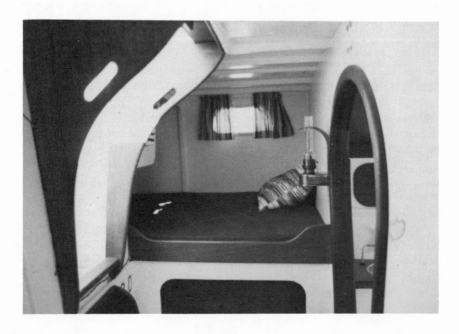

It should be emphasized that this cabin is designed for sleeping: it does not overlap the cooking, eating, lounging, and bathing facilities located elsewhere in the craft. The crew's rest is critical to the vessel's safety.

CENTRAL COCKPIT

The central cockpit is a deep, central well dead amidships. It offers great protection from boarding seas, the least chance of falling or being washed overboard, and the best all-around visibility. Because the mast is stepped in the cockpit, there is ready access to the halyard winches and reefing gear without going on deck. Mainsail reefing can be accomplished by the helmsperson alone.

There is stand-up headroom underneath the boom. All headsails are high-cut to afford a good view to leeward. In this cockpit, the crew can always tell with a glance just what is going on up in the slot between the sails. There is good visual and voice contact with all points in the vessel, above and below. Located at the "axial center of gyration," this cockpit has far better riding motion than if it were stuck out on the stern. Complete details for both owner-buildable pedestal steering and wind vane self-steering are included in the design.

The cockpit seats are six feet four inches long to allow stretching out for two, or sit-down daysailing for six or eight persons—with everyone positioned at least eight feet from the water with their weight amidships.

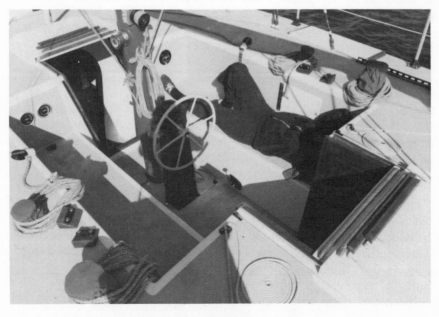

Central cockpit. (Photo by Dave Reis)

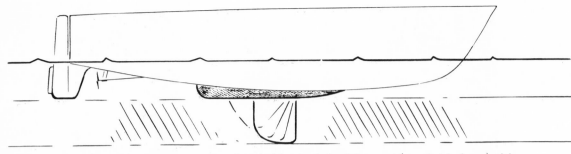

Buffer zone. The centerboard more than doubles the draft of the vessel (cross-hatched area), giving advance warning of approaching shallows. Once grounded, the "minikeel" (shaded area) offers super-strong yet sacrificial protection to the hull, prop, and rudder.

Beneath the cockpit are four stowage holds that reach the full width and depth of the hull. These holds are divided by the centerboard trunk, onto which the mast is stepped.

The forward pair of these holds is decked and sealed at the level of the trunk top. This deck is the sole of a large compartment located beneath the removable cockpit grate. In this compartment—which is completely sealed off from the hull below and generously ventilated overboard—are located all the fuels. Vapors and fluids cannot accumulate in this compartment because four large scupper-vents drain directly overside through the planking without the need for ducts. Also, any water that may enter the cockpit from above falls through the grate to drain out from the scupper-vents and through the open top of the centerboard trunk, thereby providing extremely fast self-bailing. While this boat and this cockpit may be regarded as relatively invulnerable to pooping, it is nonetheless apparent that inundation can occur in any boat. In the 34, however, cockpit water would at least be located in the center, and the huge self-bailers should allow the craft to free herself before the next crest arrives. Only two cases of total pooping of these central cockpits have been reported. Both vessels survived without capsize, and without major damage, and without repeated pooping. The cockpits drained themselves at once.

The centerboard itself is slightly buoyant, with up-and-down pendants available in the cockpit. Because the board retracts itself when it strikes obstacles or enters shallows, it provides the crew with an automatic shallow-water alarm. After turning into deeper water, the crew may lower the board again by hauling on the appropriate pendant, which is made of synthetic line. The centerboard is a truly massive foil, extending the draft from two feet nine inches (board up) to six feet five inches (board down). This deep lateral plane allows the boat to beat against open ocean tradewind seas and make good progress to windward with relatively easy motion. Yet the board may be removed for service by lifting it up through the cockpit with the main halyard, without unstepping the mast or hauling out the boat.

Beneath the fuels compartment, and divided by the trunk, are two separate holds for "heavy spares" and tools. Access to these is gained

Heavy spares hold has access from the forward cabin. (Photo by Dave Reis)

through cutouts showing in the forward cabin behind the accommodation ladder. In this space is also kept the Calamity Pack, all the zero-hour emergency equipment sealed in watertight containers. In the event of capsize, the equipment is held above water level in this location.

Like many other lockers in this design, the heavy spares hold opens athwartships so that lateral inversion of the boat would not cause the locker's contents to tumble out and be lost down through the hatches. All crucial stores are to be kept in such lockers, or in spaces that are fitted with doors held closed by finger-hooks.

Beneath the heavy spares hold, down in the deepest bilges, are placed two collapsible water tanks of about 20 gallons each. These tanks can be removed for service, or pushed aside for access to the centerboard pivot pin. Because collapsible water tanks require no vent pipes, they will better hold their contents in case of capsize. Valves in the discharge lines, located at the tanks, would allow the contents to be drawn off at the valve. Fill-pipe plumbing must be watertight even upside down.

The after stowage hold and engine room both have their access from the galley by way of large openings. On the starboard side is space for about six five-gallon plastic pails with snap-down lids for waterproof and bugproof containment of grains and other dry foods.

Below the sole of this hold is a third 20-gallon collapsible water tank, for use in dry areas or dry seasons. This brings the tankage to 60 gallons in three independent units, plus four five-gallon jerry jugs, which are used to

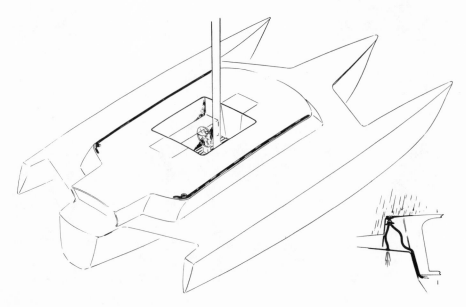

Cabin-top rainwater catchment has "Y" valve in plumbing for rinsing out salt and dirt before filling tanks. No canvas raincatcher to flog in the wind; no going on deck at night in a squall to tend buckets and hoses. Just reach up and switch the valve.

transport water aboard by dinghy and are kept full as offshore reserve. Jugs may be stowed beneath the sole in the forward sleeping cabin for best positioning of weight, with at least one five-gallon container permanently tied into the bilge. All this tankage is seldom necessary in practice, because the entire cabintop is shaped to allow guttering as a raincatcher, and may be fitted with valved plumbing leading directly to the tanks.

The after portside hold is the engine room. Any engine of 300 pounds maximum weight is prescribed, gasoline or diesel. A 30-horsepower Atomic Four just fits with side clearance, but with ample mechanic's workroom above and beneath the engine.

Because this engine room has far greater overhead space than is common in boats this size, there is room for a high standpipe muffler. This height—above the underwing—prevents a very common cause of engine damage: seawater entering the cylinders by way of the exhaust system.

The engine room can be made rather soundproof and completely vapor-tight from the rest of the hull. This is accomplished by gasketing the engine room door, fiberglassing the bilge in that compartment (no limber holes), and lining the space with fire-retardant insulation. Thus the noise and dirt of the machine may be effectively isolated. Should capsize occur, engine room contaminants will be contained herein, allowing habitation of the remaining accommodation spaces.

Exhaust goes overboard underneath the wing and so is seldom smelled on deck; but blower-ventilation of the engine space exits from the cabintop directly adjacent to the helm. This makes it possible for the crew to detect quickly any smoke or fuel vapors, or the smell of overheating.

An overhead pipe rail in the engine room is provided, and a small hoist attached, so that the engine can be removed without outside assistance. The machine is lifted from its mounts by the hoist and slid aft along the rail to where its weight can be taken on the main halyard. From there it is lifted out the hatch for overhaul on the side deck, or delivered overside to a dock or another boat.

The off-center installation of this engine does not cause the boat to steam in circles, but instead tends to cancel torque by directing its prop blast directly at the rudder skeg from a slightly offset angle. Sealed batteries are located down deep, just aft of the transmission, and hand starting may be arranged by an extended crank to the forward cabin.

Fuel tankage is 20 gallons, plus two five-gallon jerry jugs for transport and reserve. Projected speed with the Atomic Four is six knots at cruising throttle with a folding propeller, nine knots flat-out. Range is at least 200 miles in calms, with no fuel stowed within the dry hull or on deck.

In economy boats, the inboard installation may be omitted in favor of a 10-horsepower long-shaft outboard motor mounted on the transom with a vertical sliding bracket. This option is fairly successful when the owner is a skilled sailor, for the boat is designed to be managed easily under sail alone in virtually all conditions and so can be operated without dependence on the engine. On the other hand, if the owner is not a skilled sailor, perhaps the surest way to correct the situation is to install no engine at all, at least for the first season of operation in local waters. Later, an engine may be installed as a convenience instead of a crutch. If the engine is not installed, 300 pounds of water jugs should be stowed in the engine room to compensate for the missing weight, unless the craft is already laden with reserves.

Auxiliary-powered multihulls can take marvelous advantage of their engines. Narrow hull form and light weight allow motoring efficiently with a small engine and good fuel economy. Oversize engines and tanks can completely ruin sailing performance, and are not necessary anyway if the boat sails well. Careful installation of a good, small engine will greatly increase the vessel's versatility.

The position of the cockpit integrates with many other features in the boat, including the engine, as we have seen. Of course, other cockpit arrangements can be just as well integrated into other designs, and are in fact preferred by many knowledgeable sailors. The Searunner layout is just one of many that are known to be successful, but because it is so unusual, it deserves to be explained. Without losing track of this thread, let's consider other factors—such as spray, sailing sensations, weight distribution, stowage, even dinghies—to show how they all relate to the pivotal position of this cockpit.

First, there are some disadvantages that need to be understood: The central cockpit layout separates the cabins and so requires the crew to pass outside through the cockpit when going from one cabin to the other. This is

Canvas dropboard in position.

no great hardship in fair weather, but when the hatches are closed, one's transit is delayed. To avoid such delays on cold or rainy nights, some owners install canvas dropboards, simple flaps that fasten to the overhead hatch and are held down by the weight of a short piece of chain sewn into their lower hems. Thus the crew may duck from one cabin to the next, passing through the flaps, without the nuisance of removing or replacing wooden dropboards. The exceptional privacy provided by the divided layout can then be enjoyed with minimal inconvenience.

Another objection to the central cockpit is voiced by those who ask if its location doesn't tend to be wet, or vulnerable to spray. Were it not for the wingdecks, which contain the spray within the tunnels, these boats would be wet at high speed. Even so, when it breezes up, there is some spray blown into the cockpit, although less than in many multihulls because of the 34's generous freeboard.

Nonetheless, the central cockpit does have the distinct disadvantage of its forward-facing after hatchway. If this hatch is left open, spray flying aft enters the galley when the craft is closehauled.

This substantial dodger gives good shelter in the central cockpit.

The central cockpit would appear to be a natural for being covered with a boom tent or a dodger, but such canvaswork must usually divide to fit around the mast. Because of the 34's high boom, an awning can be hung beneath the gooseneck and securely attached to the shrouds, the sub-forestay, and the running backstays. If the boom tent is made fairly small and tough, with "hollow leeches" and roped edges, it will stand in the wind without flogging and so remain set while the craft is under sail, in most conditions. For use in harbor, this roof may be hung with side curtains or screens, depending on the climate. Assuming that the cover maker gives close attention to detail, such a structure will add enormously to the 34's livability in harbor. The cockpit becomes a central living room, augmenting the interior below.

A fixed pilot house is seldom seen on boats this size, for it becomes obtrusive and interferes with the operation of the boat. A variety of dodgers or Bimini tops may be used for Searunners, but they are generally more complicated than in aft-cockpit layouts because of the conflict with the mast and the staysail sheets.

To my mind, the only significant disadvantage to the central cockpit is this: The helm is located closer to the bow, thus shortening the length of the "gunsight" by which the helmsman aims the boat. This makes no difference when steering a compass course, but it makes it harder to guide the craft toward a visible destination or between navigational marks, especially for inexperienced sailors. This feature definitely requires familiarization, and if you're accustomed to steering from well aft, it never feels quite right to be deprived of a longshot view of the mast lined up with the headstay. It's different, that's all. When weighed against the advantages, it is a tolerable difference to me.

There are other interesting features in this cockpit, like the large bosun's lockers for stowage of deck gear, and the built-in insulated cooler for iced drinks. A portable workbench, with a vise, can be erected in the cockpit for routine maintenance and repair. But of equal importance to what goes in the cockpit is what goes underneath.

The sensations of on-center sailing—especially at speed—must be experienced to be understood. Among those sensations is the security one feels when the boat moves through the seaway in that surefooted manner made possible only when all the heavy stuff is located right below the cockpit where it belongs.

The designers feel strongly that the comfort and welfare of the crew are not served by locating heavy objects anywhere but deep down amidships. Accumulations of machinery, equipment, tankage, and stores all combine to make surprising tonnage. Scattering this mass out toward the boat's extremities definitely amplifies gyration on all axes. It subtracts directly from the boat's comfort, steering, speed, and safety—it subtracts from the joy of cruising. This is particularly true of multihulls, for in these craft each pound of payload constitutes a great percentage of the whole weight. Furthermore, distance cruising requires stowage holds, so why not put them in the middle where the weight will do some good? The central cockpit layout creates the space beneath for amidships stowage holds.

Nevertheless, the cruiser's expeditionary outfitting is not limited to compact, heavy stuff. The myriad light and bulky articles must find their places, too. What about the sails, the sail cover, the boom tent, and the garden hose? Fenders, docklines, life jackets, running lines, and bosun's chair? Mop, buckets, scrub brush, cleansers, sponges, and rags? Where do you put the clam fork, the casting rod, the gaff, the gill net, the crab trap, and the spear guns? Consider the stowage problem of about four sets of swimfins, dive masks, snorkels, gloves, and spears. Then come the dinghy's mast, oars, sail, rudder, and centerboard. Where do you put all this stuff?!

Certainly not all of it will fit beneath the cockpit. In the 34, most of it gets tucked away in the ama hulls. We don't like the idea of putting any weight out there, but where else can they go? If the vessel qualifies as a distance cruiser, these objects inevitably find their way into the ship. They are cumbersome things to stow, if not heavy, and the available volume in the amas solves the problem. At least these bulky articles are located down low in the amas, and not high up in the wings. But under no circumstances should these outboard hulls be asked to carry tanks, cases of cans, ground tackle, motorcycles, etc. Improper weight distribution will absolutely ruin the seakeeping qualities of the boat.

A small cruiser really needs to be a big freighter—so big that it's a bit much to ask of one hull. Traditional cruisers in this size usually have enough room for the heavy stuff, especially if the boat has a wide hull and deep

WHERE DO YOU
PUT
ALL THIS STUFF?

draft. But when the light, bulky articles are all stowed below, they tend to drive the crew right out of the cabins. In port, this accumulation is often seen stacked around the deck or dumped in the dinghy when the dinghy is not in use.

In theory, the stowage problem is easily solved by the multihull's extra hulls; but in fact, it is often compounded in designs that have standing headroom walkways in all hulls. This means that the majority of deep space (whether in the central or the outer hulls) is simply unavailable for the stowage of anything but air. It is used for the passage of people's feet. The displaced plunder usually gets heaped up in the wings, high above the waterline, where the superstructure must now be designed around it. The boat's windage and "roll center" are thereby elevated in the interest of floor space. Alternatively, or simultaneously, stowage articles are pushed out toward the ends of the vehicle where they are hard to reach, and where their weight amplifies gyration and degrades the steering properties—especially downwind steering in survival weather. A lofty mast and large sailplan further compound this dangerous progression. This unscientific approach to multihull design is simply not well suited to serious seafaring.

Now, let's face the greatest stowage problem of all: where to put the dinghy? The usual solution nowadays is to settle for an inflatable dinghy. And yet, to commute around the harbor in a rubber boat, you need a small outboard motor, since rowing the "bladder boats" any distance is a herculean job. And that's what the dinghy is for: to commute around the harbor, often against the wind and chop, hauling fuel, ice, groceries, laundry, water, and people, sometimes over considerable distances.

Many experienced cruising sailors prefer a hard dinghy, one that really

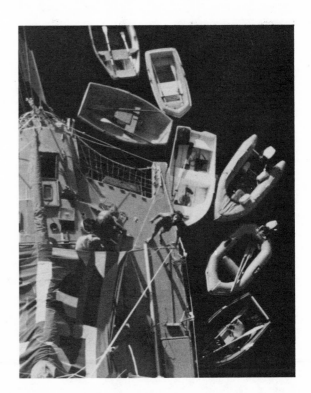

Dinghy variety.

rows and sails. The 34 has ample space to carry either type, inflatable or hard. Or, for the greatest of luxuries, one of each! The dinghy is a very important piece of auxiliary equipment to the distance cruiser; it is his link with the land. Its services are very much in demand. If one of each type is kept ready on the wingdecks, then when someone goes ashore, whoever remains aboard is not stranded. This duplication is particularly important in family cruising.

But the wingdecks are not the safest place to keep dinghies when at sea. They interfere with sail handling and may be vulnerable to boarding seas. When making ready for a passage, the 34's inflatable can be collapsed and stowed in its special wing compartment. Two such compartments are provided, one for the self-inflating, canopied life raft and the other for the blow-up dinghy. These compartments are accessible from on deck and—in the event of capsize—from underneath the wing.

The best seagoing position on this boat for a small, lightweight hard dinghy is on top of the sterncastle. Here it can be lashed upside-down in chocks and ride well above the waves, completely out of the way of sail handling. But most important, because of the cockpit's central location, the bulk of the dinghy does not obstruct the view forward from the helm. In the usual monohull the cockpit is behind the dinghy, which is stowed on top of the coachroof. The enormous blind spot thus created is about the most blatant absurdity in traditional yacht design, followed closely by dinghies that cantilever precariously outboard in davits, or dangle astern in tow.

A hard dinghy is stowed on top of the sterncastle in this 31-footer, Neegee. And the crew is snugged-down in the cockpit, well protected from all directions and with complete visibility forward from the helm. (Photo by Tom Freeman)

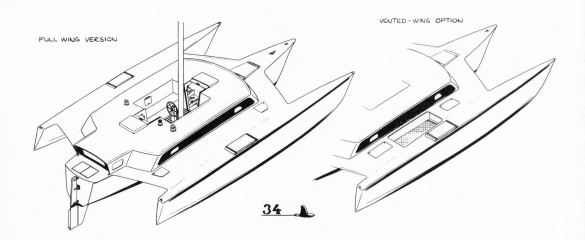

FULL WING VERSION

VENTED - WING OPTION

34

Inflatables can be partly deflated and folded in half, reducing the chore of blow-unblow, and the folded bulk may now be lashed securely to the sterncastle top.

The 34 can be built with the so-called vented wing as an option. This vent is nothing but a large hole through the wingdeck located in a nonstructural area. The hole is covered with a stout net at the underwing level and it forms a deep recess in the deck. It provides a place for throwing all manner of things—anchors, line, fenders, and loose sails—where they will temporarily stay put. A folded, half-inflated dinghy will ride safely in this recess. So will the life raft canister.

Theoretically, the vented wing serves to relieve wind pressure under the wings and thus reduce the chance of capsize. Although this theory is controversial, it is just possible that the vented wing could make the difference between capsizing and not capsizing. But the vented wing option is usually elected for aesthetic reasons, so that the crew can watch the water (and the porpoises) streak between the hulls, or for other practical reasons, such as to reduce wavetop pounding on the underwing, or to make a convenient hole in which to dump a dinghy.

Speaking of dumping dinghies, no other item of the cruiser's gear is so easily lost or stolen. The dinghy is vulnerable when tethered astern, either under tow or while the yacht lies at anchor with the crew asleep. To guard against loss, the 34 includes features for quickly and easily pulling the dinghies up onto the deck. The amas have low freeboard at the sheerline aft and the railing here is covered with a length of split PVC pipe (slick black plastic with a soapy feel). A gate in the lifelines provides the ideal place to pass up heavy objects like ice and fuel cans from the dinghy. Then the crew may board the vessel at the same position, and pull the dinghy up onto the wide, clear wingdeck for overnight storage; or transfer it to any of its three seagoing positions: the sterncastle top, partly collapsed in the wing-vent recess, or fully deflated in its special stowage hatch within the wing.

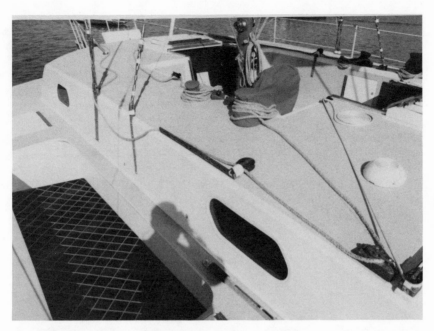

Vented wing. (Photo by Dave Reis)

A sailing dinghy, strange as it may seem, can contribute to capsize prevention offshore. Many of today's aspiring sea travelers are newcomers to boating of any kind. It is greatly beneficial if a sailing dinghy is the initial acquisition of the multihull's equipment, and is available during the construction of, or before the purchase of, the cruising multihull. Dinghy sailing is the very best training for multihullers. It gives the student experience with the nonfinite capsize, and develops the conditioning required for sailors to perceive just when the big boat is being overdriven, a situation that can otherwise be insidiously masked by the stiff stability of multihull craft.

Hours of enjoyment in the dinghy are a welcome respite from the labor of building the big boat, and thus developing simultaneously the most basic skills of seamanship. When the big boat is finally finished, the sailing dinghy will faithfully fulfill the duties of a harbor commuter, while continuing to provide fine recreation for the crew. If every neophyte seafarer were to cut his teeth (or her teeth) on a hot little sailing dink, much of the lubberly multihull management often witnessed around the harbors would cease. And it might make a major contribution to the prevention of offshore capsize.

Some sailors will want to lash a couple of surfboards to the ama bows. There's nothing better for sport, and the surfboard relieves the demand for the dinghy by younger members of the crew. Like all the other things we've somehow found a place for, surfboards need to be stowed securely for sea. The type with a removable skeg facilitates this. Low, form-fitting chocks can be mounted on the deck and the boards lashed into the chocks bottom-up.

This method of pulling up the dinghy employs a wire stretched between the hulls and fitted with a plastic pipe roller. The headsail winch may be used; no bow eye should protrude from the dinghy's stem.

"If every neophyte sailor would cut his teeth. . . ."

These chocks and lashings should be strong enough to hold even when the ama bow is being driven through wave crests. Watch out for surfboard wax, though; it makes a miserably sticky mess on deck. It melts into the nonskid and can never be successfully painted over.

After all is said and done, it is difficult to imagine another craft this size that is better suited than the 34 to carrying auxiliary vehicles. One small, lightweight hard dinghy that really rows and sails, one bladder boat, perhaps with a little outboard motor, plus the life raft, and maybe a surfboard or two, and you're pretty well covered. And none of these obstructs the view forward from the cockpit.

DECK HARDWARE

While we're here on deck, let's have a brief look at the way in which the 34's operational hardware is laid out. First, the ground tackle. Assuming that there are at least two able-bodied persons in the crew, an anchor windlass is not generally required in a multihull this size. For day hops, one anchor, usually a plough, can be kept on a bow roller at the stemhead. But for seagoing, both working anchors, each with chain and rode, are stowed in special lockers in the forward wing. These lockers drain directly downward and are sealed off from the rest of the craft so that rust and mud and harbor-bottom odor cannot permeate the accommodation. A sternhook may be kept in the similar locker (also self-draining) on the sterndeck, where it is

51

Bow roller installation.

always ready for emergency stops. As mentioned earlier, the bower anchor (for storms and other clutch situations) is stowed in the deepest forward bilge, where it may be worked through the foredeck hatch.

Each anchor is equipped with a full boat length of chain and 150 feet of nylon rode, except the bower anchor, which has 300 feet. Very often the two forward working anchors are used together, especially when anchoring in tidal estuaries. A large snapshackle is used to fasten their chains together so that one anchor may be set upcurrent and another down-current, as described in Chapter 7.

One more glance around the deck reveals that this cruiser, unlike most, has ample deck space for things like a solar cell, a wind generator, a tomato plant, a crab trap, or a lobster pot—the myriad appurtenances of cruising.

Also note that the hardware layout is clean, but complete. All halyards and sheets, winches and quick-release cleats are within arm's length of the helm. So are the centerboard pendants, engine controls, self-steering tripline, and backstay levers. The craft can usually be handled by one sailor from one place, but there is room in the deep cockpit for a gang of deck apes when desired.

Strongpoints for anchoring, towing, docking, dragging the bridle-drogue, and hoisting the boat by crane are all prescribed in the design. There are ample through-bolted cleats for large lines used in canal locks and for manhandling in emergencies.

A crab trap and a lobsterpot on deck with room to spare . . . and even below deck for seagoing.

The double-headsail cutter rig offers great power in a wide variety of sail combinations, with a minimum of sail changing. The optional sloop rig is provided for those who wish a simpler, more economical rig and sailplan. Either way, the hardware layout is carefully arranged so that this multihull can really be *sailed.*

Before we leave the cockpit, there is one more consideration that must be discussed. See those thresholds at the bottom of the companion hatches? Right there just above the cockpit sole. Well, that's about where the inverted waterline would be, at those thresholds. Judging from them, you can see that if the boat were ever capsized, there would be lots of space inside the cabins for long-term survival habitation.

I know, it's hard to think about calamity at this point, but if we talk it over now, it'll make a big difference to us if we're ever caught out in survival weather. It would be darn nice to know that if the worst should happen (or rather the next worst, relative to sinking), we'd still have a place to live. The discussion in Chapter 6 is intended to combat the major danger, which is panic.

The 34's inverted waterline would give us about a foot more space than other Searunners have, because of certain differences in construction. The amas, for instance, are completely isolated from the wings, leaving no chance for airlock to bleed through the wings into the main hull. That will help make her float higher. If we were ever to sustain damage to the underwing panels from pounding seas, water entering the wing could not run into the amas. That one has happened before. It leads to loss of stability and a lot of pumping.

In addition, the 34 has several large sealed voids in the wings. Some of those compartments that we used to use for stowage in the other boats are sealed off. They tended to become catch-all spaces, and that's no place to put the weight of things that probably belong ashore anyway. Now we seal those big voids with epoxy, fill them up with plastic milk containers, and close 'em up, except for a pop-out inspection port in the deck for each one.

These voids provide the buoyancy to make the boat float very high if inverted, but they also might come in handy in the more likely prospect of catastrophic shipwreck. If the vessel were driven on a badly breaking reef, and all three hulls were completely scuttled, she would still float with the decks well above the surface because of the extra buoyancy in the wing-voids. The central cockpit would still offer some protection from the waves. Again, the waterline would be just above the cockpit sole. We're suggesting that all Searunners, and all multihulls, be built with features like these because of the peace of mind that they bring to the crew.

And you know, it just might be a whale that someday makes us glad we've got those voids in the wings. I don't mean to aggravate the Greenpeace folks, but whales have been involved in several yacht sinkings and possibly some capsizes. In the case of multihulls, I don't think it's the whale's fault. We come zipping along with our narrow hulls, causing very little water noise to warn of our approach, and maybe jab them in the ribs with two or three sharp bows. I think they would gladly get out of the way if they knew we were coming. Maybe someone will invent a little underwater whistle to warn the behemoth. I sometimes think the ticking of our Sumlog would be enough, because whales have such incredible audio-perception. The risk is very small, but it's sure nice to be ready, because then the worry goes away.

Let's now go below again, this time down through the cockpit's after companion hatchway.

GALLEY

In the galley, the most important department of the habitat, there is one factor that takes equal precedence with organized stowage: flat counter space. Countertop area in the 34's galley measures 30 square feet, less the amount consumed by the stove on one side and the sinks on the other. That's the area of about half a sheet of 4' x 8' plywood for each of two separate work spaces. High fiddles line the edges of these counters, and canister stowage may be arranged within more fiddles at the counters' outboard edges.

The galley sink can be double or single as preferred, perhaps handcrafted of stainless steel or wood-epoxy to the desired width and depth. Ideally, the sink is set within a slightly concave countertop so the whole area will drain into the sink. Sink drains go directly overboard, well above the waterline, with no seacocks, and are of large diameter to swallow such biodegradable waste as eggshells, pineapple trimmings, avocado skins, potato parings, and lime rinds—to reduce the accumulation of garbage in the galley. We have learned that sink drains should be stoppered while the boat is running under power, to avoid the possibility of exhaust vapor entering the galley.

Water supply to the sink comes from two large foot pumps, one salt and one fresh. The cutting board may be arranged to cover part or all of the sink but with large drain holes in the board underneath the spigots. When not in use, the cutting board mounts in chocks against the bulkhead.

Also bulkhead-mounted is the teakettle "hangerupper," a device that grasps the base of a standard kettle so as to allow temporary storage of hot water up against the wall, the safest place for something heavy and hot. Two kettles are best, a large one for seawater and a small one for fresh.

The cooking stove prescribed is a three-burner bottled gas or kerosene model with oven. It fits against the hull while protruding about three inches inboard of the counter's front. A simple two-burner countertop model may be substituted for those cooks who prefer using a folding stovetop oven. Such portable ovens work very well, provided the stove burners are large enough to produce sufficient heat for baking. Kerosene is the best fuel for stovetop baking because it burns so hot. Folding stovetop ovens are not inconvenient if there is a handy bin adjacent where the oven may be stowed without folding. A gimbaled stove is not required, but good, adjustable stovetop fiddles are recommended, arranged to secure the stovetop oven as

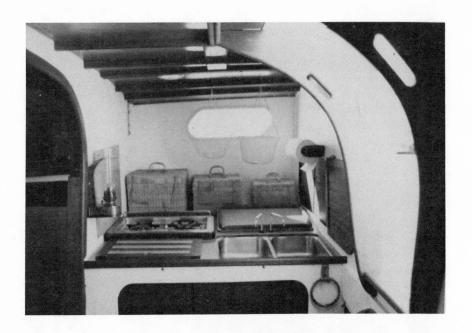

The builder of this just-launched 34, Dave Reis, found the galley counters so large that he put both stove and sink on one side . . . and left the other side available for a huge chart table. Note access to the stowage hold below. (Photos by Dave Reis)

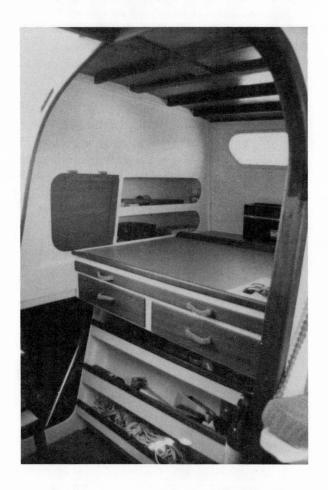

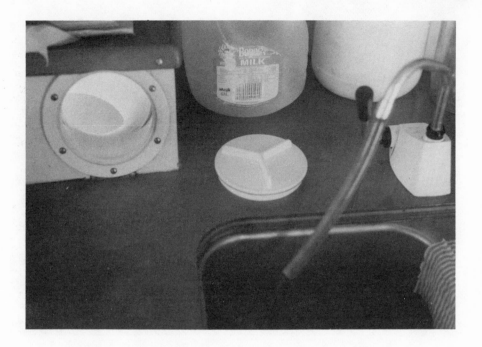

This galley has a large through-wing disposal for direct dumping of biodegradables at sea.

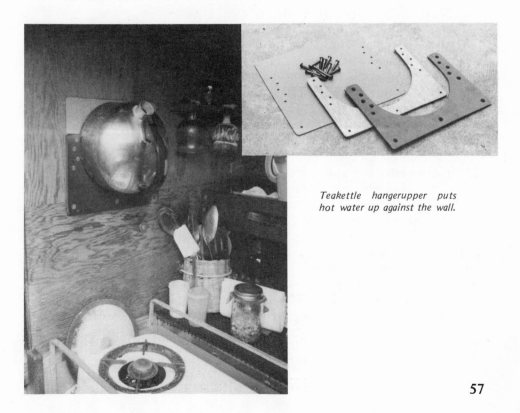

Teakettle hangerupper puts hot water up against the wall.

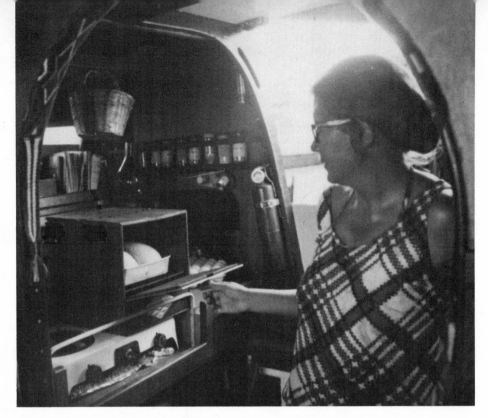

Stove-top oven requires—and creates—lots of galley heat.

well as pots and pans. Propane shutoff at the tank is accomplished in the cockpit, with a second valve at the stove for convenience.

Even though a gimbaled stove is not required in multihulls, we like to see the galley equipped with a Sea Swing cooker for one-pot specials in heavy weather. A second mounting ready in the bilge would make this simple unit available for hot meals and heat even in the case of capsize.

In the Searunner 34, each galley counter has two very large stowage bins in the wings which open onto the counter. These spaces are for keeping pots and pans, baking dishes, canned supplies, flatware, grain grinder, oven, etc. The lower starboard bin, located opposite the engine and insulated from the sun's heat on deck by the bin above, is ideal for location of the cool locker for storing fresh fruits and vegetables.

Produce that has not been refrigerated can usually be obtained from roadside stands or native markets and will keep much longer than supermarket produce, especially if stored in a dark, well-ventilated space. The 34's cool locker is generously ventilated underneath the wing by a screened trap door, which can be closed from inside. Fresh vegetables are kept here in suspended net bags or monkey hammocks for best long-term preservation. Total volume available in the cool locker is eight cubic feet, and the combined volume of all four galley bins is about 22 cubic feet.

Located beside the stove and sink are shallow bins or drawers for cutlery and utensils. Working downward from there, the hull sides are lined with

58

angled shelves with high fiddles. On the port side these shelves stop at the engine room, but to starboard they continue forward underneath the cockpit into the dry-stores hold. In all, there are about 32 linear feet of shelving, for storing cans, jars, bottles, small bags, and boxes of food. No special protection of these items is required because they are not relegated to the bilge; they are all within grasp, labels visible. Gallon-size glass or plastic jugs are kept beneath the galley sole. Six five-gallon plastic pails, with snap-down lids, are used for bulk food storage in the dry-stores hold. The major part of these provisions would remain undisturbed in the event of capsize ... kept dry and confined above the inverted waterline.

Both the engine room and the dry-stores hold are accessible from the galley. The dry-stores hold may, like the engine room, be fitted with a door, thus providing an ideal "bonded locker." In some ports, provisions can be purchased "in bond," or without local tax, provided they can be stowed aboard in a compartment to which the local customs official may attach a seal. This assures that those provisions will not be opened within that country and so may go tax-free, which sometimes makes a substantial difference in their price. The bonded locker can also be used upon entering some ports where the officials might require declaration of such items as alcohol, firearms, and medical narcotics. Thus declared, these items may sometimes be sealed within the bonded locker instead of surrendered for "safekeeping" ashore. With an inconspicuous lock, a place to attach a seal (like the lead and wire gadgets on electric meters), and hidden hatch hardware, this bonded locker could provide valuable protection in some ports. Any sealable compartment will qualify—for instance, one whole ama of the 34—but a more unlikely location with an out-of-sight seal would be better. A light fixture in this compartment, with a push-and-hold switch, is a nice convenience.

That leads us to the subject of lighting, and electricity in general. The 34 is not designed to carry a generator, so the cabins are well equipped with kerosene lamps, the standard farmhouse variety for which inexpensive replacements are available worldwide. They have generous fuel containers and give adequate light for reading if backed by a reflector. They can be mounted on the bulkheads with simple flashlight holders. They require large pie pan heat shields overhead to prevent fire, but no gimbals are needed. A mantle-type lamp, mounted at the sterncastle table, gives great illumination. The kerosene Aladdin, or even a fixed propane lamp such as the ones used in house trailers, each with shade, will give 100-watt light but must be generously heat-shielded and not left burning unattended at full brightness. Unless a vent is provided through the deck above these lamps, they can make the cabin too hot in the tropics.

All kerosene appliances can be filled easily from a standard six-gallon outboard motor fuel tank kept in the fuels hold. Fuel is delivered to the lamps by using the tank's rubber hose. The squeeze-ball primer, when located at the delivery end of the hose (and equipped with a stopper on a string) makes a convenient pump so that no pouring of kerosene is required

The well-stocked galley in the 31-foot Searunner Misumbo . . . *somewhat smaller than the 34's galley. But the boat is being* cruised, *so long-term provisioning is evident.*

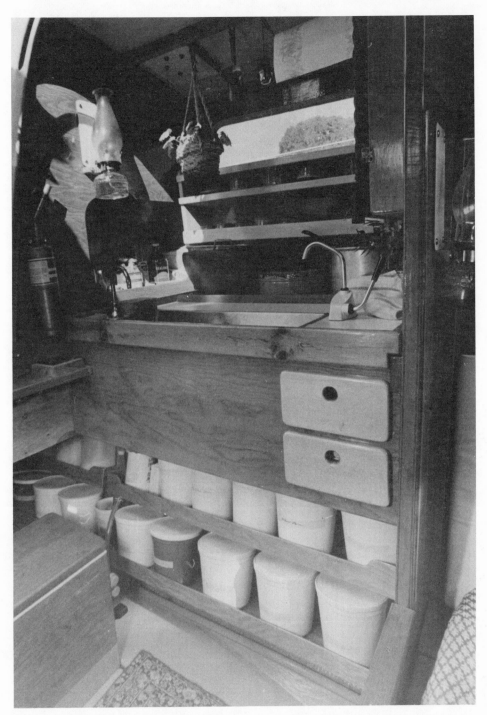

Bins, shelves, drawers, and access to the bulk stowage holds are all visible—with all the food protected from bugs and water in containers that float. (Photos by Tom Crabb)

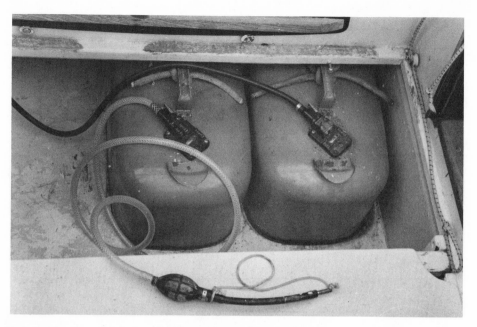

Fuels hold under cockpit is self-bailing and completely isolated from the dry hull. Kerosene is dispensed with the squeeze-ball pump directly into the lamps and stove.

when filling small tanks. The kerosene hose can be taken directly to the appliances in the cabins.

The crew soon becomes accustomed to the odor of kerosene lamps, and discovers that it is a deterrent to flying insects, especially if a few drops of citronella are added to the tank of each lamp. Mineral spirits, available at paint stores, makes a very clean-burning fuel for stoves and lamps.

The biggest bother of kerosene lamps is that they must be lighted with a match. For protecting matches (and the salt shaker) against dampness, they may be kept in a small, tight, metal box attached to the overhead in a position fairly near the galley lamp. Regular use of the galley lamp will generate enough heat to keep the matches (and the salt) dry. Alternatively, gas cigarette lighters also work for lighting lamps. (The age-old problem of the caked-up salt shaker can be solved by preparing a saturated salt solution and dispensing it from a Tabasco-sauce bottle . . . "liquid salt.")

The cruiser's preference for kerosene lighting is not just a preference for the soft and pleasant quality of the light itself; kerosene reduces dependence on electricity. The 34's electrical system is practically nonexistent; there is a compass light and a tri-pole running light at the masthead (with kerosene running lights for backup) and an optional masthead strobe. Small fluorescent fixtures in the galley and over the chart table are a convenience, used to avoid the chore of lighting a lamp when it is needed only briefly; the electric lights in this boat are not intended for reading or other sustained use. All electrical instruments, such as a depth sounder or a transmitter, should be the type that causes only small and intermittent battery drain.

Large solar cell gives 2 amps at 12 volts in bright sun. The Plexiglas cover, stored under the hatch hood, reduces effectiveness 12 percent but offers protection to the unit when a crowd is aboard.

Our aversion to electricity is shared by many seasoned sailors who value the serenity of shipboard life; who have witnessed its destruction by the noise of a generator when the thing runs, and the frustration when it won't run in a craft so dependent upon power that it is helpless without. Because the 34 is not designed to carry an auxiliary generator, nor the fuel for long periods of battery charging with the auxiliary engine, neither is she intended to support a host of pumps and fans and motors. Small electrical demand can be met by recharging during normal operation of the auxiliary engine, or by a solar cell or wind generator.

Wind generator gives 0.4 amp at 12 volts in a 25-knot wind. It mounts clear of crew but makes a howling noise. Both solar and wind units are desirable because at times the wind blows at night and the sun shines in a calm. (Photos by John Marples)

63

ICE? you gotta be kidding

No electrical or mechanical refrigeration is prescribed, although the built-in ice hold will keep a block for several days. One soon becomes accustomed to living without refrigeration when it is simply unavailable, in preference to contending with the hassles of full-time floating refrigeration. You don't have to worry about losing your freezerful of food because a small, inexpensive part in the big, expensive system (a complex, heavy, noisy system required to convert petroleum into ice) gives out at a time and place where, because you were depending on the thing, you are stranded with nothing much to eat. And a Scotch highball mixed with pure rainwater makes a very satisfying sundowner, with ice or without.

Heat, on the other hand, is something that the 34 could sometimes use more of. Multihulls are not generally well suited to cruising in cold climates, and this multihull, with divided cabins and double hatches, is one example. Nonetheless, the spaces are small enough to be warmed by the usual kerosene or charcoal cabin heaters, assuming enough heat is produced to allow ventilating much of it away, thereby controlling condensation. An occasional cold snap can be tolerated by using the galley stove and a dry bunk for respite, until the boat can be sailed into lower latitudes. Fighting the cold at sea is not something normally done for pleasure.

These minimal energy demands are designed into the 34 for the following reason: sophisticated convenience systems requiring a substantial supply of electricity are shown by long experience to detract from the self-contained and independent nature of a cruising sailboat. Seawater is such caustic stuff, and installation problems in a small boat become so extreme, that even the very best equipment installed by the finest of technicians requires a continuing hassle over maintenance, repair, and replacement. These problems in turn limit the vessel (to the degree that her systems are sophisticated) to staying within reach of yachting centers and repair facilities. Learning to do without pressure water and electric light and cold beer is, for many of us, a

"Can't we have heat in the bathroom?" asked Marjorie. So Gerard Arseneau fabricated a fine woodburning stove connected with a hot water radiator in the head compartment of their Searunner 37. This extends the sailing season in their home waters of New Brunswick, Canada. (Photo by Tom Crabb)

rather demanding adjustment. But it is not nearly as unpleasant as doing without the marvelous mobility and freedom of a real cruising boat.

So the 34's galley is not loaded with electrical outlets, and her dishrack does not tremble from the constant hum of a generator. But there is countertop work space, some solid equipment for cooking good meals underway, and an extraordinary volume of organized galley storage. The dry-stores and preserved-food capacity of this galley is adequate to last at least two months for four persons, and the supply can be greatly extended with fresh vegetables from local markets and protein from the sea.

The cook stands between the two distinct departments of the galley, cooking on one side and cleanup on the other, with six feet four inches of headroom and 12 square feet of floor space. All facilities for cooking, cleanup, and storage are arrayed within sight and reach. No other function interrupts this space. But with scarcely a step, the magic sustenance of the galley can be passed to the crew waiting hungrily in the cockpit or the sterncastle.

STERNCASTLE

Moving from the 34's galley to the sterncastle is like going from business to pleasure. No crawling under beams is required; with a slight step up and a little slouch, even a large person can pass easily through the arched portal in the main-strength bulkheads.

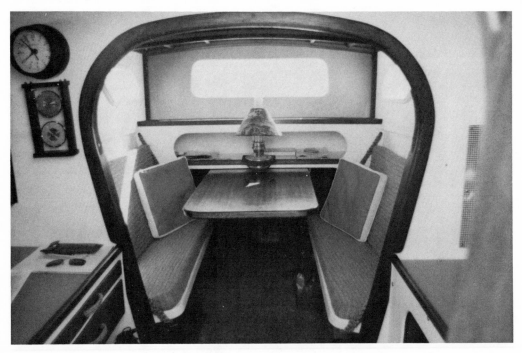

Sterncastle lounge in the Searunner 34. (Photo by Dave Reis)

When seated in the lounge, one's attention is immediately drawn to the large sterncastle window aft, especially if the boat is underway and the window is wide open.

The feature attraction is the wake, streaks of effervescence peeling away astern. This window may be left open even when the boat is driving hard to windward and spray is flying from forward. It may be left ajar in heavy rains, when ventilation is so important. Even when closed tight, this window cannot drip; its casement angles outward at the top, thus allowing gravity to carry any droplets out instead of in.

Because the window swings out to open, it is very resistant to being stove-in by waves. A plywood stormcover is recommended for use when running in storms with warps or drogues or para-anchor dragging astern. Nonetheless, we know that the design of this window, uncovered, can withstand the force of a wave breaking completely over the boat from astern.

The sterncastle is a microcosm of the traveler's own culture. Here the crew can hunker down around the table and enjoy a home-cooked meal. Outside, the ocean may be breathing hard from heavy exercise, or slumbering in calm. Inside, the sterncastle plays host to many pleasantries. A glance out the window might reveal the winking harbor lights of some foreign port, but inside, the occupants create their own environment. Books, music, cor-

The sterncastle plays host
to many pleasantries.

respondence, family and friends—all represent the crew's very own selection or creation. The place provides respite from the excitement of harsh contrasts and rapid change. Perhaps the bulkheads are bedecked with the rich and salty souvenirs of sea travelers, but the travelers feel at home.

If the dinette seats in the sterncastle are arranged with fixed stowage space beneath, there is still plenty of distance between the seats for a convertible single bunk. Optionally, the seats may be built to fold up, which provides the necessary width for a commodious double berth. When the table is slid aft, like a giant breadboard, and the mattress is rolled forward, the sterncastle double berth resembles a great floating waterbed. The whole thing can be stowed away, or rolled out for service, without making or unmaking the bed.

This quick conversion, plus the three bunks in the forward cabin, makes the 34 a weekend cruiser for four persons, even five on occasion. But for living aboard or sustained voyaging, she is best suited to a crew of two or three.

COSTS

Any boat with all these features, which will do all of these wonderful things, can't be cheap. Not cheap enough to be mass-produced and resold with the necessary margin of profit. You'll never see this 34 in a showroom because it cannot be built down to a price.

When the 34 is built and sold in other ways, the owner's investment can vary enormously. If built to order, out of premium materials, by a custom wood-epoxy yachtmaker, the craft might cost 50 to 60 thousand dollars, 1978 prices.

Based on the going rate for good, used, home-built 31's and 37's, and assuming that used 34's were available in 1978, they would be reselling for about 25 to 30 thousand dollars, ready for sea. "Ready for sea" is the expensive part. If outfitting is restricted to just weekending requirements, it would be possible to reduce the total substantially, but we can't see giving partial figures. They lead to boats ill-equipped to accomplish what they're meant for, and they lead to disillusioned clients.

A determined individual can expect to produce successfully his own 34, from plans, as a backyard project. Depending on his skill and time available, such projects take from one to five years. No carpentry or boatbuilding background is required because of the scope of the plans, but the completely uninitiated builder takes longer. His results, however, are oftentimes better than those of the builder who knows how to work fast. There is no way to predict, with any accuracy, the working hours required to complete a backyard boatbuilding project. The figure might vary from about three to over ten thousand amateur man hours. That's a lot of spare time! It is safer to speak in terms of years, and avoid the disappointment of an unattained launch date.

Predicting costs is just about as nebulous. Buying standard-grade materials and all outfitting equipment (as of 1978), the individual may expect to invest somewhere between 15 and 20 thousand dollars in a complete Searunner 34, fully found. Depending on his overall economic policy, that figure might be reduced by 20 percent, or almost doubled, without substantially affecting the suitability of the boat for her intended purpose. Based on long experience with owner-builders, this is the projected range of investment in the 34: one to five years, 12 to 30 thousand dollars. In comparing these figures with those projected for other similar designs, be assured that no firm estimates are possible because the builder is such a huge variable. This boat will cost no more or less than any comparable, complete, owner-built ocean-cruising sailboat.

A Searunner 34 at her mooring.

PERFORMANCE

Because of her accommodations and cargo space and her robust construction, the Searunner 34 does not represent the very latest in a multihull speedburner. Compared with recently built racing machines, she is relatively heavy for her sail area and her length, so the form of her hulls must include enough fullness to support her loaded weight. In this respect she is not unlike the other models in the Searunner series, all of which were designed for something besides speed.

She has a strong, powerful cutter rig. Two headsails, combined with the big, deep centerboard, explain the excellent cruising performance for which these boats are known.

But the 34 is not quite like the others. Old hands will notice a slight readjustment of proportions. She is a touch wider overall, and a bit longer-legged under the wings. The main hull is a shade narrower and a fraction deeper. The minikeel is smaller and the rudder skeg is larger—just a few minor variations on the familiar form. With another 10 years' experience, perhaps other refinements will be made.

At the time of writing, the first 34's are just emerging from their backyard boatyards, but their performance can be reasonably projected because the design is so similar to the 31 and the 37. There have been many boat-for-boat comparisons over the years, and reports seem to justify the following conclusions:

In light airs, the 34's near sisters ghost right along with hot ocean-racing multihulls of similar size. They can do this, however, only when they are not loaded for cruising. The 34 is designed to achieve the security of natural ballast, and to have the best riding motion in rough conditions when floating at her cruising load waterline.

Fully loaded, and sailing in light airs, these craft perform at least as well as loaded monohull cruising craft, and usually much better. Performance in light airs is crucial because the predominant conditions in cruising are light air and heavy load. Any sailing cruiser that will not glide along in the zephyrs is little more than a motorboat.

In the moderate winds, the 34 should compare well with good racing/cruising monohulls on all points of sail. She can be expected to outsail easily the traditional cruising designs of her size, and at least hold her own with contemporary cruising multihulls.

In strong winds, these vessels usually outsail fast monohulls, often those much larger. This is especially true closehauled, because when the wind rips and the seaway rolls, the cutter rig and the centerboard and the skeg rudder truly come into their own.

The centerboard takes credit for the fact that, given proper handling, a Searunner will come about crisply in all conditions. It's not quite like tacking a close-coupled monohull, because you have to "sail through the tack." But when this is done, the centerboard eliminates the need to back the jib or jibe around or steer backwards, as with many multihulls. And when running at high speed in steep seas, the centerboard's long couple with the skeg rudder (one is far away from the other) ensures that she will always answer her helm. It is possible to negate these claims with too much (or too little) sail, but that's not proper handling.

The 34 can be expected to achieve eight knots closehauled to windward, loaded, in protected water and hard wind, and making good about 90 degrees between tacks. Reaching, she will probably make at least 12 knots flat out, no surfing. Both the 31 and the 37, when riding well-formed open ocean waves, running hard downwind and surfing at their best, have achieved bursts of 24 knots, measured on reliable instruments.

Sailing closehauled against open sea conditions is always a real battle, but good cruising multihulls can withstand sustained hard driving against strong headwinds going as fast as the crew can tolerate. Six knots of speed with 100 degrees between tacks and five degrees leeway is anticipated upwind passagemaking performance for the 34, going against normal trades. Virtually the same speed but with 110 to 120 degrees between tacks can be maintained when well reefed against "reinforced trades" of 25 to 30 knots velocity. Even beating against storm seas and winds of 50 knots, the 34, under deep-reefed main and storm staysail, will still make good ground to windward. Many cruising craft are blown helplessly to leeward or left entirely dependent on their engines in these conditions.

These are not certified results, but neither are they wild claims. They are based on my own direct experience and on owners' reports received at the design office over the years.

Cruising speed may be determined by the skipper. The usual Searunner passage time from California to Hawaii, cruising, and self-steering, is about 15 days. But if a gang of huskies push the boat hard, and if they have steady weather, a 37-footer can make the passage in just two-thirds that time. A run of over 200 miles per day, for 10 days in a row, is really romping for an inexpensive, plywood, backyard-built cruising boat!

This discussion of performance might sound superfluous to some sailors. They may believe that a cruising boat does not need to go fast. Strictly speaking, they are right. Even though good speed is sometimes valued highly, just so you can get where you are going, there is nothing that says you've got to get there sooner instead of later. The proponents of great spaciousness for cruising might say that the 34's divided cabin layout is not commodious enough; that she has too much emphasis on speed. Conversely, those who advocate the use of speed machines for cruising will retort that the 34 has too much accommodation and cargo space, and is therefore relatively slow.

But what about safety? Surely it is not the multihull's lack of speed, nor its unexploited spaciousness, that has caused the type to be disfavored by so many experienced keelboat sailors. It is their unexploited safety. The extremely fast multihulls, and the extremely spacious ones, have each contributed the most damage to the reputation of all multihulls. Therefore, a carefully balanced design is very much in order for the type.

We assert that the Searunner 34 can be seriously considered by any sailor who seeks a high level of comfort and performance but who demands safety above all else. It is this balance that is the forte of the multihull configuration.

No one in my acquaintance has enjoyed more completely the full potential of that balance than our co-designer, John Marples. But he didn't get there by himself. Michelle Murray, mate of *Bacchanal,* has been instrumental in convincing John that speed is only part of the picture. After John's TransPac win in 1972, he approached cruising with the same hammer-and-tongs attitude that is required to win races. But there is another attitude required to "win" at cruising. In the following remarks, transcribed from a tape recording, Michelle speaks to all who must change modes to go cruising:

Michelle Murray and Bacchanal . . . *in the cruising mode.*

I just grabbed the mike from John to talk about going slow. It's a new policy of ours and I'm sure it has a lot to do with adjusting to the cruising life. When we first left the States we made fast passages—even a couple of 200-mile days and such. That was okay, but we've gotten into a much slower pace now. When the boat gets down to six knots, instead of putting up another sail, we just say, "Oh, it's all right, this is fast enough." And really, it's so much more comfortable!

This new approach has changed my whole attitude about cruising. I was getting a little bummed out—having some bad reactions to things, like when the wind increases. And about other things like always making plans and being constantly on the go.

It's so nice to slow down. We can go really fast when we have to, or when we want to play. It's so neat! But there's no need to do that all the time. Getting ready to go cruising takes such a lot of planning and work that it's a difficult adjustment just switching over to the cruising mode. I think that's why a lot of women quit cruising right at the beginning. They should stick around, and help convince the skipper that it's time to slow down.

John himself has addressed the problem in a more general way. In talking of selecting a multihull design, he says:

You know, when it gets right down to it, we really don't go *that* fast. Our passage times have been a day or two shorter than the other boats out here in the Pacific, even when we take it easy for comfort, but the difference isn't all that great. When we push hard, the degree of concentration which the speed demands is very draining for a small crew on a long haul. With just the two of us now, it's a different bag than racing with a boatload of skilled crew like the "Santa Cruz Crazies" who helped me win that race.

Because inexperience is the main problem in multihull crews, I think it's wise for a beginner to work his way through several "clunkers" before he undertakes a real "rocket number."

On the other hand, just because we're sailing in a cruising machine doesn't mean we're restricted . . . that we're always running up against the wall. When everything is right, man, we can really *get it on!* At other times it's very nice to know the potential is there.

In the Searunner 34, the potential is there, but that itself may be restrictive. She is not everybody's boat. She is too much chariot to spend her life at the dock, waiting for that occasional 10-mile splash from Woods Hole out to Martha's Vineyard. Also, there is not one smattering of tradition in her; no link with maritime heritage for those who choose to emulate the oldtime sailor's life.

Yet for someone who wishes to live the sailor's life today, this boat makes sense. It is he who may establish instantaneous communication with a craft like this. Probably he is someone who thinks of boats as tools and not as toys. There is something purposeful about these craft; they have a latent independence just waiting to be used. Recreational yachting is fine sport, and the 34 would make a fine, sporty yacht, but contemporary distance cruising is not sport. It is a formative pursuit. It takes a student on the biggest field trip in the world, and brings him back changed.

72

4

Analyzing
Multihulling's Mysteries

"Nobody knows what happened to Arthur Piver. It is the purest kind of sea mystery. He simply disappeared . . . not a trace was ever found of man or boat." That's the answer I've given countless times since "The Father of Modern Trimarans" failed to return from a coastal voyage in 1968. Even today, "What happened to Arthur Piver?" is the question most asked by boatwise people inquisitive about seagoing multihulls. And very often, they don't like the answer.

"But wait a minute," they say. "You've been telling me that multihulls can't just disappear. You've tempted me with an alternative to sinking—but then you say that Arthur Piver simply disappeared."

So attractive is the hope that Piver didn't really disappear that the case is still fraught with rumors. Folks still ask me in hushed tones to divulge his motive for self-imposed exile. Sometimes my inquisitors follow up their questions with a groping plea: "Don't tell me you don't know what happened to Arthur Piver! Tell me what you think *might* have happened to Arthur Piver."

There was no wreckage. Not from Arthur Piver's borrowed boat, there wasn't. But the Skipper's disappearance left his family and friends in a stunned state, and the multihull phenomenon itself was dashed into many drifting fragments.

When Piver was reported overdue, a massive air-sea search began. When it failed to yield results, and no sighting was reported from the populous sections of the California coastline, I guessed that the wreckage of the boat, perhaps with the Skipper still alive, would be discovered along the lonely, mountainous coastline of Big Sur, where my family and I had lived for several years. The geography, currents, and prevailing wind all suggested that something would turn up in the rocky coves or along the isolated beaches

Steve Brown '78

ARTHUR PIVER

that lined the seaboard beneath that fantastic escarpment of the Santa Lucia Mountains.

I combed the coast. I hiked along the cliffs and climbed out on the promontories to peer down into craggy cirques. I walked the beaches, overturning chunks of flotsam from the far corners of the earth, always expecting to uncover a ragged piece of blue-painted plywood, with those model airplane-like longerons attached.

Throughout my lonely vigil I contemplated the nature of my past association with this man Piver, whom I had loved, and rejected, and now wished so much to rediscover. I hypothesized that the relationship between a youth and his mentor must often end sadly; that the Skipper had been a father figure with whom I could resolve natural conflicts. I felt the weight of guilt, and the exuberance of this most important hunt. I recounted the many things that he had taught me, and resolved to honor his successes, and to avoid the pitfalls he so plainly pointed out.

I even fantasized that just beyond the next precipitous point, shrouded in the mist of surf and the odor of drying kelp, I would find him, comfortably camped on the beach with the remnants of the borrowed boat. I would approach, but while still at a distance I would shout, "Doctor Livingston . . . . "

I found nothing.

Neither did anybody else, but the rumor mill went wild with all sorts of outlandish reports. He was down in Bora-Bora with a harem of vahines; he had rendezvoused with a Russian sub and defected to the East to design silent, sailing-hydrofoil sub-chasers; he had skipped out to South America with his bundle to avoid the IRS. Indeed, a private investigator was said to have tailed him through Peru and Bolivia, coming within 12 hours of the trail. All nonsense. There was an insurance investigation, but nothing was ever found.

What is left? Thousands of Piver trimarans, and conjecture. Considering the time and the place, one imaginable circumstance that might explain the disappearance of an unsinkable boat would be collision. The pieces wouldn't sink, but if the captain of the colliding commercial craft had wished to avoid an investigation, perhaps even an international incident, he might have ordered that the pieces be picked up. What else is there to suppose?

That Arthur Piver chose to disappear? Not on your life, or his. He was far too gregarious, too competitive, too vital to bow out consciously.

"Nobody knows what happened to Arthur Piver. It is the purest kind of sea mystery. Not a trace was ever found of man or boat."

Another question I often hear is: "How did you get started designing multihulls? . . . Where do you learn about something like that?" The high-sounding name of some institute would be useful here, but there is none. All I can reply is, "Just by doing it. . . . by being a friend of Arthur Piver's in the early days."

Ah! The early days. It's true all right, I was there, and it was a great time to remember. I was fresh in from the Caribbean, where I'd been sailing in the crew of some large charter schooners, and now I was hoping somehow to acquire my own small boat. I was visiting my parents in San Francisco after several years away from home. I met Arthur Piver through a mutual friend, Don Kogut, who insisted that even though I was broke I could build one of Piver's little trimarans for sailing around on San Francisco Bay. It was 1958. I was 24, Art was 48, and the modern daysailing trimaran had just been born. I invited myself for a sail, and that did it . . . but it wasn't easy.

Piver's boat was offensive to me at first. Having learned to sail on Long Island Sound in a 51-footer, with all the traditional trimmings, I found the 16-footer *Frolic* to be the antithesis of tradition—a collection of angular plywood boxes strung together with two-by-fours and painted vomit yellow. The construction was crude, like a soapbox racer built by an adolescent. "Don't mind her looks," said Arthur. "I built this thing for two hundred bucks! So could you." The "thing" was topped off with a mast made from a large TV antenna, and transparent Mylar sails stuck together with Scotch tape. They rattled in the wind atrociously, like the sound of crinkled cellophane amplified through earphones. But no sooner had those sails filled with wind than the little boat shot forward with head-snapping acceleration . . . a performance drastically different from the schooners I had known.

Piver's attitude was also drastically different, not just from that of traditional sailors, but different from his own on land. The instant we were underway, his mature shoreside manner vanished and he behaved like a big kid. Out on San Francisco Bay the tide was running in a raucous rip, dead against the ocean swell and wind coming in through the Golden Gate. The resulting overfalls would have been perilous for any normal 16-footer, and I was aghast to see the Skipper send *Frolic* plunging straight for the meanest part. "Hope you don't mind getting wet," he grinned. And then, "Here, you steer—straight downwind."

I was hanging on, and wishing I were somewhere else, when the big kid began to sing. It was a popular nonsense ballad of the day, something about, "Feet up, pat 'em on the po-po . . . Let's hear him laugh!" and with that Arthur Piver pointed aft and whooped, "Here comes a pat on the po-po now!" We were overtaken by a steep lump, which promised to inundate our peculiar craft, but the Skipper sprang up and hurled himself against the mast with a grunt and a jolt. The boat lurched forward, catching the wave, and sped away from the curling crest just like a soapbox racer rolling down a moving hill. Piver laughed out loud all the way down, at me. I was transfixed on the tiller, spellbound with fright and delight both at once, and it must have shown in my face.

I had known and loved some fine traditional boats in the East—the sort of love affairs one never recovers from. But so alive was this offensive little craft that all at once I loved her, too. She was incredibly sensuous. I began building . . . I just had to have a *Frolic* for myself.

Or was it the Skipper whom I loved? Now comes the hard part of the story, because the answer to that is yes, but it didn't last.

Piver's boyishness out on the water was infectious, and there were several other young sailors like myself who formed a tight group of friends around the man and his boats.

During those few years around 1960, camaraderie in this group was extremely high. Half a dozen little boats were built on shoestrings, all drawn on butcher paper by the Skipper on his basement floor, and built by members of the clique. This armada of multihull apparitions regularly assaulted the San Francisco yachting fleet from its lair along the Sausalito waterfront. At that time other Bay sailors had never before seen craft that could jump from a dead stop to 10 knots in just a few boat lengths. The gusty winds, steep chop, and strong currents of the Bay provided ideal testing for new ideas. And the relatively ponderous monohulls of the day were easy prey. Often we were seen screaming along in a cloud of spray, cutting around the flanks of the monohull herd and yelling like a bunch of cowpokes on painted ponies. We were also seen limping home ignominiously, at times, with blown-out sails or broken masts or missing rudders, or all three at once. We caused a spectacle that did not endear us to the local yachting fraternity, but God, it was fun!

Our group was growing and Art began selling plans for his little multihulls, some not so little. I had been away in the mountains for a while, working in the snow and dreaming about going back to the Caribbean. In a wave of excitement I realized that a trimaran like *Frolic*, if enlarged to about 24 feet, would probably do a fine job of hopping down the coast to Panama and through the Canal into the Caribbean.

If a 16-footer could deal with that wind-against-tide cauldron underneath the Golden Gate Bridge, then I extrapolated that a 24-footer could deal with the Pacific Coast. I wanted to sail again in clear, warm water in my own boat. I remembered the good parts about Caribbean cruising, and I tried to forget about the times I'd been scared, scared of finding myself in a schooner that was going down. And to tell the truth, I wanted to ride herd on a few charter schooners.

At Christmastime, 1958, I traveled back to Marin County near San Francisco and once again met with my mentor in his basement. There I approached him with my idea—to build an enlarged *Frolic* with a small cuddy-cabin, and put to sea.

He hesitated for a long while. His face was consumed by a pensive grimace that I have since come to recognize. It was his reaction to the weighty responsibility of sending folks to sea in upstart boats. Finally he said, "Well, as a matter of fact, I've drawn up a 24-footer for a guy over in the city." He pulled out the crude drawings, which were labeled "24-foot 'Nugget,'" and said, "See, it's a big four-place daysailer. This guy Carleton Eugene wanted something that would carry four people (*Frolic* was loaded down with two crew), and I guess you could put a little cuddy on it and . . . " He hesitated again. "But Panama? . . . well . . . you know what you're doing, so . . . sure! You could probably sail it anywhere."

It is my guess that the modern seagoing trimaran marks its own conception at that moment.

The following September I sailed south in my *Nugget* with my bride. Jo Anna and I met while I was building the boat, and we soon decided to share the full adventure together. It's been quite a trip—far better for the sharing. Before we ran out of money in Mexico, and returned to California with our developing family, we were able to report to the Skipper by mail that our trimaran was definitely capable of voyaging, marvelously capable. With my background in traditional yachts, I felt confident in making this report.

The following year, 1960, Piver crossed the Atlantic in his own enlargement of the concept, the 30-foot *Nimble*. The year after that, he crossed the Pacific in his 35-foot *Lodestar,* and the boom was on.

"Boom" is the word, because Arthur Piver dramatically publicized all of these early sailings. His boat design was characterized by three traits: freedom from preconception, a great empirical grasp of sailing dynamics, and a crude but unhesitating execution of his ideas. The same features characterized his promotional campaign.

Being in the publishing business gave him access to facilities for producing quantities of leaflets, catalogs, and books. A copywriter by profession, he knew just how to cover the territory in words and pictures, and he did it with the same enthusiasm he displayed for the boats themselves. Through all of this he was a prodigious worker, in nonstop action. To aid others in pronouncing his unusual name, he'd say, "Piver, rhymes with diver." And I'd add, "Driver."

My association with the man was close. It pleased him to have me appreciate his boats because, as he wrote, "Jim was the first experienced sailor to become attracted to our designs." (Always "our," and the editorial "we," to guard against revealing the enormous ego-investment he made in his work. When writing of himself, the closest he would come to first-person-singular were his awkward references to "the Skipper.")

The Skipper's advent in my own life was absolute salvation. I'd been battering around in a state of extended adolescence when we met, hard-pressed to find something to do with myself that had direction. He gave me that direction.

He gave the same to several of our early group. It was almost as if we were disciples, helping him to build the boats, sail the seas, and spread the word.

And a hot gospel it was, for sure. Piver found a thousand ways to say it: " . . . traditional skills not required . . . no more than the cost of an ordinary automobile . . . apparently noncapsizable . . . sailed easily at 24 knots . . . seemingly immune to the ravages of the sea. . . ."

These lines were, in the Skipper's opinion, absolute truth. And in my opinion too, for that matter. I knew what he meant to convey, and I accepted that some enlargement was necessary in order to convey that truth to others. We had an honest cause. These boats were so enormously different from others that there was no describing their sailing sensations. They had to be experienced. A bit of theatre seemed quite an acceptable means to get people out on the water. And it worked. Many hundreds of cause-hungry individuals, who had no sailing experience with which to compare multihulls, did buy the plans, build the boats, and join the cause.

Our enthusiasm was interpreted by shellback skeptics as pure promotional baloney, but uninitiated landlubbers interpreted our promotion to mean that with just a pile of plywood and a pot of glue, the world could be their oyster, too! Nonsailors were so enthralled by Piver's line that they beat a path to his doorway, each with a wad of money in his hand going in, and a roll of boat plans coming out. When his regular advertisements read, "Discover WHY there are thousands of Piver trimarans," the takers eventually learned it was partly because the Skipper had done a truly fabulous job of marketing the plans. He knew his audience, and he spoke to them directly.

As this commercialism grew more obvious, it undermined the associations between the Skipper and his crew. The disciples became jealous of the success in which they had participated so loyally. They felt that the Skipper was tight on screen credits. They began to express their own acquired prowess in multihull design and sailing. And Arthur Piver reacted with a hurt possessiveness, a proprietary, sovereign claim on the very concept of the double outrigger.

This sad dissonance was accompanied by a heightened hullabaloo between the yachting fraternity and the multihull proponents. All of us involved with the new boats had discovered in them a source of identity. It was as if we were participating on an anthropological level, consciously initiating what we knew was to become a viable subcultural spur. If that sounds pompous for a mere sailboat design, consider that the boats themselves were, and are, the vehicles of a distinctive lifestyle still emerging, a philosophy purporting to be free from the ballast of conservatism—vibrant, buoyant, fast, fun. The expression of this new identity by multihull sailors, and the performance of the boats themselves (sometimes) was found rather threatening by those who were aligned with the dour caution and ritual of traditional yachting. In this charged atmosphere, Piver's potent promotional bombardment—in the magazines, at the boat shows, and on the bookshelves—was cause for a return of fire. Piver's was the voice of the prophet, the herald, the authority. It began as a bold cry in the wilderness, but it slowly developed the intonations of the sideshow barker. There was lots of able competition intent on getting equal time. In the dialogues taking place with traditional yachtsmen and within the multihull fraternity, the voice of Arthur Piver became the voice to be shouted down.

My wife and I were among those who observed and participated. We were hard pressed to make a living in the direction that the Skipper had so fatefully indicated. Art and I discussed arrangements for me to assist in the operation of his burgeoning business, which taxed the Skipper's patience because it was noncreative. But I didn't recognize the opportunity. I was young and impatient. I wanted to *design*. I felt I knew enough about the boats to generate improvements, at least in the plans themselves. I believed that I could draw plans that would remove the need for such dangerous improvisations as were going on in the backyard boatyards. After all, I was a backyard builder myself, but unlike most, I had some experience at sea. Piver's builders were not exactly encouraged to improvise, but his plans required it to some degree. For the most part, these builders knew nothing of boats and the sea. There was rampant abuse of the scant, developmental design information then available. Many people used the plans second-, third-, and fourth-hand, thus further widening the gap between the builder and the designer.

This effect was multiplied by the Skipper's suggestion that anyone, regardless of experience, could cheaply and easily build his trimaran and safely go to sea. Many neophytes have succeeded in this, but such a claim sparked unfounded confidence and insatiable expectations. Arthur's off-handed casualness toward the challenges of seafaring ("We've got more solutions than we've got problems"), and his cornball prose about "girl-infested islands" far from "the organization world," caused many of his customers to fantasize a great escape from their workaday lives ashore. When these ill-prepared Magellans tightened up the last turnbuckle and set sail, they often discovered that escaping to the ocean is a jump out of society's frying pan into the fires of reality.

This explains why there are so many atrocious multihulls marooned in the world's harbors, their disillusioned owners leaving them to the doom of disuse. Some of the early owner-built boats were truly excellent, and were sailed a long way. So many others were never finished, or still bear conspicuous harborfront testimony to broken dreams. Because standardization was lacking in the owner-built boats, the original *Frolic, Nugget*, and

Nimble designs were botched up until the poor things wouldn't go to windward, couldn't come about, and looked like holy hell afloat. The Skipper's promotional contentions continued in a blitz, but he was running on what he knew *could* be done with multihulls, not what *had* been done. The man's unbounded optimism transformed hope and foresight into hard fact within his own consciousness.

Because the Piver faction of the multihull movement was largely peopled with beginning sailors, there resulted a great rash of landlubberliness. Poor boat management in crowded waters might have gone unnoticed, or might have been accepted out of kindness toward the learning sailor, if it had occurred in what Piver called "ordinary boats." But because the multihull stood out, and because wild claims were being made for the craft in spite of evidence to the contrary (and also because some convincing demonstrations supported a sneaking suspicion that multihulls could be damned good boats in the hands of more experienced builders and sailors), their blunders inspired ridicule, even hatred, on the part of the yachting establishment. In the growing controversy there were good grounds on both sides.

The flak became thick for Arthur. The enemy had lots of ammunition— plenty of examples of bad trimarans, supposedly produced to his designs. In order to support his claims, he took up big-time racing.

With the devoted assistance of Rich Gurling, one of the original crew, Piver built two impressive racers: the 38-foot *Bird* and the 33-foot *Stiletto*. And with Rich aboard as crew, they campaigned these vessels all over the world, making voyages to Australia and England in order to arrive at the starting lines.

In spite of his determination, the Skipper never had the satisfaction of a conclusive victory at the finish. He would fly home from the races and write glowing tales of incredible runs on certain stretches of the course, and imply that if the halyard hadn't broken or the currents hadn't been deceptive, they would have . . . and so it went. His habit of writing about a failure so as to make it sound like a great success caused well-founded anger among his competitors. The flak got thicker.

He was constantly on the defensive, whether in a dockside gab or a boat show presentation. Novices were often spellbound, but the more experienced sailors—even some multihull sailors from the original carefree, fun-loving group—were sometimes repulsed. This was no longer the big kid who whooped and hollered for sheer joy, and sailed like a bronco-buster. This was an aggressive businessman preoccupied with the threat of competition and bitter about the encroachments of others on what he considered his sovereign territory, the trimaran itself.

I was the first to trespass on home ground. While Art was making a Pacific voyage in 1963 I drew the lines for my first boat, a 38-footer called *Off Soundings*. When Art returned to California I presented him with the drawings, suggesting that he might consider adding the boat to his stable. Our friendship terminated.

The maestro reacted to the impudence of his protege by kicking him out.

It hurt, but it was good for me. He, for his part, seemed to derive little satisfaction from having produced a protege, which is a shame, because his great achievement was that he produced so many.

All over the world, boatwise individuals were inspired by his enthusiasm to enter the multihull field. Not just to buy a boat and sail it, or to build a boat and sail it, but to start at the ultimate level of complete involvement—by designing a boat.

Art Piver was not alone in providing stimulus and direction to fledgling multihullers, but he was certainly the most vocal and inspiring. Unfortunately, he considered all competition in designing trimarans to be simple plagiarism. In a way, he was right. Victor Tchetchet coined the word "trimaran," but Arthur Piver produced the first one that really worked well. And he let the world know it.

Others from the early group of sailing friends began to "plagiarize." Lauren Williams, who for several years did all the drafting and a good portion of the designing of many Piver multihulls, eventually expressed to the Skipper his intention to hang out his own shingle. As Williams described the incident to me, "He took the news without any sign of emotion, and I was hopeful of preserving our long friendship. But from that moment on, there simply ceased to be a friendship, or any communication whatsoever."

Through the mid-1960s, each veteran of our original group resorted to designing his own boat. Fred Jukich, Piver's old flying, skiing, and sailing buddy, finally designed and built his own trimaran. Rich Gurling, who spent so many months at sea with the Skipper, eventually declined further invitations to crew and developed his own small racer.

Nobody, but nobody, could contest Art Piver's claim that he took his boats to sea for thorough testing. The results were always described as unqualified successes, but without the Viking-like seamanship of Gurling, there would doubtless have been some unconcealable failures.

This is why I was so surprised to learn that Arthur Piver planned to enter *Stiletto* in the 1968 OSTAR (Observer Singlehanded Transatlantic Race). Singlehanded! He had never sailed singlehanded anywhere! In my opinion, as an ocean sailor he was not a natural. Don't get me wrong—few watermen could "feel" a boat, and second-guess the moody sea, like he could. But he was impatient with the all-important details of preparation, navigation, and tactics. He was at his very best at an informal rollick, sailing for the fun of sailing. But singlehanded racing?! I saw this as a sign of desperation.

Stiletto was lying in England well before the race, having unofficially run along with the monohulls in the 1966 Bermuda race, finishing behind two-thirds of the fleet because of sail damage. From Bermuda she was sailed to England and entered in the 1967 Crystal Trophy Race for multihulls, finishing sixth. The craft was left in England while Art returned to California. (During these forays, almost the entire operation of his busy basement office was ably managed by his wife, Florence.)

In order to qualify for the 1968 OSTAR, each contestant had to have previously sailed 500 miles solo, nonstop, but not necessarily in the boat to be used for the contest. (This ruling has since been changed to 1,000 miles, and in the same boat.) Because Piver had done no offshore singlehanding, and because his boat was in England, he decided to borrow a boat belonging to one of his customers and sail it from San Francisco south to San Diego, a distance of about 500 miles in water already familiar to the Skipper.

The only boat conveniently available to him was a 25-footer hurriedly built by a serviceman who had been transferred overseas. Preparations for this qualifying passage were made while the craft lay at Kappas' harbor in Sausalito, the old familiar lair. A friend of mine who was living aboard at an adjacent dock later described these preparations something like this: "That boat he borrowed was a mess. It had hinges in the crossarms to fold for trailering, and the hinges were working loose. The hull was leaking, the windows were weak, the rig was sloppy . . . and Piver acted like he wasn't up for it. The whole thing came together like he just didn't care."

" . . . like he just didn't care." I still hear the words. But why should he? He was just trying to put an annoying prerequisite out of the way so that he could get on with the real thing.

But I believe the real thing had already gone by for Arthur Piver. The last few times I saw him, it appeared that all the controversy had taken the high-flying fun out of being who he was, "The Father of the Modern Trimaran." His health mirrored disillusion. More critical, but never mentioned, was the falling away of all his adopted sailing sons, one by one. Of the original Sausalito clique, only Bill Goodman, a crewman on the first Atlantic voyage, preserved his friendship with Arthur to the end. Although he designed and built his own trimaran, Bill in his strict, gentlemanly way never expressed any dismay at the Skipper's dogma, a hard line to which the great promoter himself always adhered.

Yes, he certainly believed every "wild claim" he made. Looking back, I can better understand the frustration he felt in trying to convey the simple truth about his boats. His early statements actually contained some reservations: "apparently noncapsizable" and "seemingly immune to the ravages of the sea." But with more experience offshore—and he had plenty—he became increasingly less cautious. Finally, he said things like, "Here are boats that the sea cannot hurt." A wild claim for sure, but it was meant as a relative truth, and he believed it. As a relative truth, I believe it, too.

Years afterward, Bill Goodman wrote of Art Piver: "He knew, I think, that he was drifting away on strange currents from the free spirit he had partly been, and wished himself entirely to be. But one's later years are often sad, and many men must swallow that bitter pill, though the dosage varies widely."

In March of 1968, Arthur Piver tacked out through the Golden Gate for the last time. I like to think of him grinning in the cockpit of his borrowed boat, aglow with recollections of riding herd on the gold-platers in that same water every summer Sunday afternoon. Or beating through the narrow sluice between Fort Point and the south tower of the bridge, against a roaring tide and a hard wind, just to let the *Frolic* show that she was well named. Then he would remember clawing out to Point Bonito and lurking there, like a barracuda, waiting to strike at the first unsuspecting inbound freighter.

When his prey came steaming up the channel, the strange yellow boat would dart out in pursuit. From the cockpit, a vital man waved to the freighter's crew, who were collected on the fantail wearing expressions of disbelief. Climbing up the ship's wake, *Frolic* "curtsied" on the stern wave's peeling crest and dived off dramatically to surf the wall! The Skipper was trimming sheets with his teeth and steering quickly to play the wave and chase the ship, and all the while he was yelling out for joy.

Surely these marvelous memories passed through Arthur Piver's contemplation as he closed The Gate behind him. Perhaps, from underneath the Cliff House, the faint barking of sea lions accompanied his musings on his many sailing friends. Together, the sea lions' barking and the friends' voices must have faded into the familiar freight-train rumble of distant surf, as the Skipper found himself for the first time alone with the sea.

Nobody knows what happened to Arthur Piver.

There are other pure sea mysteries in the youthful heritage of modern multihulls.

In several incidents only wreckage was found, with no explanation for the disappearance of the crew. In at least one other well-publicized event, "not a trace was ever found." This was the utter vanishing of Mike McMullen and his fine trimaran racer, *Three Cheers*. Mike was a former Royal Marine who had successfully campaigned *Three Cheers*, a swift 46-foot Newick design. He was very well prepared to compete in the 1976 OSTAR, and because of the combination of great sailor and great boat, he was considered a serious contender for first place against the formidable competition of much larger craft. As the starting date approached, however, Mike's closest friends noticed a change in his behavior. He became moody and irrational. Then a few days before the race, Lizzie McMullen, Mike's wife, was killed in a bizarre accident. The two of them were working on last-minute preparations of the boat, and Lizzie was electrocuted when she attempted to retrieve an electric tool that had fallen in the water.

This alone may have impaired the sailor's judgment in the race that followed, but it would not explain McMullen's prior change in behavior. He insisted on competing in spite of the circumstances, and after the start he was never seen again. It was known that he intended to sail the northern route from England to Rhode Island. On this course he would have encountered some terrible gales in the beginning of the race, and these probably would have driven him farther north, perhaps into areas of floating ice.

Serious contenders in these singlehanded contests are subjected to enormous psychological pressures. Anyone who would choose to test his mettle by taking such a challenge must surely possess strong identity and will. Singlehanding, of itself, is intensely cathartic; but when the stimulant of high-level competition and the bait of worldwide adulation are added to this quest of self, then, in my opinion, the race assumes a stuntlike quality. It would seem that only the most stable and mature of sailing's superstars can perform in these solitary rituals without suffering damaging character modification.

McMullen was apparently a stable and mature individual. He had withstood the test of competition, though never singlehanded, and had recently written the book *Multihull Seamanship* (David McKay Co., New York), the contents of which attest to his knowledge and achievement as a multimariner. Yet his usual level-headedness and companionability somehow changed as the race date approached. His behavior was described by one close acquaintance as "manic," and those who understood the circumstances said his disappearance was "not a multihull-related incident."

If indeed he sailed off into the far North Atlantic, the vastness of that unfrequented ocean would explain the disappearance of *Three Cheers*, but again we are left with conjecture alone to appraise the effect of stress on his behavior; there was the natural anxiety over such a race, combined with the tragic loss of his wife. His book, and his memory, remain as significant contributions to the multihull tradition.

There are yet additional mysterious sea stories in which the effects of competition may have played a key role. The earliest example was the 1968 disappearance of Australian designer Hedley Nicol, with two companions, in the 36-foot trimaran *Privateer*. This occurrence was documented for me by Hedley's father, Hunter Nicol, in a touching exchange of correspondence in January 1968. The best way to describe the incident is to quote directly from Hunter Nicol's first letter:

Dear Mr. Brown,

I have read your article on multihulls in the December 1967 issue of *Rudder* magazine, and note in particular your references to my son, Hedley Nicol. I thank you for your kind remarks about him.

Hedley was a good son. He was taught to be cautious, and carried this learning throughout his life. He was considered to be an excellent companion.

His work in the designing, building and sailing of trimarans was receiving attention throughout the world when, at the request of a man from the U.S.A., he decided—rather suddenly—to sail across the Pacific for the express purpose of showing his latest design in the World Boat Show in California.

Hedley had a very wide knowledge of sailing catamarans and trimarans . . . . Without any exaggeration I would consider him equal to anyone, at least in this country . . . .

Fully provisioning *Privateer* for the entire trip, and with a crew of two other experienced multihull sailors, he left the coast here on August 17, 1966. On the 19th he radioed, "300 miles out all going well love to all at home Hedley." That was the last ever heard of them.

As they did not arrive in California in time for the November show, an alert was sent out by Hedley's agent in California . . . . From weather bureau reports I later ascertained that a heavy NNE gale came up only hours following my son's radio message . . . .

On September 2, 1967, the port outrigger hull of the *Privateer* was found about two miles off the NE coast of North Island, New Zealand. This was thirteen months after departure. It was secured by fishermen and handed over to the New Zealand police, who in turn contacted me. I was able to positively identify it as the port float of my son's boat. It was found empty, floating upside down with the two hatch covers missing, and a considerable amount of marine growth on the sides and decking. Otherwise it was in perfect order, showing no sign of structural damage . . . .

A number of messages were scribed on the float, but due to the loss of time in finding it these were mainly lost. The police worked with infrared lamps to assist in the recovery of the messages, and . . . this is my reconstruction of what happened:

I believe they lost their mast in the gale . . . the sails would fill with water . . . the boat would be out of control . . . with deep swells and winds as high as seventy-five knots, the boat was turned over. After the gale subsided, an attempt was made to re-right the boat.

Hedley had previously stated that if he were ever to capsize he would cut off one float with a saw, flood the other float, and attempt to re-right the craft in this manner. Then he would attempt to handle the main hull and one outrigger as a catamaran. I now accept the position that they failed in their attempts. As a last resort, messages were scratched on the severed float, and it was cut adrift in hopes of getting assistance.

We know that the main hull and starboard float definitely would not sink, and we are hopeful that someday the wreckage may be found. Then the sea may give us the real story of what did actually happen.

This is about all I can tell you, Mr. Brown, of what I know about the loss of my son, his crew, and *Privateer*. I consider Hedley had a brilliant mind in regards to boats, and losing him at the age of 39 leaves the boating fraternity poorer. He left a sorrowing wife, one son, and one daughter, and we his parents to mourn his loss . . . .

Well, Mr. Brown, I must now draw to a close, hoping that what I have written will be of some value to you in your career among the trimarans.

With kindest regards and fraternal greetings from

Yours sincerely,
Hunter Nicol

P.S. May I mention that Hedley was never once defeated in sailing two of his own designed-and-built trimarans: *Vagabond* for 28 wins and *Privateer* for 8 wins. These were in bay and ocean races under all weathers and against all types of sailing craft.

Before the disappearance, we received with great excitement the news that Hedley Nicol was coming to California. We had heard of the remarkable sailing exploits of this most gregarious of multihull sailors. And he seemed to be a charmed competitor: 36 consecutive firsts on Australia's tough racing circuit. We also knew of his propensity to test his designs ruthlessly. He was the only multimariner to undertake a storm-wind speed trial in a large, stripped-down trimaran, pushing the craft all the way to what was essentially an on-purpose capsize. Eyewitnesses called his 36-footer, *Vagabond*, "the flying trimaran": she literally took off from the water like an aircraft and performed a slow roll in mid-air. Hedley shortly had the vessel back in competition.

His father's remark about Hedley Nicol being an "excellent companion" was widely confirmed. I for one was eager to make his acquaintance, for he had the air of being a real designer's designer—hard sailing, fun-loving, and humble. His boats were good, very good for their time.

But what could explain his impulsive decision to sail some 6,000 miles, nonstop, for the stated purpose of displaying his boat in a show? There were many Nicol designs already under construction in California; his plans were being marketed successfully in the United States. It would not seem practical to make such an arduous voyage just to accomplish a display.

Well, the multihull grapevine reported that Hedley's keen sense of competition was aroused by the bombastic claims of speed made by Arthur Piver, claims that Hedley had reason to doubt because of the performance of the Piver boats then sailing in Australia. It was said that Hedley Nicol intended to ride herd on the Skipper himself.

In a demonstrative statement of Australian pluck—that characteristic Down-Under willingness to "give it a go"—Hedley forgot the cautious teachings of his father, sailed at the height of the austral winter, and lost his life.

The mystery of the *Privateer* was contemporary with the well-publicized losses of the crews from two other Australian racing multihulls. *Vagabond*, Hedley's previous boat, was found dismembered, floating in company with a dead whale; and *Bandersnatch*, a Crowther racer, was shipwrecked in a storm on a vicious offshore bar. Both crews were lost. These incidents sparked public outrage against multihulls, a controversy from which the Australian contingent has not yet fully recovered.

I have often been amazed at the extensiveness of the multihull grapevine, and Hedley Nicol's case contains one more example. The year following his disappearance I learned from one of my clients about a conversation that took place aboard a military vessel in Japan. My friend was visiting aboard a foreign-flag frigate, and learned that the captain was a sailing enthusiast. When it developed that my friend sailed a trimaran, the frigate's first officer remarked that he had once discovered the hulk of a capsized Nicol trimaran at sea. There being no survivors, he ordered his gunners to destroy the drifting wreck, it being a hazard to navigation. Apparently the incident was never reported officially. That incident may explain at least one of the few mysterious cases in which a multihull has disappeared "without a trace."

When wreckage is found, but no survivors, the mystery of disappearance still exists. One such case was that of the *Triple Arrow*, a noble racing trimaran sailed by Brian Cooke, an experienced and respected British yachtsman. The boat was designed by Andrew Simpson, who would later refer sadly to the beautiful 50-footer as luckless.

Triple Arrow competed in the 1974 Round Britain Race, in which she was capsized by a vertical blast of wind off a cliff under which she was lying becalmed, but was recovered with prompt outside assistance. Cooke's remarkable appetite for contest led him to resume racing immediately, and he finished the two-thousand-mile course in eighth position overall!

Early in 1976 he took up a contest against time alone, in an attempt to sail singlehanded a distance of 4,000 miles in 20 days (20 200-mile days). There were no other competitors. Sir Francis Chichester, who conceived the undertaking, had previously attempted the same stunt on the same course (transatlantic from northeast to southwest) and failed to meet his goal. Cooke took up the challenge and was eventually reported overdue. Six weeks later, *Triple Arrow* was found in the vicinity of the Canary Islands, capsized again, with no trace of the lone sailor. Whether he was separated from the craft before, during, or after capsize is yet another matter for conjecture.

What motivates a man to drive himself and his craft in pursuit of such a hypothetical destination, wherein there *is* no destination; only time/speed/distance? What psychological result can one expect while performing as a solitary superstar? These questions come to mind when pondering the ironic fates of two more British sailors, Nigel Tetley and Donald Crowhurst, and their 40-foot trimaran sisterships, *Victress* and *Teignmouth Electron.*

Contestants in the first running of the biggest stunt of all, the 1968-69 singlehanded race nonstop around the world, neither Tetley nor Crowhurst finished; Tetley was rescued after abandoning his broken boat when almost home, and Crowhurst was apparently lost overboard. The evidence suggests that Tetley drove his boat to pieces in an attempt to beat Crowhurst back to England. And Crowhurst pressed his countryman to this by fraudulent reports of his own progress—indeed, he had not sailed around the world at all, but simply lurked in the South Atlantic while the other contestants ran the distance around the bottom of the globe. But on the final leg for dear old England, Crowhurst became unwilling to complete his fraud, which would surely have been uncovered, and the resultant anguish apparently drove him insane. Dual logbooks were later found aboard the drifting, undamaged *Teignmouth Electron,* one to substantiate his supposed circumnavigation and one to record his actual route—which never left the Atlantic. Notations indicate that under these stressful circumstances he lost contact with reality and stepped off into the sea.

Nigel Tetley later victimized himself in a bizarre suicide ashore. Neither boat was capsized, but the minds of both men were somehow turned inside-out.

There appears to be a fair share of nationalism involved in these contests. Robin Knox-Johnston, who eventually won the first singlehanded round-the-world race in his monohull *Suhaili,* expressed this nationalism as an aside when giving his motives for participating. Included in his otherwise reasonable explanation was the revealing admission, " . . . so the Frogs won't get it."

The face-off between the British and the French is particularly heated in these affairs. For example, the singlehanded transatlantic race is organized by the British, but the French have been first to finish three times out of five. Their recent tendency has been to enter in "monsterboats," such as the 236-foot, four-masted schooner *Club Méditerranée,* which was built especially for the race at enormous cost with funds provided by the French resort chain. After the 1976 race made it obvious that such gargantuan vessels could not be fairly classed as singlehanders, the British organizers ruled out anything longer than 56 feet. The French promptly announced the staging of their own unlimited event, the Route du Rhum, featuring some $200,000 in prizes as bait.

While the relationships between the contestants are usually quite proper, and the races have a truly international flavor, the atmosphere has become increasingly charged, like that of the Olympics, with disputes over government sponsorship, corporate sponsorship, professionalism, and nationalism. And against this background we see the lone mariner sailing off across the sea to try to beat the other guy and the other flag.

All very well, but when international rivalries are concentrated in singlehanded, nonstop ocean races, and the vehicles chosen are sometimes developmental multihulls, we must anticipate that accidents are inevitable.

More alarming to me is the fact that these highly publicized attractions tempt inexperienced individuals to undertake foolhardy voyages. A grave confusion exists in the boating public's mind between racing and cruising, especially when it comes to multihulls. I would like to see the separation made distinct, with the emphasis of each on safety.

It isn't just the sailors who find themselves involved. After Mike McMullen disappeared, Dick Newick, the designer of his boat, expressed the tensions suffered by the families and friends of those who compete in such events. "I wish it were a doublehanded race," said Dick. "I'm tired of agonizing over these guys." And then speaking for himself—but also for everyone involved— he added, "Well, if you're going to play these rough games, you can expect to get hurt."

There is another rough game in boating, which is sometimes played with multihulls. It involves cops-and-robbers competition, and may even include a little race. It is called smuggling.

In spite of the contention that multihulls are poor load carriers, and even though past experience has long since caused customs authorities to peg them as likely suspects, still there are many attempts made to carry contraband in cats and tris. Nothing in the movement has led to a longer list of broken boats and broken lives.

Incredible voyages are undertaken in this quest. The Pacific run from central Mexico to San Francisco, for instance, is over 2,000 miles long, almost all closehauled against a strong northwester. But the passage can be timed so that the craft will enter the Golden Gate on a Sunday afternoon, along with the local yachting fleet returning from a day of dipping toes in the ocean. Supposedly the ocean-weary smugglers can slip in unsuspected, eluding the coastal dragnet perhaps already on alert for their vessel.

Such was said to be the plan of one Goliath Rivers, master of the lean and hungry trimaran *Myopia*, which departed Puerto Vallarta in December 1971.

Such an ambitious passage was nothing new to Rivers; he had made the

Pacific circuit twice before: California, Hawaii, Central America. He was a real wayfaring adventurer who had endeared himself to the quiet people of many remote villages along the western seaboard. Those who sailed with him described fantastic adventures, both ashore and at sea.

Rivers was a hell-bent sailor. I once received a tape recording made aboard his 42-footer while she was running hard in a North Pacific gale; the sounds were of high-pitched vibrations . . . long, pealing wails coming from the craft as she sliced the sea, locked in and surfing for minutes at a time on mature deep-ocean waves. The crew, too, emitted wails, and shouts of fright and glee.

But on the December voyage in question, the craft was loaded down with contraband and hauled up by-the-wind for days, bashing out the miles in desperation. Rivers and one crewman, together with a dog and a monkey, were deprived of any respite by their cargo—no familiar stops along the coast of Baja, no port possible in a storm.

Furthermore, there was no prudence in their pace, no heaving-to for breakfast or to catch a steady sextant sight, for there was more at stake than the cargo. There was the race. The contest. The point of honor lay in beating *another* trimaran to San Francisco!

Cal Wursterberger, skipper of the trimaran *Dancing Barefoot*, had issued a challenge just as the two boats left the anchorage in that lonely cove on Flag Bay. Together the crews had gone up into the mountains to meet their suppliers, carrying their money and their guns, and returned by muleback with the stuff. And together they planned to enter San Francisco. But whichever boat was first to arrive off the Farallon Islands, in the approaches to the Golden Gate, would win the race. It was a serious challenge, the ultimate test of boats and wills.

Wursterberger made it, and sold his load, but admitted, "It was the hardest money I've ever made," and he later became embroiled in massive complications with the law.

Myopia was discovered weeks later, drifting upside down 130 miles west of the Farallons. The cargo was still aboard, but one outboard hull had been amputated, perhaps by a collision. Rivers and his crew were gone (perhaps taken off by the colliding vessel, to disappear under cover on account of their cargo). The monkey had eaten the dog.

So it is that the young heritage of modern multihulls has its share of classic sea mysteries. By collecting the above accounts I do not wish to imply that it is only the racing craft that have come to grief, or that all multimariners suffer exotic psychological effects. On the contrary, several cruising capsizes are recorded in the next chapter, where they are examined for the knowledge of multihull safety that was gained from their survivors.

And of course many races, and very many cruises, have been completed without capsize. Multihull sailors are often the most stable and reasonable of folks. They possess the authenticity to select something different because it is something they can truly understand and make work for them.

One cardinal example is the story of *Queequeg's Odyssey,* written by young Quen Cultra and published in 1977 by the Chicago Review Press. This account is capsulized in the first sentence of the book's preface, which reads:

> With little money and no previous experience in boat construction, sailing or navigation, I built a trimaran in a Midwestern barnyard, launched it in the Illinois River, and sailed around the world.

Cultra's story is but one of many published—and hundreds of unpublished—accounts of workaday individuals who have sailed the world in backyard multihulls. Like *Queequeg's Odyssey,* these are true-life sea stories laced with every form of honest adventure and formative experience, and as such would sound like music to Arthur Piver's ears. This was what he wanted most, "a yacht in which the common man can sail the world, but which he can build for roughly the cost of an ordinary automobile." *Queequeg* cost a bit more than an ordinary car: $6,100 in 1969, plus 25 man-months of "unskilled" labor. Like the rest of us, Quen learned his seamanship the hard way, and his vessel gave him—forgave him—that opportunity.

Another worthwhile multihull book, which makes an effective contrast to the cruising yarns, is a little volume called *Multihull Ocean Racing* by Richard Boehmer (Boehmer Publishing, Riverside, R.I.). Richard has produced a black-and-white kaleidoscope of fascinating forms: dozens of simple line drawings show many of the vessels engaged in the first decade of organized offshore competition for catamarans, trimarans, and proas. These drawings are all done to the same scale so that the viewer gains some appreciation of the stupefying variety of shapes and sizes that have put to sea in the name of multihull racing. Each of the major fixtures is described, giving details of the course and a history of the contest. Salient design features for 40 different boats are presented with the drawings, as well as race records and biographical high points of the designers and sailors.

It is in reading the biographical comments that one appreciates both the remarkable successes and the monumental disillusions that have characterized the multihull's brief history. This is indeed a dual phenomenon, with dreadful failures vying for attention with startling achievements. One cannot but realize, when reading Boehmer's book—and Cultra's too—that these are chronicles of a stormy era not unlike the early days of aviation, telling of the men and women who laid the groundwork for a time when perhaps we will again use the power of clean, free wind for transportation.

The early tragedies at sea, by their very nature, caused the public image of the oceangoing multihull to be steeped in deep, dark mystery. For over a decade, our quest to understand the phenomenon of capsize was thwarted because there were no "flight recorders," no survivors to tell us what had happened. All we had to go on was the wreckage.

5

The Castaways Came Back

Not until the middle 1970s were there several capsizes in which offshore castaways survived to tell their tales. From these we began to piece together the essence of multihull capsize; we slowly realized the enormous significance of the main difference between capsize and other forms of maritime disaster, namely, that after the capsize, the boat doesn't go away.

From the information that began to trickle in, we were eventually able to draw certain conclusions about the causes of capsize and how it could be effectively prevented; and about the aftermath of capsize and how it could be prepared for. These facets, capsize preparation and capsize prevention, are described in Chapters 6 and 7, respectively. For now, let's briefly recount the incredible tales of survival that made those two chapters possible.

There must be a hundred trimarans named *Trident* or *Triton*, but one in particular is significant to us—the Piver 31 named *Triton*, built by James Fisher near Seattle, Washington. It was a two-year backyard project, costing Fisher about $5,000 in materials. *Triton* was well built for her cost, and well used for protected-water cruises on Puget Sound during the summer of 1972.

The following summer a serious sea voyage was undertaken, its destination being Costa Rica, where Fisher planned to devote himself to missionary work.

For this venture, Fisher enlisted his wife's brother, Bob Tininenko, and Bob's wife, Linda, as crew. None of the three had any deep-sea experience. Fisher's wife, Wilma, stayed behind; she was pregnant with their third child, and it later developed on the voyage that Linda was carrying her first, a fact that she had not disclosed to her husband because she felt it might interrupt their plans to join the cruise.

Some cruise!

Having proceeded only as far as the northern California coast, they were set upon by an unusually fierce summer gale. By steering attentively for an agonizing 12-hour stint at the helm, Bob Tininenko managed to keep the bows headed straight away from the largest waves throughout the 60-knot segment of the blow. They carried a small storm jib and dragged three drogues astern, and Bob resisted the temptation to steer diagonally across the seas toward land. These were the correct tactics of multihull seamanship for the prevention of capsize.

But after the worst was over and Bob was ready to collapse, Fisher took the helm. In what was probably his attempt to run toward the coast, he allowed the boat to head obliquely across the seas, which caused it to broach wildly. After stern warnings from Bob, the vessel broached again on a particularly vicious sea, and capsized.

Now, here's the amazing part of this sea story: without having made any preparations for the aftermath of capsize, even without having acknowledged the possibility of capsize in their pre-cruise planning, two of the three persons aboard the *Triton* were still alive when rescue arrived—some 72 days later! The derelict had drifted a thousand miles since the capsize, and officials were incredulous that the stricken trimaran could go that far, for that length of time, without breaking into pieces.

The grisly ordeal of the *Triton*'s crew is related in a book entitled *Lost*, which was written by Thomas Thompson with Tininenko's cooperation, and first published in 1975 by Atheneum. But the story was not widely read until reprinted by Dell as a paperback in 1977. The account contains no direct references to capsize prevention or preparation, but it is loaded with evidence to support the suggestions that appear later in this book. *Lost* is obviously sensationalized, with references to such things as giant whirlpools offshore, and impossibilities like diving out from inside the half-filled and capsized craft while wearing a life jacket. Nonetheless, the sea saga is recommended for anyone who intends to venture offshore in *any* craft without making basic preparations for survival. They had nothing ready or planned, yet they managed to survive for 72 days. They had to cut their way into the upturned bottom of the boat with a belt buckle! They rigged a platform inside, above the inverted waterline, by drilling multiple holes in the hull and rigging a net. They scrounged up enough food and water from normal ship's stores to sustain life for a very long time. Linda Tininenko's tragic death was probably caused by the death of the fetus she carried, or perhaps she too would have made it through. Jim Fisher expired several days after the rescue, apparently because he had abused his kidneys by sporadic consumption of his water ration, following his ideological conviction that rationing, and the conservation of his energy, were not necessary. He insisted their salvation would be looked after by the Lord. The two men were in constant conflict over their religious differences, and Fisher apparently discarded a substantial quantity of food as a gesture of his faith.

Whatever conclusions might be drawn from this strange episode, one thing is certain: if the catastrophe had been a sinking instead of a capsize, there would have been no survivors. They had no life raft, no radio beacon, no tools, flares, radar reflector, capsize hammocks, medicines—they were absolutely unprepared. Twelve ships and several aircraft were sighted during their ordeal, yet except for using Linda's makeup mirror as a reflector, they were powerless to attract attention. Bob's attempt to make a torch from fuel and rags was thwarted by Jim on the grounds that it would interfere with God's will.

From sad stories such as this tale of the *Triton*, we began to learn, slowly, the positive aspects of capsize prevention and preparation. At least somebody came back to tell us what in hell had happened—what had happened in hell.

While the foregoing accounts have all involved trimarans, this is not to say that no capsizes have occurred in catamarans. On the contrary, a number of the larger cats have turned turtle, particularly in 'longshore races. Their crews were promptly rescued and no attempts were made, as far as is generally known, to inhabit the inside of these capsized catamarans.

In the 1967 Crystal Trophy Race, the 43-foot catamaran *Golden Cockerel* was capsized after her skipper, Bill Howell, raced her with one hull flying for something like half an hour, hardly a capsize to be blamed on the boat. An aerial photo of the craft revealed that she floated very high when inverted, with the entire underwing dry. The crew was standing in a relaxed manner, leaning against one hull as if it were a lamppost.

A report of this incident described how one of the crew members was below at the time of capsize, and remained below for a period long enough to move methodically through the accommodation area of both hulls to close off all through-hull fittings, thus preventing loss of airlock. It was obviously the air trapped within the hulls and wing that caused the craft to float so high.

From this revelation we can draw two inferences not demonstrated by the *Golden Cockerel* capsize because she was rescued so promptly. The first is that if the incident had occurred at a time and place where long-term survival was required, the crew would not have been able to cut access hatches in the hulls, as was done with Jim Fisher's trimaran. Any openings whatever would cause loss of airlock and rapid settling of the craft until the underwing surface might be chest-deep in water. The hulls themselves would not be habitable without cutting hatches because of the lack of a long-term oxygen supply, and with hatches cut, the resultant settling probably would not leave sufficient above-water space inside for habitation.

In the trimaran's case, it was airlock in the outer hulls that held the entire craft high enough to allow open habitation of the central hull.

Second, the catamaran crew would soon find that the underwing surface, no matter how elevated, would provide inadequate protection from long-term exposure, and would go awash in heavy weather. The logical solution to this problem (for catamarans as well as for other multihulls) is to carry life rafts for capsize habitation. But the life raft has its own special problems.

On December 29, 1974, Tony Allen capsized his trimaran, *Rebel II*, in

Australian waters. He cut a hole in the bottom with an axe and salvaged useful equipment; then he set up housekeeping in the self-inflating life raft that was tethered to the stricken yacht. Because of the extremely jerky motion caused by the tether, and the chance of sustaining damage to the raft at the point of the tether's attachment, Tony cut the raft loose the following day and went drifting away from *Rebel II.* He was fairly well supplied with rations, water, and flares, but before the first week was out, his raft began to leak air. It eventually required pumping up about 10 times per day. With his rations exhausted but his water supply holding, and with the raft slowly giving out around him, he managed to attract the attention of a passing ship by shooting flares, and he was rescued after 20 dreadful days.

Azulao was a small, super-lightweight racing trimaran with very small, experimental amas. Nick Clifton, an experienced British yachtsman, raced the boat in the 1976 OSTAR and remained in the U.S. for almost a year. On March 30, 1977, he started for home across a troubled North Atlantic ocean, and a week later was capsized while lying ahull in Force 8-9 winds.

Azulao was probably the first multihull with self-righting capabilities built in, a great credit to her designer and builder, Derek Kelsall. Her extremely small amas probably also meant she had capsize capabilities built in. The craft was supposed to have stabilizing hydrofoils attached to the amas, but these were not fitted for lack of time—another case of capsize that cannot be blamed on the craft itself.

The self-righting system planned for *Azulao* was very similar to the somersault method described in Chapter 8, but it was not tested before the race, nor prior to Nick's return passage. Only a small malfunction of the hatches prevented Clifton from pumping out the main compartment to cause rotation, and thereby performing his own recovery at sea, an achievement that would have made him a key figure in the history of multihulls.

But with the failure of the main hatch, Nick abandoned the self-rescue attempt and entered his life raft, which was tethered to *Azulao* by a short line. When the heaving trimaran threatened to damage the raft, Clifton extended the tether with a piece of inferior line found aboard the raft. The extension was parted by a heavy jerk, and the raft, with the solo sailor aboard, drifted away from *Azulao* at speed.

But before leaving the cabin of his upturned boat, Clifton had switched on his ELT (a small, waterproof Emergency Locator Transmitter, also known as EPIRB, Emergency Position Indicating Radio Beacon). This device is not strictly intended to summon assistance, but instead is designed to indicate the position of the castaway to searchers who are looking for an aircraft or a boat that has been reported overdue. *Azulao* was not overdue, but her beacon was fortunately heard, and reported. A Coast Guard aircraft eventually spotted the trimaran. There being no sign of survivors aboard, the aircraft began searching the vicinity directly downwind and spotted Clifton's raft. A tanker in the vicinity was guided by the aircraft to accomplish his rescue.

Clifton's raft was oversize, being a four-man inflatable inhabited by one man. During the three days that Nick was aboard, the raft capsized once, probably because the weight of one man was insufficient to hold it down, and most of the provisions aboard were lost. The accidental separation from the mothership deprived this castaway of access to ample provisions contained therein and also meant his separation from the ELT. No capsize hammock was included in Clifton's self-rescue preparations, but had there been some system of elevating himself above the inverted waterline inside, and had there been an access hatch for keeping watch, perhaps there would have been no temptation for Clifton to leave the shelter of the cabin and enter the tenuously tethered raft.

All circumstances considered, Nick Clifton was very fortunate to have been rescued in three days. And Tony Allen was just as lucky to be spotted after 20 days. Their chances for long-term survival were substantially reduced when they took to their inflatable rafts. This is not to say that life rafts should not be carried aboard offshore multihulls. In Chapter 6 there are more details about the selection, installation, and attachment of life rafts for nonsinking motherships.

There was no life raft aboard the *Meridian.* Only a rubber dinghy was at hand when this 35-foot trimaran was capsized by tropical storm Amy off Cape Hatteras in June 1975. The crew made attempts to employ the dinghy, but it soon became apparent that the mothership offered far better shelter than the inflatable. The two-week survival siege that followed cost the life of Rodger B. Stewart, owner-builder of the craft; but Stewart's three teenage sons and their adult friend, Clint Spooner, all were saved. The *Meridian* incident has contributed more to our knowledge of capsize survival than any other multihull catastrophe, including the curious revelation that with certain multihulls, the life raft should be the last item of survival equipment to be deployed.

My investigation of the *Meridian* incident has been one of the most fascinating episodes in what Hunter Nicol called my "career among the trimarans." Because it illustrates so well the manner in which hard facts on multihull safety have been wrested from postulation, it seems this story should be told from the start.

In the spring of 1975 my family and I were on the last lap of our three-year cruise in *Scrimshaw.* We were looking for a place to settle down on the east coast of the U.S. and so had spent two delightful weeks in June exploring the North Carolina Sounds. Having visited a pleasant community called Belhaven, we pushed on for Virginia where we had a friend to contact.

Strong northerly winds were blowing, but we entered Pungo Cut and motored for 20 miles in the lee of high trees along the straight, narrow ditch. When we emerged from the Cut into the Alligator River, we were stopped by the wind. It was far too strong to motor against with our little outboard, and we were unable to sail in the narrow channel. So we spent the night tied to the bank of the snake-infested swamp, and awaited better weather.

During this layover our radio reported several vessels missing offshore, one being a trimaran overdue on passage from Bermuda to Norfolk. An early tropical storm was raging in that area, and we were experiencing its fringes. The storm made the overdue trimaran report especially ominous, and we wondered if perhaps the boat in question might be a Searunner, one of my designs. Such are the causes of sleepless nights for those of us who prescribe small craft for ocean voyaging.

Next day the weather was worse, and the wind direction still contrary. We decided to return to Belhaven because the town had been preparing for a lively Fourth of July celebration. We joined them.

Later I would learn that the Fourth was the day Rodger Stewart died. He was diabetic and had gone six days without insulin, because neither of the two vials of insulin carried aboard *Meridian* could be found after the capsize.

Later that week, with the help of our friend in Virginia, we found a place to try living ashore; it was in the Tidewater area on the southern Chesapeake. The transition from boat to house was rather hectic, and shockingly expensive. And all through early July we kept hearing radio reports of the search for the lost trimaran. The search had an on-again, off-again quality that was confusing, and there seemed to be a good deal of hubbub in the press. It later developed that the Coast Guard had suspended the search on July 7 after combing a large chunk of the North Atlantic, but the families of the crew had exerted substantial pressure, through their elected representatives and friends, for the search to be resumed. In effect, their argument said, "They cannot have sunk! You can't just quit looking for them, because they've got to be out there!" And they were.

The search resumed for two more days, but without results.

Finally on July 15, the news was full of reports that the *Meridian* had been found with four survivors, but that Dr. Stewart had died of diabetes and been buried at sea.

The boat was not a Searunner, but the survivors were residents of the Tidewater area. Jo Anna and I remarked together, "We've got to talk to those people," and through a contact known by our original Virginia friend, we were put in touch with Mrs. Pat Stewart, wife of the deceased, who kindly referred us to the crewman Clinton Spooner.

In a fascinating series of tape-recorded interviews, it was Spooner who constructed a detailed report of what had happened. Because of his interest in sailing and in multihulls, he strove to analyze his unique experience, and offer conclusions to affect the future safety of seafaring in capsizable—but unsinkable—craft. The following is transcribed and paraphrased from several sessions with Clint Spooner.

"We continued on through Saturday night (June 28) with the fair wind picking up a little so that we made very good time. Rodger and his son Gordon dropped the genoa on their watch, about 9:30 that evening, and replaced it with the working jib. Keith and I came on at eleven, and about one in the morning we dropped the mainsail and continued under just the working jib. It was still very comfortable sailing and we proceeded at six or eight knots with absolutely no problem.

"We monitored the civil defense radio station in Maryland, WGU 20, and they had no warnings. They merely said a low pressure area had formed off the North Carolina coast and was headed northeast. At this point we were still 350 miles at sea and figured it would have long passed to the north of us before we approached the coast. There was no hint of any high winds associated with this low pressure system.

"During my watch the seas picked up considerably, and the wind was building and shifting into the south. When I turned the helm over to Dr. Stewart at 3 A.M., we were making good progress, surfing at times up to about nine knots, but there was no concern. However, when daybreak came we could see the size of the swells—maybe 10 feet crest-to-trough, and rather steep—and we were a little concerned at that point. I monitored WGU 20 and they just had the same tape-recorded weather report. Our wind had increased to about 35 knots, still from the south, but we didn't think there was anything to be concerned about, so we continued on westward toward Cape Hatteras.

"About nine in the morning it was getting to be work steering down those waves, so we took down the working jib and put up the storm jib.

"The radio stayed with its 'low pressure' report until about ten-thirty, at which point they changed the tape to say that it was a 'weak tropical depression' headed east. Well, that meant we were headed right for it! The 'tropical depression' part meant that we might be in for trouble, but they did not call it a tropical storm or a hurricane, so we still weren't overly concerned.

"Around noon things were kicking up rather badly, so we put out the tire drogue, a 14-inch tire on a single nylon line, tied directly to the main hull stern. We also got out an anchor and line, and made that ready in case we wanted another drogue. We also tied a piece of nylon line around the wing, front-to-back under the wing and over the deck just to serve as an extra hand-hold (in case of capsize).

"Rodger and I had talked about it before, and there was some uncertainty on the rotational direction of revolving storms ... Rodger had said they rotated in a clockwise direction, but I seemed to remember that hurricanes rotate counterclockwise. It bothered me enough that I went below and looked it up in Reed's Almanac, and sure enough, it said that 'cyclonic' storms in the southern hemisphere, like typhoons, rotate clockwise, but hurricanes in the northern hemisphere rotate in a counterclockwise direction. With the wind from the south and our being headed west, that meant we were steering straight for the eye!

"Since the storm was headed east, according to the radio, we figured we could go north and the thing would pass below us and we'd have no problem. So we jibed the stormsail over and ran off to the northward on a broad starboard reach. I took the helm at about two o'clock—it was gusting over 40—and I tried to work the boat north by angling down the waves. This was difficult because they were very confused, coming not only from the east but from the north and south as well. Sometimes they would add, or combine to produce a very high wave, and other times they would subtract to make quite a trough that we would dive down into.

"A couple of times the tire drogue came up and surfed along behind us on top of the water, and we would accelerate quite rapidly . . . so we added more rope and some chain to the drogue . . . I guess we had 200 or 250 feet of line on the drogue and it stayed down fine . . . helped ease the steering considerably.

"But approaching three o'clock or so, it became harder and harder to steer down the waves . . . it was blowing up to about 60 and you could feel the wind grab the boat . . . and at times it seemed to be lifting the main hull enough to make her pound underneath the bottom . . . sort of a helpless feeling . . . .

"The two younger boys, Keith and Gordon, were down below; Gordon was back in the stern bunk.

"I was at the helm when we capsized. A large wave from the east lifted us up and we broached slightly to starboard . . . the wind got underneath the starboard wing and we just went right on up . . . we skated along on the side of the port ama for a few seconds and continued a slow roll right on over . . . I remember the mast hitting the water and we were falling out of the cockpit and the boat landed on top of us.

"Those of us on deck were wearing safety harnesses with C-clip connectors at the far end of our lifelines. My lifeline was short enough so that I could not go overboard, and now I was being dragged along underneath the boat . . . the deck bounced off my head a few times and dazed me a bit . . . I drank a fair amount of salt water and at that point I thought that I had pretty well had it.

"Luckily, the boat rocked on a wave and a little gulp of air came in underneath the deck and allowed me to catch a breath . . . and collect my thoughts. I was able to release the C-clip and set myself free.

"When I came to the surface I saw young Rodger, the oldest of the boys, holding on to the line that we had tied around the wing. He was trying to pull himself up, but we later realized his lifeline was still attached underneath and was holding him down. His father was behind him, trying to push him up. I scrambled up on the wing, and just as I turned to help young Rodger, the two other boys popped up. They had dived out of the cabin together, and they made it to the wing. I pulled them up, and then managed to release young Rodger's lifeline, so that he and his dad could climb up on the wing.

"The first thing we noticed was that the boat was floating very high, very high. The wing was well clear of the water so that the waves were not breaking badly over us. The wind was blowing across the boat so that we were fairly well sheltered by the hulls. Even though the waves were 30 to 40 feet high, and the wind was probably a steady 60 knots, we were not in any immediate danger.

"But our natural concern was that the boat would sink eventually . . . the boys inside had reacted with the ingrained 'let's get out of here' reflex because they naturally assumed the boat was going down with them trapped inside.

"Rodger and I told them that she would not sink completely, but that she might slowly settle enough to just wash us off, so we decided to go inside somehow and get the inflatable dinghy and whatever rations and supplies we could grab.

"Our first problem was to get into the hull. We were standing very securely on the wing, and of course nobody wanted to dive underneath again, so Dr. Stewart and young Rodger got out their knives and, little by little, managed to carve a hole in the side of the hull. They were able to cut through the fiberglass and rip it back, and then they scored the wood continuously for quite a while. I was surprised that they were able to work like that, but the boat was very stable. Once the cabin was half-filled with water, the motion stabilized a lot, and the boat was actually riding more smoothly than before the capsize.

"Finally the skipper was able to kick a hole in the plywood planking, and he reached inside and found a winch handle; with that he enlarged the hole enough to crawl inside. We were all concerned about him going inside the boat, in case it should sink or something, but we were still floating very high.

"Inside he found his tool chest and a saw, and enlarged the hole, and he also cut another hole on the opposite side of the hull. These were to allow us emergency exits, no matter what happened. Then we all got inside the boat, and we put the younger boys up above the water. The underside of the stern bunk was dry and reasonably comfortable at that point.

"Still wondering how long the boat would float so high, we got the inflatable dinghy out of its stowage position in the wing. Dr. Stewart dove into the wing and found the air pump, and we took the dinghy out onto the wing and pumped it up. I had real difficulty with this because it seemed the threads on the pump wouldn't fit the dinghy. But we finally got it inflated.

"About that time the boys noticed that the water level had risen and was flooding into their bunk level at the transom. Dr. Stewart and I felt by now that the boat would stay afloat, and in fact it never settled any further, but the boys wanted to be ready in case it sank. So we got them into the dinghy, together with some provisions we had gathered up. However, the waves were now washing through the tunnel and sloshing the dinghy around rather violently. I held on to the dinghy and the boys got in and bailed, but whenever a big wave came by, it would try to swamp the dinghy.

"By now we were all getting very cold, and we were able to determine that the boat was not settling any deeper, so the boys got back inside the main hull. We lashed the dinghy on the wing, rather securely we felt, but neglected to bring those provisions back inside. We sort of wanted everything ready to go, just in case we had to abandon ship.

"Then Dr. Stewart and I tried to make preparations for getting through the night. I prepared the space in the stern bunk by putting one of the settee cushions up there, which kind of got me up out of the water a little more. It gave me a space of about 20 inches between the bunk bottom and the keel. But there were some transverse braces supporting this bunk, which poked up underneath the cushion and eventually caused me a lot of grief from bedsores. In time we all got painful, running sores and rashes.

"The skipper rigged up some platforms for the boys and himself by bracing loose floorboards across the main cabin, with everything sort of suspended on the bottom of the dinette table . . . he managed to make space for all four of them to huddle together to keep warm. We pulled a lot of stuff out of the water to use for cover to conserve body heat. I spent the first night in the fetal position inside a trash can liner. Later we cut up the genoa and made covers for us all.

"We were fitful during the first night. It was very hard to overcome the suspicion that at any minute the boat might settle deeper. Even though it never did, the claustrophobia of huddling in a slot above the water, with the wind and waves roaring by outside—all of that was hard to overcome. From my position I could see the two hatches cut in the sides of the hull, and every big wave came sloshing in through those holes, giving the impression that the place was filling up. So each time a big sea rushed in, I would wait for things to subside and then call out to the others that the water level inside had not changed. We eventually realized that the boat's natural buoyancy, combined with all that air trapped in the outboard hulls, was holding us up like that. Later on we got smart and boarded up those holes and cut new hatches in the uppermost portion of the hull's bottom. But in the meantime the tremendous sloshing and strong currents inside tore up the interior and I'm sure carried off a lot of useful items—probably including the EPIRB and the insulin. We later dived through the whole interior and never found them. Either one might have saved the skipper's life.

"That first night we also lost the provisions that were in the dinghy, and later the dinghy itself broke loose. These circumstances just kept mounting up on us . . . .

"We figured we were about 180 miles due east of Cape Hatteras when we capsized on Sunday, June 29. The first two days and nights we couldn't do much of anything but just hang on because we were still in the storm—it was still terribly rough.

"We were very fortunate to have some fresh water left in a small container, and one five-gallon jug too—although some of that was lost with the dinghy. So Monday we made some Tang and ate some Pop-Tarts that we found floating around in the cabin. Tuesday we shared a can of corned beef hash, and it was amazing how much our stomachs had shrunk already—we could hardly finish it.

"Dr. Stewart didn't seem concerned about going without insulin. The rest of us were all very much concerned, but he said that he could make it for about a week if he didn't have anything to eat, and if he just rested . . . he said that we shouldn't worry . . . .

"Wednesday afternoon it started to clear off and Thursday was a beautiful day, so we all crawled out and were warming ourselves, all wrapped in

Dacron in the morning sun, when we saw our first ship. It came up from the south and passed about four miles away from us . . . .

"It was at this time that we tried to use the flares and smoke bombs and found that they simply failed to function! Signal flares made by Olin and marked 'for marine use' had gotten wet and wouldn't work. Smoke signals made by Survival Systems, Inc., also failed to operate at all. The sad truth is that most of that kind of stuff is simply not waterproof . . . it would have to be kept absolutely dry until nearly the time of use.

"But we flashed our signal mirror and waved a red sail bag, and when the ship came abeam of us, it appeared to stop. We were all tremendously excited. We were under quite a bit of pressure, timewise, because of Rodger's condition, and we assumed the ship had stopped and was putting out a lifeboat to come and get us. However, as we learned from all the five ships that eventually passed us by, there is an optical illusion. When the ship comes abeam, it only *appears* to stop.

"Later that day we heard airplanes, but we never actually saw a plane, except for high-altitude contrails. If we'd had the EPIRB, or a good radar reflector, the search planes almost certainly would have noticed us on their radio or radar. But we were absolutely helpless to make ourselves known.

"Later I did put together a radar reflector made from a drip-pan from underneath the stove. But we had no way to elevate the thing above the wavetops . . . no poles or spars to use for a mast or a spear. We tried fishing and made a short spear, but had no luck at all, even though we could see plenty of fish . . . .

"Thursday afternoon Dr. Stewart began passing in and out of consciousness. The boys and I felt that we had done everything we could. Here he was, six days since his last insulin, and he was lapsing into a diabetic coma. He had worked very hard in the beginning, trying to improve our situation—all at a time when he probably should have been conserving his strength. He performed beautifully for his boys for as long as he could. He was in some pain Thursday evening, so the boys administered codeine tablets, and he rested comfortably after that. With all of them together, he died in his sleep sometime early Friday morning—the Fourth of July.

"He was buried at sea according to his stated wish. But it was a very difficult task for us all. We wrapped him in Dacron, tied a battery to his ankles, said a few simple words over him, and lowered him down into the sea . . . .

"Our survival routine continued for another week, but of course we had no idea of how long we would have to hang on. We rationed the food carefully, and the water too. We tried to catch rain, without much success: salt spray contaminated any collection system we tried, because we couldn't get it up high enough. We stood watches whenever the days were not cold and wet: otherwise we tried to conserve ourselves down below. We were all getting pretty weak, and our skin was so soft that it didn't take much to rub a hole in it. But the weather was generally pleasant—a little chilly, but not bad. It was fairly comfortable at night once we got wrapped up in the Dacron . . . .

"Sunday afternoon I got pretty discouraged. I felt that there was nothing more to be done in effecting our own rescue. We'd made the boat as visible as we could by nailing up all sorts of brightly colored objects. A yellow horseshoe lifebuoy was fastened to the tip of one daggerboard, which was sticking up out of the amas, and half of the red sail bag was nailed to the highest part of the main hull, along with the makeshift radar reflector. But we were without any good means of signaling. Even the mirror was turning black.

"When I turned in that night I felt cheated; here I was in the prime of life. I had just secured a position with a prestigious law firm, my wonderful wife was right with me in the same profession, and all of a sudden I was staring at the end of the road.

"And those three brave boys, suffering through their father's death. We had somehow survived that awful storm without drowning, and now we spent these endless days just staring at the beautiful ocean, slowly starving, and nobody knew we were there! I promised myself that night that if I ever managed to get out of this predicament, I was never going to take my life for granted. I would live with a reverence for life itself, and be thankful for the experience of learning just how precious it can be. And I went to sleep thinking about John Denver's song, *Poems, Prayers and Promises*. The words kept running through my mind. Something about, 'It's really fine to have a chance to hang around.'

"Monday morning dawned bright and clear. I remember waking up and looking out the hatchway there and seeing the red glow of the sun as it came up. And I thought, 'Hot dog! This is going to be the day.' I could feel it. And I prayed, 'Please God, if we're going to be rescued, please let it be today.'

"The boys were thinking the same thing. Keith passed me back a third of a cup of water, which was the breakfast ration, and I slowly crawled out to greet the day. About mid-morning it was warmed up enough for the boys' morning watch. (If it wasn't warm and sunny, we had to stay below, because in our condition we just couldn't tolerate any cold at all.) It was warm, so they watched the horizon for ships.

"Around noon the boys went down below, and I took over. I decided to take a little nap out there in the sun, hoping the ultraviolet would help cure my sores. But before lying down, I took one more glance around the horizon and I thought I saw something to the east of us. I squinted very hard and could see the narrow hull shape of a ship. Since it was so narrow, that meant it was headed fairly close to us.

"So I put on my pants, grabbed what was left of our signal mirror, and began signaling the boat. After 10 or 15 minutes of that, it became apparent that this one was going to pass quite close. I called the boys from below so that we could go through another one of our drills. They came up reluctantly, because we had been through this before, with great disappointment. But I gave Rodger the fire extinguisher and Keith the mirror, and I went to my bunk for the 30-30 rifle. As the ship approached, within about a mile, Rodger discharged the fire extinguisher and Keith flashed the mirror and I fired the gun. Then we waved the red sail bag, the ship went right on by, and the boys started back down below. But as Keith was crawling down the hatch, he said, 'Boy, that ship has changed course.' It appeared to have turned to head straight away from us. We were looking right into the sun, so I stowed the rifle, sat down on the hull with the signal mirror, and kept on flashing.

"All of a sudden I noticed that the ship was getting bigger! So I squinted real hard and sure enough I could see the *bow wave.*

"At this point I started pounding on the hull and yelling to the boys, 'Come on up and look at this! Come and have a look at our ticket home!'

"So they all came up through the hole and . . . the emotion was pretty heavy . . . crying . . . we were all pretty excited . . . tremendously relieved and . . . it's hard to describe . . . ."

Sandy Spooner and Pat Stewart later told us of their first two weeks in July. It was evident that the families ashore endured the same anguish, even if not the same physical privation, as the castaways themselves. Dealing with the press and the Coast Guard were at least as frustrating as the incidents at sea. And the suspense of not knowing what has happened is maybe worse than knowing, and waiting for what's going to happen next.

The survivors' recovery period, after rescue, was greatly facilitated by Sandy and Pat. The Stewart boys contributed to Spooner's report, and emphasized several aspects of survival and preparation. Their subsequent recovery from the death of their father demonstrated a resilience that would have made him very proud.

Pat Stewart cooperated completely with our attempt to gain all pertinent information. She remarked, "I was very lucky. I could have lost my entire family. And the story must be told, because if Rod had lived, the first thing that he would have done would be to publish a complete report."

When the *Meridian* story was told, as a series of three articles in *Multihulls* magazine, Sandy Spooner revealed the forward-looking attitude of all involved when she said, "It was as if our existence had been subjected to some gigantic interruption, but I think Clint is ready to put this thing behind him now so that we can all get on with our lives."

In the weeks following the rescue, several commercial vessels reported sighting the *Meridian*. She was drifting to the northeast, still whole and still habitable. Some eight weeks following the capsize, the hulk was actually picked up and taken to England. She had weathered at least one more cyclone and was still basically intact.

From analyzing this and other capsizes, we now know that what happened to the *Meridian* can be effectively prevented. And we have also learned a great deal about how to prepare for capsize if it comes. These preparations will promote long-term survival of the crew in a relatively comfortable and safe habitat, while also providing the castaways with the means to attract attention to themselves. Both objectives can be accomplished far more effectively from the mothership than from a life raft, inexpensively and with uncomplicated equipment. Furthermore, these preparations can be made with the confidence that the modern multihull is structurally capable of providing a very long-term capsize habitat. Even with tons of water inside, and storm seas outside, it remains intact.

Although Dr. Stewart had modern emergency equipment on board—radios and pyrotechnics and inflatables—it was not technology that brought the survivors home. It was a sharp-eyed Greek sailor named George Fafoutis, second mate of the *Elinora,* who spotted something among the waves that he could not identify. And it was the *Elinora*'s captain, Nicos Fafoutis, the mate's brother, who was willing to interrupt his ship's passage and investigate.

And it was something else. It was *Meridian* herself. When the Greek freighter came along, *Meridian* and her survivors were still there. And they were willing to help extrapolate conclusions for all of us who sail the deep sea in multihulls. This time there was no conjecture—there was a living, talking crew.

6

Capsize Preparation

The multihull capsize is a new kind of maritime disaster. It bears some similarity to a sunken submarine with men entrapped, or a lost space capsule. The novelty of an accident in which survivors are provided shelter and sustenance by the wreck itself, but are castaways just the same, leads the mind to conjure up all sorts of horrors. It also gives the press its chance to play to the public's ghoulish curiosity. In recent years, however, real progress has been made toward the understanding of offshore capsize. Like any calamity, it can be prevented, and yet certain preparations must be made to meet it if it happens.

A multihull capsize is not by itself an ultimate disaster. There is a wide gap between capsize and actual loss of life. Given proper preparations and equipment, and a suitable capsize survival technique, turning over is not nearly as threatening—as final—as the familiar once-and-for-all finish of a boat that's sunk!

Yes, there is always the life raft, and in a monohull it represents an important chance for survival. We also carry life rafts in multihulls, but in case of capsize, we prefer to stand by our upturned vessel, our mothership. Many multihulls are habitable when upside down. Besides better shelter and more space, we've got lots of stuff on board that could not be carried in a raft, like full cruising stores and lots of fresh water and plenty of flares and several good lights. We can elevate the radar reflector and the emergency radio beacon. We've got the ship's medicine chest, clothing, and something to read (albeit soggy) while lying in our capsize hammocks. We've got fishing tackle, diving gear, and tools. There's a snug, raised position for the person on watch, and the big boat has a better chance than the raft of being spotted.

All of this assumes proper preparation to prevent the loss of precious stores and equipment (which would be gone in the case of sinking). In a capsize, it is just possible that our only immediate loss is mobility.

To regain mobility, there is the old option of "taking to the longboat," and the new possibility of "somersault self-rescue." We'll examine in detail in Chapter 8 some very interesting multihull survival and salvage techniques. But for now, let us agree that castaways from any marine disaster are largely dependent upon attracting the attention of another vessel. The chance of doing this, and the chance of there being somebody alive to rescue, is somewhat greater in a multihull than in a life raft.

If that makes capsize survival sound like a Huck Finn adventure, please forgive me. I've never been in a capsize, but I've had my feet deep in the bilge of a sinking monohull and there's nothing cute to be said about it. The chance of a multihull capsize may be at least as great as the chance of a monohull sinking . . . but a capsize doesn't have to be as great a *threat* as a sinking. With the lack of finality in capsize, we contend that the two are equal hazards. One is new and sensational, the other is old hat. Both can be largely prevented, and each can be prepared for. At zero hour, given my choice between capsize and sinking, I've got my druthers, and I submit that self-righting and nonsinking are both valid concepts.

What is it like to be floating upside down, offshore, in a capsized multihull? What exactly does one prepare for?

Although in 20 years of multihull sailing I have never capsized, I have fortunately been able to draw upon the experiences of others. The example of the *Meridian* (Chapter 5) illustrates very well the main areas where preparation is necessary.

106

"It lacks the finality of sinking out at sea."

The first area is psychological. The very thought of zero hour is almost too threatening to ponder. A great curtain comes down around the cranium when dread of disaster intrudes itself. While planning a boat, or a boat trip, the necessity for safety preparations tends to spoil the pleasure, and so it is often blocked out.

However, any responsible mariner will find the weight of his responsibility difficult to bear if he knows that precautionary measures have been omitted. This pressure can ruin an otherwise pleasant, safe trip.

The first step, therefore, is to get oneself in a frame of mind that will raise the curtain on this problem. The preparations themselves are the only way to attack that underlying dread and put it in its place, so that the plans and the trip can then continue unencumbered by the threat of maritime catastrophe. This is the only approach that really *solves* the problem, so that the offshore sailing experience can be enjoyed.

Having made this psychological breakthrough, the other precautions to be taken are pure nuts-and-bolts. They are easy to perform and not especially expensive. Following is an attempt to examine the several types of capsize preparation, to allow the individual skipper to make decisions based on his own boat and his own pocketbook.

Wherever possible, both minimum and maximum degrees of preparation are described in hopes that at least *something* will be provided in each category. Just a little forethought and a few inexpensive preparations, if made for all offshore multihulls, can result in an entire fleet of vessels that possess ultimate safety, not just ultimate stability.

1. YOUR BOAT'S CLASSIFICATION

Is your capsize survival procedure life raft-oriented or mothership-oriented? This depends on the nature of your boat, primarily on how high she

107

would float in the event of capsize. Questions also to be considered are: how long will she float at that height, and is there space inside for long-term habitation above that inverted waterline?

Boats equipped with a great deal of foam flotation at or near the deck will certainly float higher than those without, but the usual buoyancy comes from large volumes of air locked within inverted spaces. A major difference between the usual catamaran and the usual trimaran can be seen here. Assuming that the catamaran has no through-hull fittings or other openings in its hulls or underwing, it would trap a great volume of air upon being capsized. Or, if openings exist, the crew may be able to close through-hull fittings promptly upon inversion. However, such airlock spaces will serve as habitation only temporarily, until the oxygen inside is consumed by the inhabitant(s).

The trimaran, in contrast, rarely has underbody openings in its outboard hulls. After capsize, airlock in the wings and outer hulls will provide flotation, while the main hull remains available for habitation. Hatches for ventilation, light, and access may be cut in the trimaran's central hull without disturbing other airlock spaces.

Any multihull that has enough foam flotation, or airlock flotation, to cause the capsized craft to float at approximately its underwing level, and that simultaneously offers enough above-water space inside to provide long-term habitation for the crew, can be said to be CLASS I—HABITABLE.

Any multihull that does not meet these requirements of above-water space and fresh air supply for long-term habitation, but that has enough flotation to prevent total sinking, can be said to be CLASS II—NONHABITABLE.

The essential difference between these two types of multihulls is that in Class I the survival procedure is oriented toward living inside the mothership, while in Class II the survivors must inhabit a life raft that is attached to the mothership. In both cases, the crew has access to the contents of the big boat. (Some very light-displacement monohulls might qualify under Class II if given enough flotation to prevent total sinking.)

The Class II vessel, because of its complete dependence on the raft for habitation, requires a good raft, self-inflating, ruggedly constructed, with a canopy, and plenty big enough for all the crew.

The Class I vessel, because it serves as habitation, may—at a minimum—be equipped with a light-duty raft or perhaps rely on an inflatable dinghy or even a hard dinghy, or both, for backup.

However, some overlap exists between the two classifications. Most Class II vessels could be upgraded to Class I by providing enough foam or trapped air buoyancy. In any multihull, unused voids could even be stuffed with plastic milk containers. Boats classed as habitable could be rendered uninhabitable by structural damage (such as in a capsize caused by collision) that has violated the airlock. A first-class life raft, and plenty of flotation, are therefore advised for all offshore multihulls. Nonetheless, the separation of the two classifications still exists. Some multihulls certainly will not provide long-term habitation if capsized, and others probably will. This distinction will influence capsize preparations.

So, decide which type of multihull you have to prepare, habitable or nonhabitable.

2. THE RAFT

Selection of your life raft may be influenced by the vessel's classification and by finances. A good, big, rugged raft, accessible from both the deck and the underwing, is preferred for any offshore multihull. But the Class I owner who is strapped by financial or space limitations may elect to substitute an inflatable dinghy, or a lightweight aircraft-type life raft, or even a good rigid dinghy, but each must be equipped with some kind of canopy or tarpaulin.

The life raft is the last thing brought into service in Class I survival, but nonetheless something must be provided to back up the mothership in case she is rendered uninhabitable by fire or collision.

Logic says that it is foolhardy to sail anywhere in a Class II multihull, or in any sinkable craft, without a good, rugged life raft. The same goes for Class I, except that simple capsize would probably leave the crew with a better place to live—the boat herself.

Installation of your raft is influenced by such factors as space and the crew's experience in skindiving. Ideally, there will be a special built-in compartment in the wing, or in some other secure position, where the raft is safely stowed, accessible from both the deck (in case of fire) and from under the wing (in case of capsize).

Some life rafts have automatic ejection/inflation features that are marvelous for boats that can sink, but not necessarily advantageous for boats that can capsize. The automatically inflated raft might be caught underneath the boat.

" ... Selecting your liferaft ... "

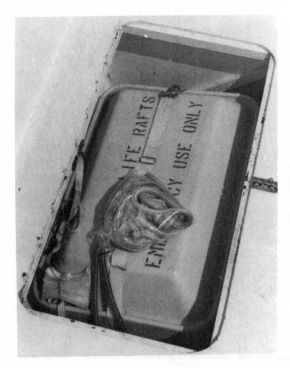

Special life raft compartment in the wing of this trimaran gives access from on deck and from under the wing. Note the duplicate tethers, each rigged to pay out without snarling.

Some multihulls have nets between the hulls to which a life raft can be lashed when the vessel goes offshore. The raft can be reached by cutting through the net from underneath. This makes a good raft installation for boats without divers in the crew and/or without underwing access to a special life raft compartment. However, for any exterior installation, a good canister or some other protection is needed to protect the raft from sun and salt.

Factory inspection of the raft is assumed; it is wise to inflate a new raft and inspect it to familiarize yourself with this critical piece of equipment. Many life rafts have proved faulty in design or construction, so look yours over carefully before installation. Repeated inflation with the CO_2 cylinders is discouraged, however, because the gas entering the chambers can freeze-damage the adjacent material. So inspect your raft by blowing it up with mouth or pump. Examine the valves on the cylinders for signs of corrosion, and inspect the fabric wherever it is creased.

The most critical component of the raft's equipment is its tether to the mothership. Some lightweight, inexpensive rafts do not have attachment points of adequate strength to withstand shock loads on the tether caused by heavy seas. And the tether itself must be attached to the mothership in a manner that will resist chafe.

If your raft has questionable attachment points, consider rigging a harness around the raft so that the tether pulls from behind. Some manufacturers offer towing eyes, which can be attached firmly at the factory, or even by the owner.

The tether itself can be secured to the mothership by an eyebolt adjacent to the raft's stowage position, and be flaked or stuffed in a plastic bag to allow paying-out without snarling; coiling the tether is not advised. All sharp surfaces in the vicinity should be rounded off to guard against chafe.

A 50-foot length of premium nylon, half-inch diameter, is suggested for the painter because nylon greatly resists chafe. Wire cable can be used if the boat offers special chafe problems.

The length of this initial tether can be extended with a similar length of smaller nylon to provide shock absorption. Within a large loop of the small tether, tie a 10-foot length of 3/8-inch-diameter best-quality "bungee" shock cord. A farthing weight (any 5- or 10-pound weight like a short length of chain) can be installed midway in the tether to further absorb shock. Hand-holding the tether in the raft might be required in extreme conditions. Two complete tethers would be more than twice as good as one.

Attention to this detail, especially for Class II boats, could make the difference between surviving with the aid of the mothership and trying to make out with the raft alone. Worse, if no provision is made, the tether could cause damage to the raft, like tearing at the attachment points.

Not enough is currently known to say which is the best system for retaining attachment to the mothership. Drifting downwind on a very chafe-resistant, elastic tether is one approach, but another is to lash or "spiderweb" the raft between the hulls. A catamaran that is floating high on airlock but that does not offer habitation might be a likely candidate for the spiderweb approach. "Wash" conditions in the inverted tunnel need to be appraised. Suitable elastic line (like a full spool of heavy nylon cord) and multiple attachment points, located on the raft and on the sides of the hulls, would be required. This system would retain intimate contact between the raft and the main boat . . . .

The tether and/or the spiderweb is your link with the mothership, so make sure it is secure. At least three cases in which the raft became separated from the mothership were caused by inadequate tethers.

Finally, Class II vessels, especially those without divers in the crew, may benefit from having all emergency equipment and supplies packaged together and attached to the raft. Class I vessels may elect instead to stow this package inside the boat, but away from fire-risk areas. A detailed description of this "Calamity Pack" appears later in this chapter.

Notice that it is in respect to the life raft, its installation and attachment to the mothership, that Class I vessels are considered superior to Class II. In Class I, the raft is the last alternative, and remains unused while the big boat provides habitation, thus avoiding the danger of the crew becoming separated from the mothership.

But there just might come a time when the crew would wish to separate from the mothership. Before the days of inflatables and unsinkables, disaster was prepared for by carrying at least one longboat aboard every ship. This was a seaworthy sailing skiff. Many sinkings and mutinies were survived by sailors who made long deep-sea voyages in the longboat.

One attribute of the longboat not usually shared by inflatables or unsinkables is mobility. Bladder boats and capsized multihulls are not generally capable of hoisting sail and setting off for the nearest land downwind.

To compensate for this shortcoming, there is at least one life raft on the market that is designed to be sailed. Proponents of this craft have demonstrated its effectiveness at sea. Called the SSD Sailaway Life Raft, it is sold by Survival and Safety Designs of Oakland, California. The proprietor, George Seigler, has spent 52 days at sea testing the prototype, sailing from California to Hawaii! Yet Seigler is the first to equate capsize with a plane crash in this way: "I would never leave a capsized multihull in a life raft unless forced by circumstances. It is just like flying in a disabled aircraft . . . you don't bail out if there's the slightest chance of coming safely back to earth."

A large multihull may be capable of carrying a rigid dinghy designed for ocean voyaging as a lifeboat. It must be sturdily built to withstand the battering it would surely receive should its mothership capsize.

Multihull designer Dick Newick has proposed that a standard inflatable life raft could be mounted between two special inflatable pontoons, and rigged with sail. The raft would provide good shelter aboard a mobilized inflatable catamaran longboat.

One man who has chosen this alternative is Phil Weld, survivor of the capsize of his Newick-designed *Gulf Streamer* (*see* Chapter 7). For Phil's new boat, *Rogue Wave*, Newick designed a seaworthy sailing kayak, which is stowed securely in chocks beside the cockpit coaming. This position makes the kayak accessible in the event of capsize. *Rogue Wave* also carries an SSD Sailaway Life Raft.

Rogue Wave *with longboat fixed to cockpit coaming, where it is available in the event of capsize.*

Phil contends that only under the most unusual circumstances would it make sense to vacate the mothership. However, the occasion might arise when at least one member of the crew should have mobility, for instance, if the mothership drifts past an inhabited island, or drifts away from shipping lanes into a vast reach of ocean after receiving no response to the EPIRB. The skipper might conceivably decide that someone in the crew—perhaps the youngest, strongest, best sailor—should set off in the longboat to summon assistance.

These several factors of selecting and installing the life raft and the longboat are listed at the end of this chapter in the Capsize Preparation Checklist, along with all the other preparations that follow.

3. TOOLS

In the event of capsize, and regardless of the vessel's capsize classification, some means of cutting access hatches in the hull(s) is required. Tools for this job must be readily available.

Something as simple as two hatchets, one secured inside the boat and one outside, will suffice. If conditions permit, a somewhat neater hole can be cut with a drill and a keyhole saw. If heavy fiberglass or fasteners need to be cut, the saw should have hardened teeth to retain sharpness. The piece of hull cut out can be used to form a hatch cover, and later—should the boat be recovered—it would be useful in patching the hole. (Deciding *where* to cut your capsize hatch is covered in item #5.)

The most elaborate preparation would be to construct a waterproof hatch in the boat's bottom that can be removed with wing nuts. The chance of capsize being remote, this step seems a bit extreme but nonetheless reassuring. A complete lack of access is the opposite extreme, and very unnerving. If nothing else, prepare a sharp, cheap hatchet by coating its edge with silicone sealant and secure it with soft wire to the boat's transom or underneath the wing.

It is imperative to have a lanyard on every tool; tie on a stout nylon cord with a loop large enough to slip over the user's head, and long enough to allow using the tool at arm's length. The danger of losing survival equipment is so great that this advice can scarcely be overemphasized. Care in using tools, together with lanyards, is essential.

Stowage of the ship's tools is a matter for consideration. The outstanding advantage that the mothership provides, by virtue of not sinking, can be largely negated if precious items are washed out the hatches after capsize. Tools, food, water, medicines, and survival gear should be stowed to stay in the boat, even upside down.

Hand tools can be kept conveniently in high-quality plastic fishing tackle boxes with latching lids. Two boxes are more convenient to move about than one large, heavy box. If the boxes are not overloaded with heavy tools,

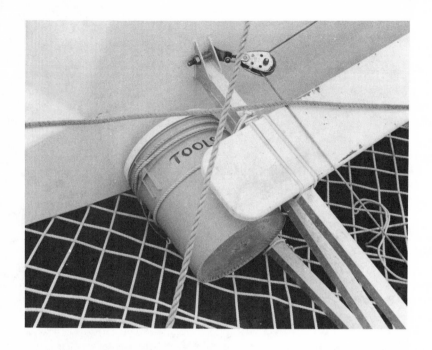

Two methods of attaching emergency tools and swimfins outside
the boat, accessible in the event of capsize.

possibly they will float. They may be routinely stowed in a compartment that would prevent loss after capsize, preferably above the inverted water-line.

A very minimum of preparation, like providing a hatchet outside and considering capsize when stowing tools inside (latching the lids of the tool boxes by habit), could make a tremendous difference in the lot of the castaway. The survival literature is full of examples of extreme hardship and tragedy that could have been avoided by the presence of a few simple implements.

4. CALAMITY PACK

One thing is clearly established by reports of those who have capsized: no matter what emergency equipment is carried, be it the most elaborate collection of sophisticated goodies or the simplest handful of Boy Scout backups, all items should be packaged together, kept dry, and secured carefully against loss. And every member of the crew must know where they are.

The primary function of calamity items is to summon rescue; the secondary function is to increase your chances of surviving, relatively well and happily, until rescue arrives.

Equipment for attracting rescue includes such basics as lights and flares, and proceeds through radar reflectors and emergency radio transmitters. These items can be vulnerable to water damage, so their packaging is very important.

To suggest a list of rescue items is to invite such reactions as, "That's

Hey Regie — how does Montecello '59 Sound? With chicken?

totally inadequate," or "I can't possibly afford all that fancy stuff." But the experience of those who have capsized offshore indicates that there is a logical minimum of equipment that should be aboard. The following list may be applied to boats that sink as well as those that capsize.

Lights. At least one good *waterproof* flashlight, with best-quality unused batteries replaced each season, belongs inside the Calamity Pack. One small handlight for use inside the boat, and one large sealed-beam lantern for flashing signals outside is a more acceptable minimum. The inclusion of a small xenon strobe is logical. The mothership should be equipped with at least one "man-overboard" strobe secured in the cockpit or on a man-overboard buoy, plus another sealed-beam lantern for navigation. If these "outside" lights are recovered after capsize, they will make a valuable addition to the lights in the Calamity Pack.

All kinds of lighting devices exist that could be used in emergencies, from small disposable units to the ones with five-year idle-storage capacity, and others with built-in, squeeze-operated generators. One useful kind of light for capsize preparation is the chemical type, which gives off a bright glow when two chemicals are mixed by breaking a seal inside a small vial. Known as Cyalume lights, these simple gadgets operate for about eight hours on catalytic action, and they are nontoxic if ruptured. Several of these, strategically secured with tape in each cabin of the boat and stored in the Calamity Pack, would provide illumination inside for emergency work.

Flares. Pyrotechnic signal devices gain their effectiveness from several factors: size, brightness, elevation, and duration. Therefore, the best flare for attracting rescue would shoot a very bright ball of smoke and fire very high into the air and keep it there for a long time; thus the parachute flare. The best of these are the large hand-held jobs with skyrocket propulsion, not the pistol-fired type. Trouble is, these big flares cost almost thirty dollars a shot! At least three, stored bone dry in the Calamity Pack, are strongly recommended.

A good supply of smaller flares fired by Very pistol and/or the little hand-held Roman candle jobs are also recommended, but these all offer less brightness, elevation, and duration.

It would be easy to invest two hundred dollars in a supply of pyrotechnics, and some sailors will understandably balk at the expense. So, in the interest of getting some kind of flares on board every offshore multihull, let's consider the good old inexpensive highway flares. These devices, available anywhere auto accessories are sold, have one strong point besides low cost: duration. They will commonly burn for 15 minutes, something no small rocket can do. However, they dribble molten sulphur while ignited, and would be very threatening in any boating situation, especially aboard an inflated life raft! They are not designed to be hand held.

But to serve as backup for a normal selection of flares, a dozen highway flares would give real duration to your signaling capability. A flare handle

CALAMITY PACK ITEMS

Waterproof lights and strobes are each equipped with a lanyard. The lanyard provided with the EPIRB radio needs to have a loop tied in the end for slipping over the head, to prevent loss. The EPIRB's bracket also has a lanyard, and several nails or screws are affixed with masking tape to allow securing the bracket in an elevated position, to receive the EPIRB. Pyrotechnics each have their own waterproof wrapping. Longer metal tube is a "flare handle" for extending highway flares. Also note the large orange banner and orange paint. Net material and nails for the capsize hammocks are at left, with a large spool of stout nylon cord.

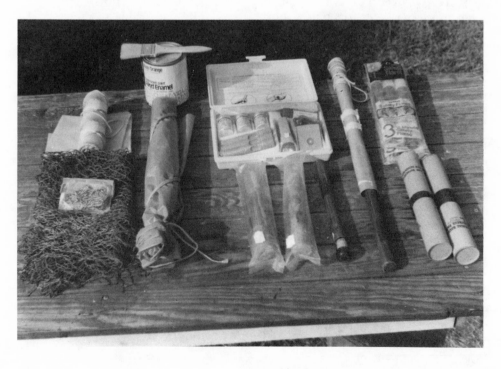

can be packaged with them to make them safer to use. This can be a simple aluminum tube about three feet long and slightly larger in diameter than the flares, so that it can be pinched in at a point about three inches from one end and the flares can be jammed in securely. The tube should also be equipped with a lanyard for lashing it to a longer object for even greater extension. Perhaps a few pre-drilled holes in the tube, and several nails attached with tape, would facilitate making this extension.

Shooting flares can be tricky business, and many cases of burns and fires have resulted. It is advisable to practice on land with one flare of each type. *Face away from the wind,* sit or kneel in a stable position, and use both hands. Wear gloves, or wrap your hands in protective material if possible, and extend the device to leeward of your boat. A pair of gloves packaged with the flares makes a lot of sense.

The best time for attracting rescue is at night. However, of equal importance are day smoke bombs or smoke rockets. At least two of these devices is a minimum; six would be more reasonable. Several types are available: hand-held, pistol-fired, and rocket-propelled smoke signals. A few of each probably would give the best selection, and the bigger the device, the larger the resultant cloud of colored smoke. Some of the most productive are those made for use by skydivers to mark their descent. Elevate the smoke flare by attaching it to an oar or pole to increase effectiveness, because it is not very effective anyway. As seen by castaways, it appears to produce a huge cloud of smoke, but it is not especially noticeable from a great distance. A fire extinguisher makes an inadequate substitute.

Many pyrotechnics available from yacht suppliers are not waterproof. Even those marked "for marine use" are pitifully vulnerable to moisture. It is sometimes possible to order commercial grade or "military-spec" flares from the same manufacturers, but in spite of pressure-testing, even these should be protected carefully until ready for use. A splash of water will not render them inoperative, but long-term stowage in damp conditions finally takes its toll. Highway flares are fairly well sealed in wax and plastic, but anything on a boat is subjected to dampness. Pyrotechnic materials are hygroscopic, meaning they attract moisture in vapor form, which can penetrate packaging much better than moisture in liquid form. Therefore, absolutely waterproof storage for the flares is very much in order. Plastic pails with snap-tight lids make suitable containers (they can sometimes be obtained free from restaurants). It is wise to package the lights and flares in their own individual waterproof wrappings—double bags to make sure—before placing them inside the container.

Because of the protection and suspicion that these fancy signaling devices deserve, other simpler types of day signals constitute an important adjunct to the night-time stuff. Such simple items as a signal mirror (the type that will not turn black from water damage), a large orange banner, water dye-markers, and bright orange paint will all be wisely included in your Calamity Pack. Special Day-glo orange paint, packaged with a cheap brush attached, can be used to decorate the upturned portions of the hulls, greatly increasing the chance of being spotted. Real survival orange can be seen at amazing distances.

During normal cruising, most skippers will want a supply of flares handy to be used to prevent collision or attract attention in any clutch situation other than capsize. These "right-side-up" flares should not be asked to serve double duty: they should not be the only ones on board. In the event of capsize (or sinking), they will probably be wet or inaccessible. There should be two supplies in two separate locations—near the cockpit and in the Calamity Pack. If this is beyond your pocketbook, then perhaps it is best to store all flares in the Calamity Pack and do your cockpit signaling with a good spotlight, which is required there for navigation anyway.

Radar Reflector. If a search is in progress for a capsized multihull, the radar reflector will contribute enormously to the chances of a successful search. The reflector should be well elevated above the surface.

Several collapsible or compact reflectors are on the market, and the old-fashioned intersecting-squares design works about as well as any. A war-surplus model still available, made of Monel screen stretched across a collapsible frame like a square umbrella, provides the largest reflecting surface for the least weight and windage, but this kind of reflector is old and requires care in handling.

Radar reflectors can be handmade easily out of sheet aluminum, or out of plywood covered with aluminum foil glued on with contact cement. In fact, one of the most foolproof and inexpensive reflectors can be made from a large net bag or sail bag that is stuffed full with scrap aluminum foil. Old offset-printing plates, disposable pie pans, and regular kitchen foil can all be loosely crumpled and stuffed into the bag. A nylon lanyard woven into each end of the bag will serve to secure it so that it cannot swing. Thus, you can provide an emergency radar reflector by simply including a suitable bag and a roll of foil in your Calamity Pack.

For maximum effect, the radar reflector should be elevated as high as possible, at least six feet above the surface. A pole to raise it two or three times this height (see item #8) can also serve to lift a banner, lights, flares, etc.

Perhaps the best time to put a radar reflector in the Calamity Pack is when providing one for the mothership, which should have some form of reflector fixed permanently in the rigging. Two reflectors can be bought or made at the same time and one assigned to the Calamity Pack.

EPIRB. The Emergency Position Indicating Radio Beacon (also known as ELT, Emergency Locator Transmitter) is the most sophisticated and expensive item required for your Calamity Pack. These radios have been used for years in private aircraft, but only recently have they become common equipment aboard private boats. Boating models have built-in flotation, not separate flotation collars. Considering how easily equipment can be lost in emergency situations, built-in flotation is critical. Also, a lanyard with a loop must be already on the EPIRB so that before using it, you can tie it to yourself (the same goes for anything small, like a knife or a light or a mirror).

In operation, the EPIRB transmits a tone on the VHF international distress frequency that can be used by rescuers to home-in on the castaways. This can bring help by attracting attention from a passing ship or plane, but that is not their actual purpose. Don't be misled by advertisements reading, "... ELT brings help fast." Phil Weld expended two units without results when his *Gulf Streamer* capsized in the Atlantic. There were contrails in the sky while the beacons were operating. When Russell Brown's proa was scuttled by a collision with flotsam, he used his unit for six hours almost within sight of Cape Canaveral, and nobody responded. There are many such cases. The truth is that commercial craft do not routinely monitor the VHF frequency broadcast by EPIRBs. (Also, about half of the EPIRB signals to which the Coast Guard does respond are false alarms!)

Commercial vessels and aircraft use a different frequency, 500 Mhz, for their own distress communications. A distress call on 500 Mhz actuates an alarm on commercial craft within range. However, no inexpensive, portable 500 Mhz beacons are available at this time. One British-made "Gibson Girl" unit, with hand crank, will do the job, but it costs about $1,200. When the public realizes that this type of beacon is what we should have, then perhaps the demand will increase and the price decrease. The commercial shipping and airline industries have no desire to go into the search and rescue business, so they will logically resist development of this equipment for private use. However, with reasonable fees set for rescue and salvage services, and a heavy penalty levied for false alarms, perhaps the 500 Mhz private distress beacon would become practical.

In the meantime, the contemporary VHF units are viable equipment. They do summon assistance in some cases, and they certainly contribute to location of boats reported overdue. With an overdue report, commercial traffic in the area is alerted to monitor VHF, and they should be able to determine the general location of the broadcast. Then the searchers can compare the EPIRB tone and the radar echo (assuming the distressed vessel is equipped with a radar reflector) to pinpoint the castaways even in thick weather or darkness. By itself, the VHF distress signal is not especially directional, and not nearly as effective for pinpoint location as radar. Therefore, it is the combination of the EPIRB and the radar reflector that gives best results. They belong together.

Depending on temperature, the batteries installed in EPIRBs will only broadcast for a few days. In some situations, it might be wise to operate a unit only intermittently, or when contrails or ships are within sight. Because VHF transmission is line-of-sight only, there is little point in expending the battery in a very remote stretch of ocean with nobody around to listen. The beacon might better be used only when potential rescue is within sight or sound, especially if the castaways are well ensconced in a good, long-term survival habitat with plenty of provisions.

120

For installation aboard the usual monohull, the EPIRB comes equipped with a special quick-release bracket that is mounted near the main hatchway so that the radio can be grabbed as the craft sinks. But on most multihulls, the EPIRB belongs in the Calamity Pack.

The bracket can be used to mount the radio in a secure, elevated position on the capsized vessel. Several nails (or sheet-metal screws for a fiberglass boat) can be attached to the bracket with masking tape so that the bracket can be mounted to the hull or the keel or the rudder or the extended centerboard. Such an installation should produce a stronger signal, and if due care is taken to protect the radio against loss while the bracket is being installed (by fitting a lanyard in advance), then the chances of retaining the radio are substantially improved.

In a capsize situation, the EPIRB should come out of the Calamity Pack and be actuated only after everything is under control.

In Class II boats, when the crew is inhabiting the raft, it is wise to keep the EPIRB (and the entire Calamity Pack) aboard the raft until such time as the skipper is convinced that contact with the mothership can be maintained. From that point onward, the mothership can be used to mount the EPIRB, banner, lights, radar reflector, etc., just as in Class I, even though the crew is inhabiting the raft.

Provisions. Most of the provisions on board a multihull could still be available to the crew in case the craft should capsize. Proper stowage is required to prevent loss and water damage to the food, but even without proper stowage one assumes that some of the vessel's cruising provisions would remain aboard in good condition after capsize.

It is nevertheless advisable to include some emergency provisions in the Calamity Pack. Class II vessels, especially, should have food and water attached to the raft, and Class I crews may want to assemble a few provisions for easy access and consumption. Some food and water will assist the crew in their performance of the initial survival procedures. After things have settled down, the ship's cruising stores can be assessed and organized. Perhaps even the stove can be used.

To go all the way with emergency provisions, as would be necessary for sinkable craft, a complete survival rations kit may be purchased or assembled and attached to the raft. The opposite extreme is to do nothing about capsize provisions. Somewhere in between, it is a simple matter to collect a few cans of meat and fruit, perhaps a quart of peanut butter, a bag of cereal, seeds and nuts, a gallon of water, a can opener and a spoon, and place them in a plastic pail with a tight-fitting lid. Tie the parcel to the boat (Class I) or to the raft (Class II) and go on about your business knowing that you have given yourself one more hedge against disaster.

Inside this food parcel might be a good place to put miscellaneous needs. Any special medications needed by the crew? How about a spare (old) set of eyeglasses for anyone who can't function without? A first aid kit, basic navigation tools, and some morale-boosters, like a small radio, some eating

Calamity packs with lanyards for attaching to the mothership or to the life raft.

goodies, a deck of cards, a harmonica, might come in handy. Some extra tools could be useful: pliers, baling wire, nails, tape, cord, matches, two knives with lanyards . . . just knowing that the stuff is in there will be solace in the night.

Survival Suit. While normal foul-weather gear should still be available to capsized castaways, additional protection will be needed, especially in the cold waters of higher latitudes. Commercial fishermen sometimes use survival suits that are like large, loose-fitting skindiver's wet suits complete with hood, hands, and feet. Such gear would probably be too bulky to include in your Calamity Pack, but it could be stored in a secure place.

One suspects, however, that the survival suit would find itself in use on cold nights while cruising; it could be a valuable piece of gear for the watchkeeper, whether capsized or not. Its normal stowage place should protect it from loss should capsize occur.

Commercial-grade survival suits are rather expensive, but there are substitutes to be considered if funds are low. Snowmobile suits could be used. Other insulated work clothes, such as one-piece padded overalls, would be cheaper yet. These substitutes would soak up water and would not keep a swimmer afloat. But for standing watch, or lying in your capsize hammock, any heat-loss protection at all, wet or dry, could be very welcome.

A condensed list of Calamity Pack items appears in the Capsize Preparation Checklist at the end of this chapter.

5. EMERGENCY ACCESS HATCH

Deciding where to cut the access hatch, in advance, involves a little crawling around in the bilges while imagining what it would be like with everything upside down.

For Class II vessels, simply decide where to cut in order to gain easy access to provisions inside. Avoid large structural members and cabinetwork. Because some Class II craft may float high on airlock but settle lower upon violation of the airlock, cut the hole as high as possible on the upturned hull, hoping to have some air space inside after the craft settles. Or, if the water is warm and you can skindive, perhaps you will elect not to cut a hatch, but to dive for the mothership's contents instead. If a capsize has occurred near shore, or in a well-traveled sea lane, and the conditions permit (or if the crew is inhabiting a well-provisioned raft), the skipper may elect to postpone cutting an access hatch as long as possible. Of course, easy access to the raft would be required. A ready-made hatch in the underwing providing access to the cabin would further reduce the immediate need for cutting a hole in the hull's bottom. Finally, if a hatch is to be cut, there is a strong temptation to put it down low, near the underwing, so that when the craft is recovered she won't have a big hole below the normal waterline. However, in any protracted survival situation, these alternatives are inadequate. Unless the hole is made up high, in the very bottom of the hull near the keel, then a person coming and going through the hatch will get wet. Furthermore, waves washing over the underwing will slosh inside and disturb the peace, giving the occupants a false impression that the mothership is sinking. But the most important reason for a high location is this: the capsize hatchway is the cockpit of the stricken vessel. It must provide an elevated, sheltered position for the watchkeeper. Standing a constant watch, day and night, will do more to ensure rescue than anything else. Once rescued, you can concern yourself with repairing the boat!

Oh! Fred, please don't violate the airlock.

Because of the importance of the watchkeeper, his position inside the boat should be carefully considered when selecting a site for the hatch. With just a bit of forethought you can probably arrange a seat by propping a floorboard between a drawer on one side and a shelf opposite. The seat should be located about 30 inches below the hatch so that the watchkeeper can sit with his eye level just above the "deck." Nearby there should be some kind of shelf or cubbyhole where the supply of lights and flares, and the signal mirror, can be kept high and dry and handy.

If the hatch is cut with one edge against a frame or bulkhead, then the radar mast (item #8) can be stepped in the hatch and fastened to that frame or bulkhead, to serve as a hand-hold for entering and leaving the hatch, and also as a grab-post to steady a person standing on the hull outside.

The hatchway may at times require a cover. If the hole has been neatly cut and the piece saved, some fabric may be nailed along the edges to make it a good hatch cover. Fabric alone, such as a piece of carpet or upholstery, will keep out spray and wind if it is secured against loss. Nailed to the hull along one edge, it might also shade the watchkeeper from the sun.

The minimum size for hatch openings is about 12 by 18 inches. Eighteen inches square is better, and a large person in heavy clothing needs an opening 18 by 24 inches.

All of these factors should be considered when deciding on the hatch site. The spot can be marked or memorized for location from inside, but how are you going to find it when cutting from outside, perhaps in the dark? One way would be to locate the hatch in relation to some feature on the outside of the hull: "one foot aft of that through-hull fitting," or "just forward of the centerboard slot." When the boat is built, it may be possible to locate a through-hull fitting exactly at one edge of the proposed hatch site. If the fitting is made of plastic, and the keyhole saw is sharp, the fitting provides a logical "keyhole" at which to begin cutting.

Otherwise, you may have to chop a small hole so that you can reach inside and feel around to get your position. This is why it is important to select the site for an emergency hatch in advance. It can be marked or otherwise prepared, and everyone in the offshore crew should know exactly where it is to be located, and why.

Some multihulls have one end of the interior separated from the other, or one entire hull built apart from the other, thus prohibiting access to the whole interior from just one capsize hatch. Watertight bulkheads or central cockpits might mean that two hatches must be cut in a trimaran, one forward and one aft. In catamarans, perhaps one hatch in each hull would be in order.

This may seem like a frivolous exercise in chopping holes in your boat, but consider this: two hatches provide cockpits for two watchkeepers. If there are enough members in the crew, two hatches will allow standing double watches. And in any rescue situation, eyes count.

In spite of massive efforts at great expense, the Coast Guard's record of success in locating multihull castaways is not impressive. Search aircraft from

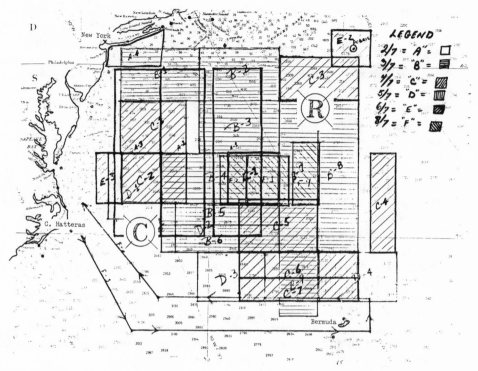

Plot of fruitless missions flown in search of Meridian. *Large "C" indicates approximate position of capsize; "R" represents position of rescue.*

three service branches were involved in the *Meridian* search. While some of these military missions are commonly flown for routine training, when the planes are actually looking for a vessel reported overdue, their cost is laid to that particular search. By this accounting, the *Meridian* search was said to have cost $400,000—and the results were zero. Huge tracts of ocean are sometimes combed to no avail. This is largely because modern search-and-rescue procedures depend on sophisticated equipment and have their best chance of succeeding when the target is also technologically well equipped, with an EPIRB and a radar reflector! To date, few multihull castaways have been suitably prepared to give the Coast Guard a good chance in the search.

Several widely publicized capsize rescues have been made by commercial vessels purely by chance: the freighter or the fisherman just happened to be coming along and some sharp-eyed sailor on the bridge spotted the raft or the upturned boat. Usually several ships are sighted by the castaways before they are spotted in return. Equipped with lights, flares, radar reflector, and EPIRB, their odds of being noticed by the watch of a passing ship are greatly increased but still slim, unless the castaways themselves stand watch. Commercial shipping is not generally known for its vigilant surveillance of the sea, but in spite of stories to the contrary, many ships do maintain full-time visual, radar, and radio watches. The castaways' problem is to

125

attract the attention of someone who is watching, or who is supposed to be watching, and that can best be done when the passing ship is first noticed by the castaways. Then they can go into their program of flashing mirrors or lights, waving banners, and shooting flares and smoke bombs. If these signals are noticed by a commercial vessel's crew, even from a great distance, they will step over to the radar, and the radio, to seek some confirmation of the visual distress signal—which would not have been made in the first place without someone on the stricken multihull standing watch.

To hypothesize, let's say that one of the two watchmates on your capsized multihull notices the mast lights of a ship, hull down over the horizon. You fire a rocket and light up a highway flare. Someone on the bridge of the ship says he thought he saw a rocket. The mate steps to the radar screen and, sure enough, he gets a radar echo from the same direction. The radio monitor, turned up from its standby volume, is bringing in the beep of an EPIRB, also from the same direction. The mate decides to awaken the captain, and together they decide to check you out.

Rescue eventually arrives because someone in your crew saw those distant lights.

So, standing watches from secure, elevated positions—the more the better—is the best opportunity castaways have of being rescued. Remember this when selecting the location of the access hatch(es) in your Class I multihull. With a little forethought, some sort of perch can also be arranged for the watchkeeper on a Class II boat.

And while you're crawling through the bilge, imagining what it would be like with everything upside down, take heart. If fate should ever take you out beyond the ragged edge, your situation will be somewhat superior to that of the sorry sailor who finds himself scanning the horizon through the sea-level peephole of a solitary canopied raft.

6. CAPSIZE HAMMOCKS

A capsized Class I vessel offers shelter to the crew, but what kind of shelter? Where do you sit or sleep in a boat that's upside down and half full of water?

The old sailor's hammock seems to be the handiest solution for several reasons. It is light and cheap and easily stored away until needed. It may be secured in a variety of positions. It is relatively comfortable. Lying in a hammock beats crawling into a shelf or squeezing underneath a bunk or curling up on the bottom of the dinette table. All of those are alternatives if no hammock is available, but a hammock is much less likely to cause bedsores and seawater boils.

Most of the smaller Class I multihulls will not offer enough space for swinging-up full-size hammocks for a large crew. But there will usually be compartments where a small platform of netting can be secured between cabinets and frames to give space for all but the watchkeeper to rest their weary torsos. Space might be tight, but one's appendages can project into an adjacent locker or the neighbor's hammock. A little inventiveness and a few materials can render even the smaller offshore multihulls habitable when upside down.

A platform can be fashioned from several yards of nylon purse net (about 1 3/4-inch stretched-mesh size) bought from a fisheries supplier and cut into pieces roughly equal to the platform spaces available in the boat. A small hammer and a supply of small, stout nails can be packaged with the net. The nails will be driven at close intervals all around the platform space, and the net simply hooked over the nails to outline the desired platform. This net is amazingly strong if it is fairly new; discarded net is unsuitable.

More elaborate preparations are of course possible. Tailor-made hammocks or net platforms to fit the spaces available, with attachments installed in the boat, make a lot of sense.

Or, at the very minimum, the skipper can look around in his bilges and simply imagine, in advance, how he would erect some kind of "nest" for his crew in the event of capsize. Even with warm water and a big boat, something must be arranged that will get the crew up out of the water and into a semirestful position. Otherwise, you would be better off in the raft.

The raft, incidentally, might serve as a comfortable "annex" to the mothership in fair weather. Spiderwebbed in the tunnel or suitably tethered to leeward, it could be used to take the pressure off the accommodations in the "main house," and provide an outpost for privacy or fishing. The same applies to any kind of dinghy. But only in the mothership can you relax in a hammock.

Please don't misunderstand. I'm not trying to paint an unrealistically rosy picture of capsize survival. But relative to surviving a sinking, there are some obvious benefits.

Do you feel a draft?

7. TUNNEL LIFELINES

Clinging to the underwing of an upturned multihull is difficult, if not impossible, in all but calm conditions. Some sort of lifeline is imperative.

A line tied longitudinally around the wing from one end to the other each time before the vessel goes to sea provides a means of climbing up on the underwing in case of capsize. Something to grasp at a higher level would also be needed, so a few eye-strap fittings should be installed on the hulls near the normal waterline. If lines are attached to these while cruising, they will vibrate noisily, in the water, so they should be attached to additional eye-straps located on the underwing, and moved to the waterline eye-straps if needed.

Safety harnesses, of the type worn by sailors on deck, could also be used to fasten oneself to these tunnel lifelines. However, all harnesses must be equipped with snap hooks *on both ends* of the tether line. This is imperative in multihulls, so that a crew member attached by a harness at the time of capsize can release himself easily. The rollover is said to be rather gentle, but being caught underneath the boat with your tether attached at its far end could be quite distressing. Some seasoned sailors suggest that a safety harness is much more likely to be worn, and thus used, if it is sewn in to your foul-weather slicker or float-coat.

Lacking proper tunnel lifelines, any available cordage could be slung around the centerboard or keel or rudder, or even around a speedometer pickup or a propeller shaft, depending on the boat. Chopping holes in the hulls to secure lines around framing inside is not the best idea, especially if it would violate the airlock! Sturdy eye-straps, installed in advance, with lines available outside, are obviously preferable. In locating the eye-straps on the hulls, consider where the fasteners will fall inside. It seems easier to install them with through-bolts in open panels of planking rather than to try hitting framing inside with screws. Consider placing them so that they might be used to spiderweb the life raft, and where they would serve as attachments for guy wires to support the radar mast.

8. RADAR REFLECTOR MAST

A spar readily available without diving would be invaluable for elevating the radar reflector and other signaling devices.

Usually there will be small spars already available someplace on the boat; a spinnaker pole or a whisker pole is ideal. If you have a sailing dinghy, the dinghy's mast can be used. Even a fishing spear would do. A good diver might remove the boat's boom. But the best radar mast is probably one that is intended for the purpose: a stout piece of aluminum tube, about as long as the underwing, secured thereto and available without diving. The ends of the tube can be prepared for your specific stepping procedure, your radar reflector attachment, your guys, and even a halyard. For example, several holes could be drilled near the base of the pole, and large nails stored inside

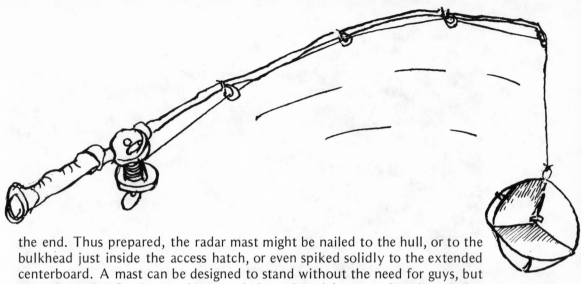

the end. Thus prepared, the radar mast might be nailed to the hull, or to the bulkhead just inside the access hatch, or even spiked solidly to the extended centerboard. A mast can be designed to stand without the need for guys, but a good supply of nylon cord is nonetheless advised for guys. Standing rigging on the radar mast can support a raincatcher as well. A sail strung up between the guys can funnel rainwater into the hatchway, where it can be collected free of salt, and without even getting the crew wet.

Two lengths of telescoping tube would give you more height. Some dinghy masts and whisker poles are designed with nesting sections. These would perhaps be best of all, if stored for easy underwing access when the vessel goes offshore. (For real elevation, a radar-reflective kite or helium balloon might make a sensible addition to your Calamity Pack. Any kite or balloon, so long as it is orange, would be easily spotted on the distant horizon.)

Other spars could also be very useful for other purposes. Long bamboo or fiberglass fishing rods might be used for waving flags or extending flares, as well as for fishing. A very valuable spar to have aboard would be the skindivers' "Hawaiian Sling"—a long, sometimes telescoping pole with a barbed gig on one end and a powerful rubber sling on the other. An ordinary spear gun would be valuable for spearing fish or birds.

(Speaking of fish, a drifting platform like a capsized multihull apparently attracts ocean fishes. They congregate beneath, and even swim inside. Getting them to bite on a hook is tricky, so a small gill net or a spear would perhaps bring better results.)

9. COLORING

Blue or green bottom paint is less visible than red. If the boat has a boot-top stripe, it might as well be bright. Orange underwing surfaces improve the boat's chance of being spotted from the air. As noted earlier, a small can of Day-glo orange paint, stored in the Calamity Pack with a brush, can be used to decorate the boat after capsize, making her much more noticeable.

Nonskid paint on the underwing surface is of questionable value. It would certainly improve the footing for the castaways, but it might, if sharp, damage a raft secured by spiderweb to the underwing. Perhaps a suitable compromise is to apply narrow strips of nonskid paint along the edges of the

Five-foot capsized scale model has two access hatches in the main hull and is floating high on air locked in the outboard hulls. An inflated life raft is secured by a spiderweb to multiple attachments on the raft and on the hulls. The radar mast elevates the radar reflector, the banner, and the EPIRB. The hull is decorated with orange paint. With these features provided and deployed, castaways could survive for months inside the mothership and/or in the raft.

underwing, up against the hulls, and wide areas of nonskid near the ends of the wing, away from the raft's logical position.

The life raft canopy should definitely be a bright color.

A detailed record of the boat's coloring would aid in search operations, so the checklist at the end of this chapter has a space for recording your boat's coloring.

10. STOWAGE

What would happen to all the stuff stored inside your boat if it was suddenly turned upside down? Certainly a lot of it would fall out, run out, and tumble around inside. However, with the very simplest of preparations, much of this precious material can be saved.

The critical items—such as the Calamity Pack, fresh water, and food—can be stored in containers that keep seawater out and also float. Stowage compartments with openings lying athwartships can be used to advantage. Even better, lockers with doors can be fitted with finger-hooks or turnpegs. The bilge compartments where valuable emergency materials are located

130

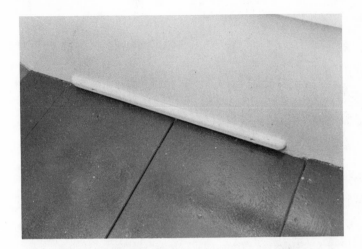

To prevent bilges from spilling their contents in case of capsize, floorboards can be secured with one end beneath strip (top) and the other end with turn-pegs (bottom).

(such as fresh water in plastic jugs) can have their floorboards equipped with turnpegs also.

Water currents inside a capsized multihull may generate a pumping action that can draw even floating items out through the hatches, so don't leave important things unattached. A monkey hammock, secured in the bilge of each cabin, would serve well for gathering up loose items after capsize to prevent loss. Good, strong hatches are needed to resist being opened by water action after capsize.

Fuel and drinking water will run slowly out of their tanks if the boat turns turtle. Freshwater tankage should therefore be augmented by separate, small containers. Offshore reserves can be kept in jugs that are not completely full, so that they will float. At least one five-gallon jug can be tied to a lanyard. Tank water can be saved from running out if there are valves in the plumbing. Water tank vent tubes can be led deep into the bilge—deeper than

Bulk provisions in this hold can be protected from loss with a simple storage net that is hooked into place during major storms.

the tanks—to prevent drainage through the vents upon inversion. These vent tubes are then available as drinking straws. Collapsible water tanks can be moved around after capsize to make more habitation space in the bilge.

Fuel tank vents exit overboard, of course. While there may be no apparent reason to save the fuel, its loss could make an awful and dangerous mess, so valves may be installed in the fuel tank plumbing. In the absence of flares or lights, fuel could be used to make a torch for signaling, assuming that the boat is not swimming in the stuff and that some dry matches have been kept in the Calamity Pack.

Engine oil could also make a miserable mess, unless it is confined by design to the crankcase or to a legitimate engine room. Battery acid would quickly become diluted to a harmless state, but the vapors caused by mixing seawater with battery acid could be very dangerous to the inhabitants of a sealed hull (no cut hatchway). Other contaminants, such as discharge from a holding tank, could also cause portions of a Class I boat's interior to become uninhabitable. Therefore, confinement of these contaminants should be considered part of capsize preparation. If you find you have a mess on your hands, the raft could serve for temporary habitation until things inside the boat are brought under control.

Food and equipment should be routinely stowed to ensure that they will still be there when you want them. Whatever is put away in a plastic jug or bucket will float, and just about everything else that really matters can be secured against loss by design and construction of the stowage spaces.

132

Diving skills are very useful to capsize castaways—much more useful than to the survivors of a sinking, unless of course their boat has sunk in quite shallow water. It would be good for someone in the crew of every offshore multihull to be a skindiver. This skill comes in handy in normal operation and maintenance, and in case of capsize it allows the castaways to make full use of the mothership's contents. After things have calmed down, a diver can wriggle through rigging and search flooded portions of the hulls, popping up to make use of airpockets. Air tanks and scuba training are not necessary. Just a bare introduction to the use of swimfins, mask, and snorkel would be of great value for everyone in the crew. Practice in a pool, and then you can all play the game of swimming underneath your boat wherever she is normally moored. Anyone who can swim underneath his multihull from one side to the other could dive to its contents if the boat has capsized.

A permanently installed boarding ladder will do much to encourage swimming and skindiving from the boat, and thereby induce the development of those skills. The ladder would also be a great advantage in man overboard recovery. If your multihull's design happens to include a nearly vertical transom and a relatively flat afterbody, then a permanent boarding ladder mounted on the transom would provide a means of climbing out of the sea even if the boat were upside down. The ladder then is the ideal place to attach tools for cutting the capsize access hatch.

In the case of capsize, swimfins are marvelous tools; they increase the swimmer's power by up to 40 percent. It makes sense for multimariners to keep a pair, with a mask and snorkel too, stored with the Calamity Pack. Knowing how to use them adds an element of great enjoyment during normal cruising, and can also bring a sense of confidence—even of invincibility—to those who sail in unsinkable boats.

Almost all of the capsize preparations discussed in this chapter are appropriate for monohulls, too. Sinkable vessels don't require capsize hammocks or access hatches or underwing lifelines, but they sure can use a life raft and a Calamity Pack. Even many of the storage considerations apply to all boats. With food and equipment well organized for easy access, and protection from water, much of it could be quickly gathered up in case of any kind of disaster.

Multihull sailors may wish to memorize a projected chronology of steps to be taken immediately after capsize. Every case would differ according to the circumstances, the type of multihull, and the degree of preparation. Nonetheless, certain basics will apply.

The immediate concern is for the crew. Take the head count. Assist in extricating anyone who may be caught underneath the boat. Get everyone aboard, and administer first aid if necessary. Anyone who is inside the boat at the time of capsize should stay inside, and pound on the hull to indicate his position. The impulse to "abandon ship" must be resisted strongly. If claustrophobia develops, busy yourself with gathering up floating objects . . . a critical step. Those outside should not try to enter the craft by diving unless the head count shows somebody missing. Rig the tunnel lifelines.

The second concern is for the boat and her contents. Anyone inside should take immediate steps to secure the ship by closing tank valves and any through-hull fittings that could cause the loss of airlock. The main electrical switch should be turned off. Items floating inside should be gathered up immediately to prevent loss.

If your multihull is Class I, you would next cut the access hatch, make sure the ship is secure inside if no one has done that, and rig the capsize hammocks. If your multihull is Class II, you will go directly to the raft. Pay close attention to its tethers and/or its spiderweb attachment.

After all of the above is accomplished and everything is under control, it is time to carefully install the EPIRB, erect the radar reflector, and perhaps fire off a rocket.

To help avoid panic, this simple list can be kept in mind:
(1) Take head count
(2) Administer first aid
(3) Rig tunnel lifelines
(4) Secure ship
(5) Retrieve stowage
(6) Cut access hatch or secure life raft
(7) Occupy hammocks or occupy life raft
(8) Install EPIRB and switch-on if communication is likely

Every sailor must acknowledge the remote possibility of a slow roll or a quick sink. Never was this ultimatum more manifest than to Dougal Robertson, author of the classic *Survive the Savage Sea* (Praeger Publishers: New York, Washington). After an attack by whales, his ketch, *Lucette,* sank within minutes: "I caught a last glimpse of *Lucette,* the water level with her spreaders and only the tops of her sails showing. Slowly she curtsied below the waves, a lady to the last. She was gone when I looked again."

These things happen. They always have and they always will. But the chance of disaster, whether it be sinking or capsize, is so remote that the risk is quite acceptable—IF basic preparations have been made. In all probability, your capsize preparations will never be put to the test. But once made, adequate preparations yield perpetual benefits in peace of mind.

EXPLANATION OF CHECKLIST FORM

A capsize preparation checklist is provided on pages 136-137. The multihull skipper should fill out one copy to keep on board. It is recommended that

Hey Ed, we gotta mothership!

maintenance of emergency equipment be recorded, and that the form be reviewed with all crew members before each offshore voyage.

A second copy should be completed and filed ashore as a record of how the vessel is prepared for capsize. Knowledge of preparedness aboard is very useful to search-and-rescue authorities, should the vessel ever be reported overdue.

After the skipper has read the foregoing discussion of the items on the checklist, he should be able to select among the various alternatives to suit his boat and his resources.

If your multihull is designed, built, and operated to include a reasonable accumulation of capsize-prevention features (*see* Chapter 7), and is also fairly well prepared for capsize should it come, then you can sail offshore with as much confidence as any sailor in any boat.

CHECKLIST FORM
For Capsize Preparation

Vessel's name_____

Owner's name_____

State registration or documentation no. _____

Description: Length _____ Type _____

    Design/class _____ (for colors, see item #9)

1. *CLASSIFICATION*
   - ☐   Class I, habitable when capsized
   - ☐   Class II, nonhabitable when capsized

2. *LIFE RAFT INFORMATION*
   - ☐   Heavy-duty life raft (describe)_____
   - ☐   Light-duty life raft (describe)_____
     Year of purchase and last inspection_____
   - ☐   Inflatable dinghy (with cover?)
   - ☐   Hard dinghy (with cover?)
   - ☐   Seaworthy "longboat" (describe)_____
   - ☐   Raft installed for easy access when capsized
   - ☐   Raft secured inside boat
   - ☐   Suitable life raft tether(s) provided
   - ☐   Materials to spiderweb raft in tunnel provided

3. *TOOLS*
   - ☐   Emergency hatch-cutting tools, with lanyards, secured inside boat
   - ☐   Emergency hatch-cutting tools, with lanyards, secured outside boat
   - ☐   Routine tool stowage arranged to consider the possibility of capsize

4. *CALAMITY PACK*
   - ☐   Calamity Pack attached to raft
   - ☐   Calamity Pack secured inside boat
   - ☐   Lights (list those in Calamity Pack)_____

☐ Flares (list those in Calamity Pack)_____

_____

☐ Radar reflector (describe)_____
☐ EPIRB (note due-date of battery replacement)_____
☐ Provisions (in Calamity Pack)_____

_____

☐ Survival suit on board (how many?)_____
☐ Medicines_____

5. *EMERGENCY ACCESS HATCH*
   ☐ Waterproof opening in bottom of boat
   ☐ Location of capsize hatchway planned (how many?)_____
   ☐ Seat and shelf for watchkeeper(s) arranged

6. *CAPSIZE HAMMOCKS*
   ☐ Capsize hammocks, with attachments, provided (how many?)_____

7. *UNDERWING PREPARATIONS*
   ☐ Underwing attachments installed for tunnel lifelines
   ☐ Attachments installed to spiderweb raft in tunnel
   ☐ Nonskid paint (away from spiderwebbed raft's position)

8. *RADAR REFLECTOR MAST*
   ☐ Spar for radar reflector mast provided (approximate
     elevation)_____

9. *COLORING*
   Sails _____   Deck _____
   Superstructure _____   Topsides _____
   Underwing _____   Boot top _____
   Bottom paint _____

10. *STOWAGE*
    ☐ Stowage of supplies and equipment arranged to consider the
      possibility of capsize
    ☐ Plumbing valves to save tankage and prevent loss of airlock
    ☐ Five-gallon water jug tied into bilge

7

Capsize Prevention
by Design and Seamanship

Ocean cruising is normally a very sedate endeavor. Calms and light airs often prevail, and at times the operation of the vessel gets to be very boring.

But there are other times, however rare, when one regrets ever having complained about a boring calm. On these occasions the crew must decide what degree of danger happens to accompany the excitement. For inexperienced sailors, the danger is often overestimated, and fear complicates the picture by impairing the performance of the crew. Navigation becomes suspect. The most common kind of accident may result: the boat is stranded or stacked up on the shore.

We have seen that the multihull is inherently forgiving in shipwreck accidents, and so the "ragged edge" between disaster and survival is rather broad.

By contrast, the most uncommon kind of multihull accident that might result is capsize. The "ragged edge" can be broadened here, too. By making use of what is now known about prevention, the chance of capsize in a multihull can be reduced to just about the same as the chance of sinking in a monohull.

Capsize prevention and sinking prevention are separate problems, but both are approached from the standpoints of design and seamanship. Strangely enough, the appropriate measures in each case aren't a whole lot different in the end.

CAPSIZE PREVENTION THROUGH DESIGN

Certain multihull designs are less likely to turn over than others. Beam, height, sail area, windage, and weight distribution can all be arranged in combinations to yield a significant accumulation of resistance to capsize.

138

One would think that it doesn't take a whole lot of mumbo-jumbo to predict which of two contrasting multihulls is more likely to get dumped under threatening conditions. Unfortunately, a glance at the elevation of their superstructures, their overall beam, and the height of their masts doesn't always tell the story.

There are some "invisible" design preventives, and some that are controversial. For instance, the relative capsize resistance of the catamaran versus the trimaran has been argued both ways. So has the concept of submersible amas for trimarans. Some say that ama shape and size have something to do with resistance to capsize. I have my own preferences, as do other designers and sailors, and since these opinions differ widely, it suggests that such features are not crucial to capsize prevention.

Which kind of multihull is more vulnerable to waves and which is more vulnerable to wind—these are interesting questions. Catamaran proponents sometimes say that trimarans are more vulnerable to waves, because their small hull is to leeward, and the spacing between this ama and the main hull is less than the distance between the twin hulls of an equivalent catamaran.

139

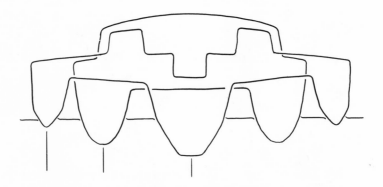

Comparison of relative beam between the author's central-cockpit trimarans and the typical cruising catamaran shows that the trimaran has greater overall beam (above) and the catamaran has greater spacing between the hulls (below).

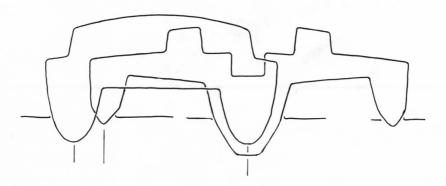

Therefore, wave crests passing from abeam are thought to generate greater heeling and greater rotational momentum in the tri than in the cat.

Conversely, trimaran proponents claim that catamarans are more vulnerable to wind. Their overall beam is less than that of an equivalent trimaran, and because the large hull is to leeward, it cannot depress, so the windward hull lifts up instead, and over you go.

I personally believe that these arguments amount to little more than academic backbiting. Probably there have been more catamarans capsized by heavy gusts in flat water than there have been trimarans flipped by huge seas in a calm! These considerations become meaningful only when the designer can guarantee the separation of the seaway from the blow—which he cannot do, so multihulls must be designed to resist both at once.

Some sailors guard against wind-caused capsize with gadgetry. Several types of automatic sheet-release devices have been used on multihulls, with varying degrees of success. Some depend on (undependable) electricity, others operate with springs or elastic or by pendulum. These gadgets appear to be worthwhile, especially when used in conjunction with self-steering,

LEFT: Home-made mechanical sheet release has two adjustments for wind force and sail area. Coarse adjustment is determined by the number of turns of the sheet around the winch, and depends on whether the sheet is wet or dry (smooth winch drum required). Fine adjustment is provided by tension on the vertical bungee, which is set into the cam cleat below. Barrel bolt is used to lock out the automatic feature, and the arrangement of the cleat, the hinge, and the winch is such that the sheet passes very close to the level of the hinge axis. RIGHT: Depending on the current wind force, sail setting, and sea conditions, adjust the number of turns of sheet on winch, and the bungee tension, until the hinged cleat begins to lift . . . then tighten bungee slightly. With increased strain on the sheet, as in a sudden gust, the sheet slips on the winch and pulls up on the hinged cleat until the sheet is released by pulling out from the top of the cam-action cleat. This device responds to wind force only, not heeling angle.

when the crew may not be so alert, or in "williwaw" conditions, such as sailing in the lee of high land, or in squalls, and when flying the spinnaker.

But any device that is supposed to release a sheet that first wraps around a winch only works if the winch has a non-sandblasted or unknurled (smooth) winch drum to prevent the sheet from binding on the winch under strain. Furthermore, the ability to release may depend on the number of turns of the sheet around the winch, and whether the line itself is wet or dry, a situation that can be changed insidiously by a dollop of spray.

One gadget that definitely works, but is not automatic, is the cam-type quick-release cleat. If correctly mounted in a position sloping toward the helmsperson, this simple device adds great convenience to sailhandling and allows the crew to quickly dump the wind from any sail. Even so, sailors know that sheets will "override" on winches at the worst times. The less expensive Clamcleats should be avoided for this reason. If insufficient turns have been taken around the winch, and there is a sudden, great increase in sheet tension (as in a gust), the sheet may slip on the winch and become

141

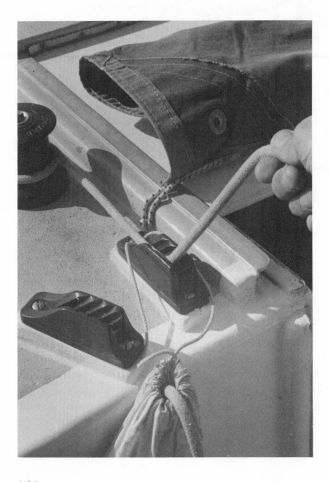

ABOVE: "Riding shotgun" on a multihull sheet in gusty weather. Nonautomatic release is facilitated by correct position and angle of the cam cleat. The cleat must be tilted downward toward the helm. With a quick tug, the helmsman can release the sheet instantly, and slack away with control, to prevent "backlash" tangles on the winch. This particular arrangement of hardware is much more important than any automatic-release feature. However, if the craft is to be operated often under self-steering, then some form of automatic release becomes important. LEFT: If insufficient turns are taken around the winch to prevent slipping, these Clamcleats can jam the sheet, requiring a hard yank upward to release ... not for multihulls. However, the same manufacturer has devised a quick-release model triggered by a separate line that can be led to any position in the craft. (Note drawstring bag for storing sheet.)

142

dangerously jammed in the Clamcleat, preventing quick release. Self-tailing winches also can delay release. But the cam-action cleat, correctly mounted, will allow the helmsperson to ride shotgun on the sheet when he or she is alone in the cockpit in a squall. Even while seated on the opposite side from where the sheet is grasped by the cam-cleat, the crew can uncleat with a slight tug on the sheet and continue holding tension or slack away with control, thereby preventing overrides and tangles. Such a cockpit hardware layout is advised for any boat.

However, gadgets are not adequate preparation for the inevitable occasion when the crew is dopey and the big sails are set and the boat is jumped on by any combination of conditions that threaten a knockdown. Gadgets must be used with caution, or, better yet, distrust. They offer no substitute for the more basic features of design that will help the craft recover from one hell of a blast of wind and wave. We'll have some examples of such recoveries later.

Sail area is an obvious variable in capsize prevention. While the largest sails can be reefed, or handed all together, it is still the larger, more complex sails that are the most difficult to reef and hand. And, once their area is reduced or removed, they still leave high, heavy masts exposed to the wind.

No sailboat, and especially the multihull, should venture offshore without reefing gear that has been well tested beforehand. Multihull mainsails require at least three rows of reefpoints for offshore work. I personally prefer roller-reefing because it offers infinite adjustment of mainsail area. There are many occasions when multihull mainsails are roller-reefed so deeply that the sail emblem is down to the boom. The design of the rig, the hardware layout, and the degree of protection for a sailor working on the foredeck and in the cockpit should all be arranged to encourage reefing. Storm jibs should be very small.

Even given provisions for sail area adjustment, it is my own opinion that modern multihull design is producing more and more vessels that, for their weight, are dangerously over-Dacroned. The ratio of sail area to boat weight, in any kind of sailboat, is the best indicator of how fast she will go, and how stable (or unstable) she will be. Extra-light sailboats with extra-high sailplans are unstable—it's that simple. Whether or not the ballast is removed and replaced by outriggers makes little difference. The light-displacement keelboats can't get away with it—they must carry modest sailplans.

And neither can the flyweight multihulls get away with it! Their instability is not as obvious as the monohull's, because it is masked by great initial stiffness. But their resistance to capsize can be cut short at a very thin ragged edge.

The extreme variation in stability found in today's multihulls is illustrated in a table of values calculated by James Wharram's design assistant, Hanneke Boon, for a variety of seagoing cats and tris. According to her calculations, the proportion of sail area to weight was found to vary all the way from about 100 square feet of sail, per ton of displacement, to over 500 square feet. Relative to their weight, some offshore multihulls carry five times the sail of others.

AUTOMATIC SHEET RELEASE <small>Patent Pending</small>

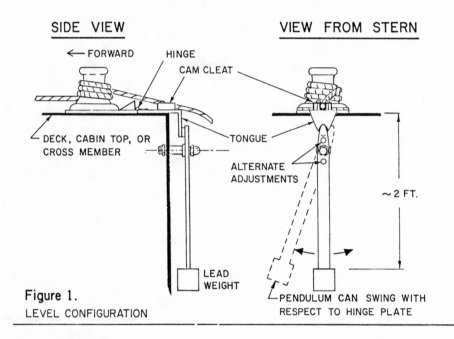

SIDE VIEW

← FORWARD HINGE CAM CLEAT

DECK, CABIN TOP, OR CROSS MEMBER

TONGUE

ALTERNATE ADJUSTMENTS

LEAD WEIGHT

VIEW FROM STERN

~ 2 FT.

PENDULUM CAN SWING WITH RESPECT TO HINGE PLATE

Figure 1.
LEVEL CONFIGURATION

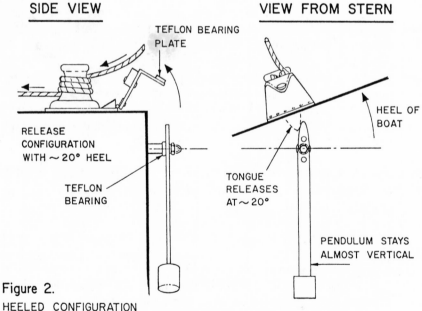

SIDE VIEW

TEFLON BEARING PLATE

RELEASE CONFIGURATION WITH ~ 20° HEEL

TEFLON BEARING

VIEW FROM STERN

HEEL OF BOAT

TONGUE RELEASES AT ~ 20°

PENDULUM STAYS ALMOST VERTICAL

Figure 2.
HEELED CONFIGURATION

Catamaran designer Hugo Myers offers a pendulum-operated sheet release that activates with heeling instead of wind force. Release may be influenced either way by gyration of the vessel in a seaway.

TYPE	LENGTH O.A.	BEAM O.A.	WEIGHT	SAIL AREA (sqft) WORKING RIG	SAIL AREA (sqft) LIGHT W. RIG	BEAM/LENGTH RATIO HULL	BEAM/LENGTH RATIO OVERALL	SAIL AREA/TON	STATIC STABILITY KNOTS	STATIC STABILITY FORCE	DYNAMIC STABILITY KNOTS	DYNAMIC STABILITY FORCE
Cat	40'	13'	1.0 ton	370	500	18:1	3.0:1	370 sqft/ton 500	22	5-6	12	3-4
Cat	29'	16'	0.9	456		9:1	1.8:1	507	22		12	
Tri	62'	33'	7.36	2300	4500	15:1	1.9:1	312	25	6	14	4
Cat	37'	20'	1.38	610	1185		1.8:1	442-(1107)	25		14	
Cat	35.5'	18'	1.78	700		12:1	1.9:1	393	27	6-7	15	
Cat	43'	16'	4.0	1030	1606		2.6:1	257-(401)	27		15	
Cat	35'	16.5'	2.45	600	690	12:1	2.1:1	245-(282)	28		15.5	
Cat	30.5'	13.5'	2.0	496	544		2.3:1	200-(272)	30	7	16.5	4-5
Tri	35'	26'	2.45	880			1.3:1	358	32		17.5	
Tri	33'	24'	1.78	592		12:1	1.4:1	333	35	7-8	19	5
Tri	31.3'	24'	1.92	650		7.5:1	1.3:1	338	35		19	
Cat	35'	15'	2.5	456	670	8:1	2.2:1	182-(268)	35		19	
Cat	30.5'	13'	2.5	362	544	9:1	2.3:1	145-(218)	37	8	20	5-6
Tri	32'	20'	2.0	440			1.6:1	220	40		22	
Tri	42'	27'	2.5	530	658		1.6:1	212-(263)	42	8-9	23	
Tri	49'	30'	3.25	761			1.6:1	234	42		23	
Tri	54'	34.5'	6.4	1800		11:1	1.6:1	281	42		23	
Tri	46'	27'	3.4	871	1172	12:1	1.7:1	256-(344)	44	9	24	6
Cat	35'	15'	4.0	456	573	8:1	2.3:1	114-(144)	45		25	
Cat	35'	16.5'	2.75	400		13.5:1	2.1:1	150	45		25	
Cat	43'	18'	5.0	800	1400	16:1	2.4:1	160-(280)	45		25	
Cat	45.5'	20'	4.0	660	935	14:1	2.3:1	165-(234)	45		25	
Cat	35.5'	17'	2.25	415	627		2.0:1	184-(278)	45		25	
Cat	30'	15'	4.3	485	628		2.0:1	113-(146)	47.5	9-10	26	
Tri	80'	38'	18.5	2260	3490		2.1:1	122-(189)	50	10	27	6-7
Tri	60'	31.2	6.0	1200	1700	12:1	1.9:1	200-(233)	57		31	7
Tri	42.5'	24'	6.38	665		6:1	1.8:1	104	58		32	
Tri	63'	34'	6.0	1190			1.9:1	198	60	11	33	7-8

Wharram's table of stability values for various multihulls.

Using an ingenious formula that accounts for the shock load of gusts of wind, and that includes the factors of overall beam and the height of the sailplan's centroid, Hanneke has produced a figure representing dynamic stability (as opposed to static or dockside stability) for each of 28 oceangoing multihulls, expressed in terms of the wind force predicted to capsize the vessel under full working sail. Results range all the way from Beaufort Force 3 to Force 8! Very wisely, the dynamic stability figure refers to mean wind velocity, but it allows for gusts of 40 percent greater than the mean, which could generate a shock load equal to twice the numerical value of the gust.

But what is the right stability for a blue-water multihull? Wharram draws a bold line across the table that rejects 17 of the 28 vessels tabulated. He suggests that minimum oceangoing stability means the multihull can carry all plain sail in Force 6—24 knots of wind—without reefing, and still withstand a gust of 40 percent greater force—about 35 knots, or Force 7 or 8. I consider Wharram's cutoff line reasonable.

Of course, there are many factors affecting stability that cannot be included in a basic table, and it would take a lot of capsizes to test the accuracy of Hanneke's formula. But if her values are even halfway accurate, we are looking at an incredible range of stability in contemporary multihulls. There are various ways to express numerically the effects of sail area on a multihull. The naval architect's sail-to-weight ratio is one. Another is to express unreefed capsizing sail force as a percentage of displacement. Then there's the new Bruce Number calculation, and Hanneke's dynamic stability factor. They all mean approximately the same thing, and with today's light materials and the growing lust for speed, these values for some boats are approaching incredible extremes. It almost seems as if their conglomerate could be better termed a "capsize index."

But that's not the whole story. To prevent capsize, one does not design the multihull with too much sail for its weight, or too little beam for its sail. And clearly, the rig should be easy to manage to encourage sail reduction as the wind increases. But there is another principle of multihull stability so obvious that it has gone almost unnoticed. Taken straight from monohull design, it is the ballast-to-weight ratio; it normally refers to the percentage of the vessel's total weight that is concentrated in the ballast keel. "But multihulls don't have ballast!" you say. Wait just a minute.

Generally, the lighter a monohull's total weight, the greater the percentage of that total that must be designated for ballast. As a rough rule, the cruising keelboat weighs about twice as much as the cruising multihull, because from 30 to 50 percent of its weight is concentrated in lead ballast alone. The multihull simply leaves this burden in the ground.

But here's the important point: another large chunk of the total weight of any cruising craft is its cargo, in the form of machinery, tankage, equipment, and stores. Theoretically the multihull sailor usually wishes to get along with less. Nevertheless, a cruising multihull must be designed with enough bottom on the hulls to carry the unavoidable accumulation of things needed even for spartan cruising. And it needs this weight to be safe.

Here's why: because the cat or tri is so light, each pound of cargo constitutes a relatively large percentage of the boat's weight, and in fact can approach the same proportion usually allotted to ballast in a monohull. If this cargo is located deep amidships in the multihull, it becomes "natural ballast."

"Keep the heavy stuff down low" is such a familiar rule that it seems to go without saying. But because of the multihull's comparative lightness, the heavy stuff is comparatively *very* heavy, and its location in the ship becomes extremely critical. The most obvious approach to capsize prevention is to capitalize on this fact.

Natural ballast may explain the infrequency of capsize among serious cruising multihulls. These boats carry a fair amount of weight and a conservative sailplan. Trimarans with deep main hull bilges provide central stowage holds for heavy cargo. Catamarans without large bridge-cabins carry natural ballast down in the hulls instead of in the wing.

My own suspicion is that the trimaran, by virtue of its central hull, offers

NATURAL BALLAST

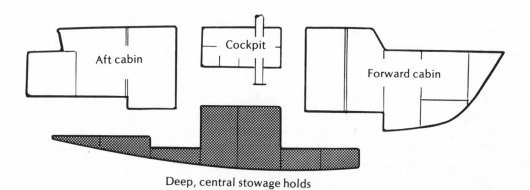

Deep, central stowage holds

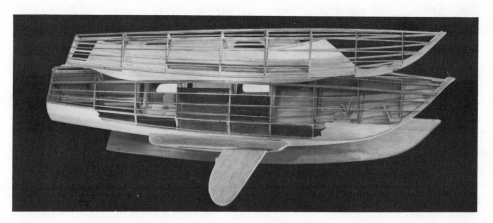

In this model by Dick Crockett of a central-cockpit trimaran, all the darkened areas of the main hull bilge are stowage holds for the deep, centralized concentration of cruising payload ... "natural ballast." (Photo by Dudley, Hardin and Yang, Seattle)

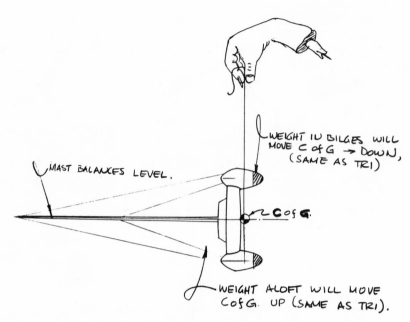

Skip Johnson's explanation of the multihull's single center of gravity.

the best chance for maximizing natural ballast. Skip Johnson, whose designs reveal careful treatment of this issue in both his trimarans and his catamarans, has reminded me that no matter how many hulls there may be, there is still only one center of gravity for the entire vehicle. Nevertheless, the deep-hulled cruising trimaran has the potential to achieve a somewhat lower center of gravity than other configurations.

Hugo Myers, whose specialty is designing fast catamarans, has emphasized that trimarans are vulnerable to breakers from abeam because of their close hull spacing. When the main hull is heaved up by a crest, the rotational momentum is said to be greater than with a similar-length catamaran, whose overall beam will be less and hull spacing wider. In addition, the trimaran has a small hull to leeward. Some trimarans may indeed have tripped over their leeward hulls, and rolled on over, especially boats with very low freeboard at the ama sheer. Once the deck is underwater, any leeward momentum becomes tripping momentum.

But natural ballast must be reckoned with. Whether the catamaran's cargo is divided between the outer hulls or elevated in the bridge, that high, wide weight distribution must amplify rotational momentum. The trimaran, with weight centralized down low, and amas that aren't too small, would seem to have as good a chance as any multihull in dealing with waves approaching from abeam.

This argument emphasizes the value of fully buoyant amas for trimarans. And it also challenges the wisdom of heaving-to in storms when the waves are approaching from abeam.

Comparisons show approximate payload
distributions (shading) of the typical
cruising catamaran and the central-
cockpit trimaran at progressive angles
of static heeling.

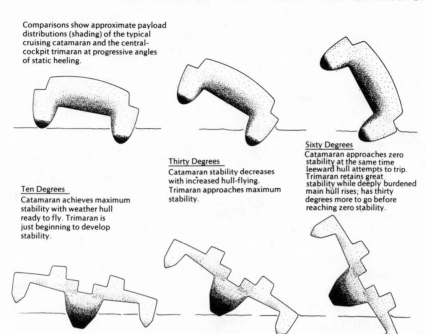

Sixty Degrees
Catamaran approaches zero
stability at the same time
leeward hull attempts to trip.
Trimaran retains great
stability while deeply burdened
main hull rises; has thirty
degrees more to go before
reaching zero stability.

Thirty Degrees
Catamaran stability decreases
with increased hull-flying.
Trimaran approaches maximum
stability.

Ten Degrees
Catamaran achieves maximum
stability with weather hull
ready to fly. Trimaran is
just beginning to develop
stability.

STATIC HEELING ANGLES
(Wind-caused capsize)

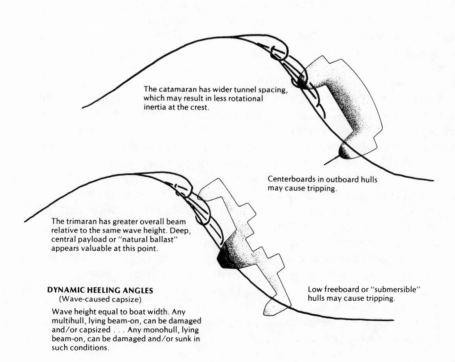

The catamaran has wider tunnel spacing,
which may result in less rotational
inertia at the crest.

Centerboards in outboard hulls
may cause tripping.

The trimaran has greater overall beam
relative to the same wave height. Deep,
central payload or "natural ballast"
appears valuable at this point.

DYNAMIC HEELING ANGLES
(Wave-caused capsize)

Wave height equal to boat width. Any
multihull, lying beam-on, can be damaged
and/or capsized . . . Any monohull, lying
beam-on, can be damaged and/or sunk in
such conditions.

Low freeboard or "submersible"
hulls may cause tripping.

Again, this cat-versus-tri dilemma may be mostly academic, or aesthetic, or epidemic, but it's not scientific. All that's certain is that both will benefit from having all the weight down low.

Let's consider a different multihull, a racer with shallow bilges and precious little cargo to concentrate anywhere, and a large, high sailplan to boot. To achieve dazzling speed, the weight of this craft is absolutely minimized. Yet it differs profoundly from the ultralight monohull whose proportion of ballast to weight must actually increase as the boat gets lighter. The racing multihull attempts to leave out as much ballast as possible. It sails offshore with minimal boat weight, scant natural ballast, and maximum sail. In the pressure of competition, capsize prevention mainly rests with the crew. Doesn't it always? No, because oceangoing crews must be allowed to make mistakes.

The cruising faction owes a giant debt of gratitude to the racers for showing us the price of making mistakes in a boat that's far too light for the sail she carries around. Cruising in such a boat is a mistake in itself.

It may sound very strange to hear a multihull designer arguing for weight, and I hasten to say that overloading is possible, and regrettably common in multihulls. Besides hurting performance, it is a primary cause of structural damage and even capsize. I'm not arguing for more weight. I'm saying that a cruising boat must be designed to carry a cruising load while still floating at her intended waterline. She must have more hull underneath to accommodate that load without pushing the underwing dangerously close to the wavetops.

The high-performance raceboats have shown us many other things, such as how to build cruising craft that are really strong. Structural problems, at least among the cruisers, are pretty much a thing of the past. The racers have shown us how to build the cruisers light enough to allow for more pounds of payload, and fast enough to be fast as cruisers go. The lighter the boat, the more security is gained with natural ballast; the more favorable the ballast-to-weight ratio, the faster we can safely go.

So it is that while much of what we know about capsize prevention has come from monohull design and experience with racing multihulls, the cruisers are in the best position to benefit. With our capacity for cargo we become safe, while simultaneously achieving a new level of cruising performance. That suggests the multihull really belongs as a cruising craft. But as the threat of capsize continues to reduce one's chances in a race, perhaps the speed machines will adopt what we've learned—from them.

One final case in contrast is the ponderous "sailing houseboat" multihull, which usually has plenty of ballast but carries it positioned in a high wing-bridge or superstructure. Sometimes even the engine and tanks are located in the wing. Their much-touted roominess usually means deep aisles and passageways, which reduce the deep-down space available for heavy stores. Inexplicably, such craft sometimes have high rigs and narrow overall beam. When several of these features are combined in a single boat, the cumulative effect is predictable: those boats are known to survive a venture offshore only with the very best of handling and luck.

Bob Puffer in the hatch of Misumbo.

A great sailor can do just about anything with a not-so-great boat. But when the sailor makes mistakes, or when he is powerless to do *anything,* then he'd like to have the design of the boat—indeed, the boat herself—take charge. The following three incidents involved vessels that I regard as capsize-resistant designs, and the sailors could do nothing but leave it to the boats.

The first is a description of an extreme thunderstorm encountered by Robert Puffer in his 31-foot trimaran, *Misumbo.* Bob had singlehanded northbound around Cape Hatteras in June 1977. Upon arriving at a latitude just south of Norfolk, Virginia, and being only some 20 miles offshore, bound for entering the Chesapeake, he noticed a grave blackness developing in the western sky in late afternoon. His radio reported warnings of severe thunderstorms and a tornado watch, so he handed all sail, cleared the deck, and waited. During this time a "vigorous local disturbance" had moved down the James River and pasted Norfolk like few squalls on record. Winds of 97 knots were recorded at the airport, and a large party-fishing boat, the *Dixie Lee,* was capsized by the storm, resulting in 14 drownings. This front moved seaward and nearly overwhelmed *Misumbo.* Bob described the phenomenon like this:

The sky grew very dark, almost nighttime-dark, and at the same time the water turned a bright iridescent, swimming-pool green. It was very strange and very beautiful, yet I felt a strong emotional depression. As the wind began, the water surface seemed to boil or effervesce—it was sort of leaping up like hot fat, and the boat naturally turned to lie ahull.

When the big wind hit, it was like some kind of collision; she heeled over with a snap. The starboard float went right down to its deck in the water and the rest of the boat just reached for the sky. The wind didn't moan or wail, it screeched, and I couldn't breathe.

I grabbed the helm and somehow got her headed off downwind. The next thing I remember, the Sumlog was reading 16 and 17—under bare poles. Off we went like that, with the sky very dark and the surface all flat and streaky and the boat going like crazy. All I could do was hang on. I thought about the drogue, so when the peak subsided, I engaged the self-steering and got the bridle and the tire out astern. But by then the show was over.

Extreme gusts on flat water, incidentally, have been responsible for a number of multihull capsizes. The theory goes that the wind velocity on the surface is greater in flat water than in rough seas. Bob's squall gave ample opportunity for a pure wind-caused capsize, but the boat resisted. One might ask what would have happened if the sails were set! But actually, a bit of sail might very well have helped to get her headed off the wind before the blast arrived.

Concerning pure wave-caused capsize, few multihulls have had a better chance to be flipped by a single breaker than Tim Mann's 37-footer, *Spice.* Tim had acquired considerable experience on the California coast, and he has since crossed the Pacific in *Spice,* but this one wave really put the two of them in trouble.

While entering the harbor at Tomales Bay (north of San Francisco), Tim suspected his boat would surf as usual if caught by a breaker, but suddenly a swell of truly huge proportions made up astern. As it rolled in from the northwest, it felt the bottom and commenced to steepen. The crest curled high and collapsed directly on the boat. Water pressure pinned Tim against the helm, and when his lungs finally found air, he saw that his central cockpit was filled to the brim. And he could see his bows emerging from the avalanche:

. . . . he saw his bows emerging. . .

Bacchanal.

"She popped up spewing water in all directions and trying like hell to surf at the same time! She took a slightly diagonal attitude on the face, water still pouring off her decks, and so help me, we *caught* that wave! We came bounding down and surfed right into the harbor."

Spice was not undamaged. She lost her self-steering device, her dinghy, and assorted deck gear, and the main hull had two feet of water in the bilge. Tim's companion hatches were not completely closed by dropboards. The designer was amazed and relieved to learn that the sterncastle window held, and that the craft had not capsized.

It is in competition that the chance of capsize is probably greatest. This is because in racing, the *combination* of strong winds and big waves is most likely to be accompanied by very high boatspeed. The 1972 Multihull TransPacific Race from California to Hawaii was sailed by John Marples and his crew of hell-bent surf-riders in John's 37-footer, *Bacchanal*. Their corrected time was 8.7 days, a record for the course. It was during this race, however, that our third and most dramatic account of knockdowns occurred.

As an example of the kind of sailing that is required to compete in such events, *Bacchanal* was being driven at a speed that the crew described as "continuous surfing." The now-famous designer Bill Lee was the tactician in *Bacchanal*'s crew, and perhaps the most gifted helmsman aboard. Once the boat had reached the trades, Bill discovered that she could be guided among the seas so as to always keep the bow pointing downhill, never losing the added help of gravity by running up the back of the wave ahead. This was done by "hopping" laterally to the next trough ahead, and to the side, thereby maintaining or exceeding the speed of the seaway—never being overtaken by, or attempting to overtake, a major crest. This tactic was dubbed "chasing holes." It required a working boat speed of at least 15 knots to be "plugged in," and the standing instructions to each wheelwatch were inscribed in grease-pen over the speedometer: "DO NOT SAIL ON UPHILL WATER."

CAPSIZE PREVENTION BY DESIGN AND SEAMANSHIP

At the halfway point in the race, the navigator, Jim McCaig, announced that they might be on their way to a corrected-time win. After dinner that night, the crew was enjoying a bit of a halfway toast in the sterncastle when the helmsman asked for relief so that he could join the party. The new helmsman came up from the cabin lights and grasped the wheel in the midst of a pitch-black, 15-knot pell-mell surf. Because his own multihull has a tiller, and because of other things, he corrected the wheel in the wrong direction and threw the vessel into a wild, chattering broach. The entire leeward ama and much of the wing were driven completely into the sea. This was accompanied by a drastic deceleration, the spinnaker flogging aloft, and the crest overtaking from abeam. Marples later described the incident very simply: "We had one bad spinout. The boat was punched underwater edgewise, she popped back up, and off we went. All of us were shaken up."

They were very lucky. With the wind and the wave working together, and with the speed and the broach working together, but with just the boat working alone—nobody helping her at all—she recovered from that knockdown.

It seems to require a combination of design features either to invite or to prevent capsize. The natural ballast factor—accompanied by a broad beam, large ama hulls, reasonable sailplans, low windage, and modest accommodations—yields seafaring multihulls that are extremely safe. They have a substantial accumulation of anticapsize features. They seldom win races, but they often place. We have learned that they can recover from colossal knockdowns, and in the next section, we shall see that they are able to withstand a gruesome kicking around by a very nasty ocean and come through on their feet.

Natural Ballast at Work. Tattoo, *Brent Whipple's 31-foot trimaran, rounds up to a williwaw off the island of Maui. The vessel's course approaches from the left, as evidenced by the wake. The gust hits, causing maximum heel and spray, as the helmsman steers to luff. The leeward ama is not submerged, and the main hull is glued down by cruising payload concentrated in the deep bilges. Multihulls must be capable of withstanding such gusts, which often occur in the vicinity of high land or squalls. (Photos by Mike Kenney)*

CAPSIZE PREVENTION BY SEAMANSHIP

Caution is essential to seamanship, and speed sometimes runs counter to caution. A conflict thus results between ocean racing and good seamanship, especially in multihulls because they can be made to go so fast.

For example, in the 1976 OSTAR, 40 percent of the fleet did not finish. Four of the first 10 boats home were multihulls, which were pushed on at speed through gales and fog and ice—singlehanded. Very small multihulls can compete with very large monohulls in these rough games.

Therefore, again let the difference between multihull racing and multihull cruising be distinct. The well-publicized crackups of raceboats have no relevance to the safety of cruising craft designed for stability and sailed with reserve. Just as safety is not the essence of the race, neither is speed the essence of the cruise.

A slow raceboat is senseless, but a fast cruiser can take unique advantage of the fact that speed *sometimes* constitutes safety. Her skipper has more options. For instance, he can better afford to wait for good weather; he can sometimes outmaneuver squalls; and he can better evade the force of storms. Possessed with the necessary judgment, he can use speed to advantage in avoiding darkness at the harbor mouth. Speed helps when running inlets, and when dodging traffic. The prudent use of high speed, twice or even three times normal cruising pace, is not available to those who cruise in slow vessels.

But how fast is safe? Some experienced multimariners contend that the safest way to handle storms is to run off downwind at high speed, thereby avoiding encounters with the largest waves by simply running away from them. This is a useful tactic only when a good, fresh crew and lots of searoom are available. Also, note that running downwind in a cyclonic storm can take the vessel toward the anticipated path of the storm center.

Nevertheless, the lightweight multihull can often use its potential for high speed to accelerate away when approached by heavy water, reducing the power of the blow. Narrow hull forms offer less resistance, reducing the chance of being tumbled stern-over-bow on the face of a giant breaking crest. A wide, deep hull develops huge resistance when pushed through the water at high speed, which may cause the monohull cruiser to trip over the drag of its own underbody, dive its nose, and pitchpole.

Multihull cruisers also have speed to use upwind, provided they are designed with adequate lateral resistance. Some designs can make fast passages against strong headwinds, and can beat away from dangerous obstructions to leeward in very heavy weather. A fast cruiser's ability to claw off a lee shore for the security of open water and to run off at speed before overpowering waves offers definite safety advantages.

The safest approach to multihull seamanship is the skipper's decision to use his speed potential as a safety margin. If he knows his craft to be capable of high speed in rough water, then he knows that it will handle threatening conditions safely at reduced speed, while retaining the liveliness to accelerate away from heavy blows.

Excessive heeling, pounding, and spray, and steering difficulty, are all signals to reduce speed. There is something spellbinding about a mad multihull dash, but if the sky is black and the crew is green and the boat is going like the devil, one can bet that the skipper's safety reserve is being spent on thrills.

The prudent use of speed, then, is a matter of multihull seamanship, and when sailing offshore it should not be confused with the thrill of a mad dash or the lust to win.

When heavy weather threatens, the multihull skipper can choose his speed, but he must also select the direction in which he wants to go, relative to the direction of the storm.

Sailing closehauled in storm conditions is possible in some multihulls, but it is unwise to continue beating into head seas that leave the boat dead in the water, without steerageway. A good inboard auxiliary used with storm sails will allow the craft to continue closehauled longer than with sails alone. Use only enough power to maintain steerageway. If the propeller's blast is directed at the rudder, steerageway can be maintained even if the boat is momentarily stopped by a colliding crest. Outboard motors and between-the-hulls propellers are useless in these conditions.

Attempting to sail a reaching course in breaking seas is not advised, for the boat is even more vulnerable to structural damage and capsize than when lying ahull. If a beam reach must be held in heavy weather, an alert helmsperson may be able to steer with enough adroitness, while sailing at enough speed, to avoid the larger crests by zigging up to let one pass ahead, or zagging down to run away from another. If the craft is equipped with a centerboard or other retractable foils, it is wise to retract them. If the boat gets slammed by a steep wave from abeam, she will try to slide sideways, but with keels or daggerboards extended—especially if they are located in the outboard hulls—the vessel may trip on the leeward foil, increasing the chance of capsize.

The simplest choice is to drop sail and allow her to drift naturally, usually sideways to the wind and sea. This tactic is called "lying ahull," and most boats do a marvelous job of handling themselves in this position—in most conditions.

However, among sailors who have experience in "survival storms," there is considerable disagreement over whether in extreme conditions lying ahull is preferable to running off, which is simply sailing downwind with the storm. By running off, the boat presents her ends to the power of the waves instead of her sides. Steering is often facilitated by dragging long lines or objects astern.

When waves are breaking severely, running off is the more logical tactic for multihulls, especially if the waves are of such power (and this is rare) that exposing her more vulnerable side surfaces to the crests threatens the boat with structural damage or capsize. Wide, flat surfaces of lightly built multihulls are not well suited to withstand the force of waves jumping aboard from abeam. Interestingly, damage is sometimes caused on the

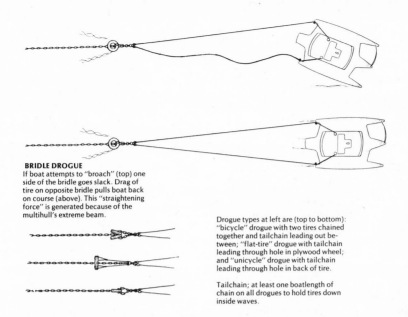

BRIDLE DROGUE
If boat attempts to "broach" (top) one side of the bridle goes slack. Drag of tire on opposite bridle pulls boat back on course (above). This "straightening force" is generated because of the multihull's extreme beam.

Drogue types at left are (top to bottom): "bicycle" drogue with two tires chained together and tailchain leading out between; "flat-tire" drogue with tailchain leading through hole in plywood wheel; and "unicycle" drogue with tailchain leading through hole in back of tire.

Tailchain; at least one boatlength of chain on all drogues to hold tires down inside waves.

leeward side when the boat is picked up by a curler and thrown onto her downhill side. This can capsize the boat, and the same phenomenon has been responsible for many monohull sinkings. The ends of a boat are designed to take the beating, not the sides.

But the craft will naturally try to lie beam-on to the storm, so the crew must maintain control in order to present the bow or stern. Downwind steering qualities now become indispensable. Multihulls with lots of lateral resistance, and with deep rudders, have crisp steering. The monohull's tendency to roll going downwind hampers the helmsman trying to keep the vessel running off, and lines or drogues tied to the stern of a heavy monohull craft and streamed to windward may offer insufficient resistance to counteract the boat's tendency to turn broadside.

In this respect the multihull can take advantage of its wide beam in a unique way. A rope bridle is used to attach the storm drogue to the outboard hulls; thus the resistance of the drogue, as it is dragged through the water, is delivered by the bridle to the outboard extremities of the multihull platform. This exerts a powerful straightening force that tends to hold the craft end-on instead of allowing her to turn sideways.

The amount of resistance required of the drogue depends on the size of the boat. Small multihulls 25 to 30 feet long need an automobile tire weighted down with a boat's length of chain. Larger boats can use two or more tires chained in tandem. Alternatively, a small, rugged parachute sea anchor can be used.

If no drogue is prepared, the boat's anchor, complete with chain, may be streamed astern on the bridle. Any object that will cause resistance can be dragged, but the weight of chain is advised to prevent a buoyant drogue from being hurled at the boat by passing crests.

If great lengths of line are used as drogue material, it is wise to keep both ends of each piece attached on board, or to the bridle junction, to prevent twisting damage to the line. A rugged swivel is needed at the bridle junction to prevent a revolving drogue from winding up the two parts of the bridle. The bridle lines themselves can each be at least 150 feet long, or long enough to put the drogue in a wave trough while the boat is on the crest. Recent information indicates that nonstretch line (anything but nylon) profoundly increases the bridle's effectiveness. Sampson's "Powerbraid" has the right combination of properties for the bridle drogue: low stretch, great suppleness for handling, fairly high strength, and fairly low cost. There is some evidence to suggest that drogue lines of 200-300 feet are necessary for riding out great storms.

A properly arranged drogue will allow the boat to progress downwind at less than surfriding speed and with good directional control, sometimes without being manually steered by the crew. However, if there is insufficient searoom, or if the boat's destination lies in a direction contrary to the wind, a larger parachute may be employed, with bridle, to virtually stop the boat while also holding her end-on. Like the drogue, the parachute should be streamed on the bridle over the stern of the multihull. (If it is streamed by the bow, the boat doesn't lie-to as well, and it may be thrown backward and damage the rudder.) Experience has shown that this parachute arrangement offers a distinct advantage over lying ahull in threatening seas.

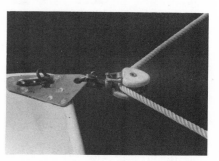

LEFT: Tire-bridle drogue has nonstretch lines each about 150 feet long. Swivel is chained to tire. Streaming aft through the hole in the tire is the "tailchain," about one boatlength of anchor chain, to hold the tire down. The anchor itself, or more tires, may be added for larger boats. TOP RIGHT: Special stern locker for storing drogue shows bridle and junction ready to receive tire and tailchain. Bridle lines are ready-rigged to snatchblocks on outboard sterns before the vessel goes offshore. BOTTOM RIGHT: Very strong hardware is installed on bows and sterns to receive snatchblocks for bridle lines.

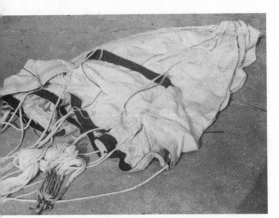

Bridle lines, 150 feet each of floating, non-stretch line like Sampson "POWER-BRAID," minimum 1/2" diameter.

Flounder Plate, 1/4" aluminum with three 7/16" holes to receive 3/8" shackles.

Swivel, 3/8" size, greased.

Flounder Plate, as above, with 5 holes.

Wire Harness, three pieces 8 feet long of 5/32" stainless 7 x 19 wire, with thimbles at top, spliced with nicopress sleeves.

Plywood Wheel, inside tire (15" wheel for 14" tire) made of 1/2" plywood with holes to suit.

wire runs through tread here

Flat Tire, commensurate with size of boat (14" tire for 30-foot boat) with holes cut to drain.

Tailchain, at least one boatlength of chain (1/4" chain for 30-foot boat) to hold tire down inside waves.

ABOVE: This very rugged parachute is currently available from Defender Industries for less than $30. A diameter larger than 10 feet gives diminishing returns as a sea anchor. This is for use in "holding station" as an alternative to heaving-to when there is limited sea room.

RIGHT: Flat-Tire Drogue. For boats 35 feet and larger, this configuration gives the most resistance for the lowest cost, lightest weight, and fewest stowage problems.

Even in more moderate weather, drogues are used simply to improve the comfort of the crew while running down a blow, or to reduce the need for steering.

Using the bridle-drogue requires that someone in the crew be willing to go on deck and set it. This process can be reduced from a struggle to a cinch by preparation before the passage is begun. Strong deck hardware should be built into the boat, and strong lines (as strong as the boat's anchor lines) should be on hand. The whole works can be rigged, ready for use, before going out to sea. If the bridle is not ready-rigged, a single drogue from the main hull stern, or centerline, is recommended for its simplicity. One suggestion for drogue preparation is to coil the two parts of the bridle in separate coils shaped like figure-eights, so that there is no twisting. Each coil can be bound at the waist with light string. The bridle junction can be assembled, ready to receive the tire. Everything is then stowed near the stern

ABOVE LEFT: Bridle junction for flat tire drogue used homemade "flounder plates." Plywood disc goes inside tire to increase drag. ABOVE RIGHT: This large tire is a used racing "slick." Its flexibility and light weight, combined with its bulk, make excellent drogue properties ... if used with a long, heavy tailchain. BOTTOM: Flat-tire drogue ready for use. Note that wires should pass through the corner of the tire's tread to prevent them from shifting position, thus allowing the tire to tow edgewise. Bridle lines can be endless to prevent ends being lost overboard. Figure-eight coils shown are bound with light string and tossed out with the drogue to unwind safely in the water.

of the craft with the ends of the bridle lines already run through snatchblocks on the sterns. These lines should be eye-spliced or knotted with bowlines in both ends to give equal length. To deploy the drogue, attach the tire(s) and tailchain, secure the bridle ends to the cockpit winches, and then jettison tire, chain, and coils all at once, to avoid the risk of the crew becoming entangled in the lines as they run out. It also ensures that the drogue will set itself automatically with both lines pulling equally, for dead downwind running.

During preparation of the final draft of this book, we learned of the first recorded capsize of a Searunner trimaran. The incident is related here because it may well have occurred *as a result* of difficulties encountered when deploying the bridle drogue.

The 40-foot *Mara*, with Bill Quinlan and David Lucas aboard, sailed from San Diego in July 1978 bound for the Galápagos Islands and the South Seas. Quinlan had very little seagoing experience, and Lucas had none, but they were aware that this voyage required them to sail the chartered multihull in the season and the area for Eastern Pacific hurricanes.

At a point some 500 miles southwest of Cabo San Lucas, Mexico, on July 13, 1978, *Mara* was struck by Hurricane Fico. According to U.S. Weather Service records, this was a major hurricane. At the time and place of capsize, the storm had a sustained wind velocity of 95 knots, with gusts to 120 knots.

After having steered *Mara* downwind until he was overcome by fatigue, Bill Quinlan then attempted to rig the bridle drogue. Because of the extreme conditions, deployment went badly. David Lucas later said:

"The wind and spray were so bad that we couldn't breathe or open our eyes. We were wearing plastic bags over our heads in order to operate on deck. At times we were surfing at 17 knots with no sail up at all. The waves seemed to be about as high as our 50-foot mast, and we had lots of solid water breaking into the cockpit. When the waves came aboard, I would hook my arms around the rigging and brace myself in the cockpit, but the force of the water pulling on me was so strong that my arms got all chewed up. (*Mara*'s cockpit is located 18 feet from the stern.) Bill had a bad time of it rigging the bridle lines in that awful stuff, and once he got them out we couldn't really see them. But it felt to me like the tire was pulling from the side of the boat . . . tangled up or something. Then it seemed like we were going in circles. I couldn't tell what was happening but we couldn't control the boat. Finally, she did a big, slow roll, both of us dropping down into the water from above, and we ended up in the air pocket formed by the cockpit, with the boat on top of us. Bill tried to dive into the cabin, but the motion was so bad that we felt she was going to break up, or sink, or something. He said, 'I gotta get out,' so we both swam from underneath and climbed up on the wing. . . . Later we found the drogue lines were incredibly twisted and tangled . . . I can't remember if there was a swivel at the tire or not."

Because the craft was not prepared for capsize habitation, the survivors entered their life raft, but only with great difficulty. No special hatch to store the raft had been built into the wing, so the raft was lashed on deck. Quinlan dived several times to extricate it, and was injured in the struggle.

Now catastrophe multiplied, for the raft was the type equipped with a large water-ballast tank on the bottom for stability. The weight of this ballast, combined with the extreme motion, caused the raft's small tether to snap, and the castaways drifted away from the mothership. Furthermore, the ballast tank did not prevent the raft from capsizing several times before the storm abated. Most provisions were lost and the flares were soaked and failed to operate.

After five days of surviving in the raft with minimal provisions, Quinlan became depressed by their predicament. He realized that their chances had been drastically reduced by the separation from *Mara*. Believing that David

161

Lucas, his 18-year-old nephew, could survive for a longer time alone with the remaining rations, Quinlan, 31, expressed devotion to his companion, slipped out of the raft, and swam away.

Two days later the raft was spotted by a fishing boat, and Lucas alone was rescued.

This tragic sequence has left me greatly saddened, and increasingly convinced that the elements of seamanship must be more widely employed in multihull seafaring. The threat imposed by great storms is common to all boats, as is the means by which they can be avoided. But certain other facets, like capsize preparation and drogue deployment, are unique to multihulls. It is contingent upon the multimariner to make use of these special differences in his craft.

Bill Quinlan and David Lucas were simply not aware of these facets of seamanship, and they are not alone. Many offshore multihulls are operated by beginning sailors who are bound to learn their seamanship the hard way. Because the results of this learning are sometimes tragic, I have spent the last two years collecting information on multihull safety for this book. Two years seems like a long time, and for *Mara*'s sake it was too long. I feel great frustration when supposing that if this volume had been available to Quinlan and Lucas, they might still be cruising the South Seas together.

A basic understanding of major weather phenomena is a prerequisite for cruising in any boat. The Coast Pilot volumes contain sailing directions for all areas of the world, and each volume includes excellent meteorological descriptions of the area to which it applies. When planning a passage along Mexico's western seaboard, for instance, the skipper who familiarizes himself with the local conditions, by reading the Sailing Directions, will be warned about the notorious Gulf of Tehuantepec. Mariners crossing this gulf in the fair season, the winter months, are advised to prepare for the so-called *tehuantepecer.* This is not a summer hurricane, which would be relatively easy to avoid; it is a hard gale that frequently blows over the isthmus from the Caribbean side and is funneled out into the gulf through a low, Venturi-like pass between high mountains. In this area, calms can turn to gales in short order. All sailors will want to be prepared for heavy weather, and avoid leaving large, light-air sails set while the cockpit is unattended.

In addition to this weather knowledge, the multihull skipper can prepare his bridle-drogue in advance. All it takes is two stout lengths of nonstretch line, a husky swivel that is greased so it will really revolve, adequate chain, shackles moused so that they cannot come open, a tire or two, and the proper deck hardware for handling the lines. Then, if he does get "blown out" by the *tehuantepecer,* all he has to do is step to the stern and dump the drogue. Such simple preparations might have saved the *Mara* and Bill Quinlan. Without these prior considerations, how can any drogue materials be deployed when the storm is so fierce that the crew must cover their heads with plastic bags.

With the two bridle lines leading from the junction at the drogue up to snatchblocks on the outboard sterns, and then to the primary winches in the cockpit, the sailor can control the length of each bridle part. If seas are breaking heavily, he will adjust the two drogue lines to exactly the same length, so that his multihull will run dead before the storm, straight down the waves. However, if conditions permit, he can adjust the drogue, and the helm or the self-steering device, so that his multihull will crab slightly sideways on one broad reach or the other, as desired, working laterally away from the path of the *tehuantepecer.* Crabbing should be given up if quartering seas begin to jump aboard. The boat's own wake seems to aggravate crests approaching from the quarter, causing them to steepen and break more severely, whereas running dead down allows the vessel to hide behind a path of smooth water sometimes created by the bridle-drogue.

Experience has shown that drogues are marvelously effective when used in combination with a small storm jib. Conversely, they have proved ineffective *without* the storm jib. It is necessary to carry enough sail to keep the vessel moving at four or five knots even in the troughs. It is the resistance of the drogue being dragged through the water that generates the desired steering control. So carry sail with your drogue.

Besides giving steering control, the drogue also controls speed. Running off in severe storms without a drogue, even under bare poles, the multihull tries to overtake the wave ahead. This is to be avoided because, instead of the bows climbing up the back of the wave ahead, they may dive in.

A more subtle, and probably more dangerous result of running off at extreme speed is the phenomenon of sailing "over the falls." If the craft is really ripping along in the trough, at the same speed as large waves ahead and astern, those waves may diminish in their normal, undulating life cycle and leave the multihull running right along with a newborn giant developing beneath. If the boat is sailing at such speed—near 20 knots—that she happens to keep pace with this developing wave, then when the crest steepens and breaks, over the falls you go.

In normal tradewind conditions, this is the most ecstatic of all sailing sensations, but in storm seas it can lead to foundering, tumbling inside the wave. This phenomenon is completely different from dragging the drogue and being overtaken by breakers that kick the boat ahead of harm's way.

When running off in any boat, drogue or no drogue, there is the danger of pooping, being boarded by a steep, overtaking crest. Cruisers with large cockpits at the stern may unwittingly admit the intruders with open arms, which explains why their skippers are loath to attempt running off. Once the vessel is burdened with a cockpit full of water, her stern is depressed and therefore very vulnerable to the next crest. Repeated pooping can break down the companionway or cockpit bulkhead and swamp the multihull or sink the keelboat.

If the multihull's drogue is of the proper size, the boat will normally take some slop over the stern. But because of light weight and high buoyancy, a real multihull pooping is rare, especially if the cockpit is located away from the transom. As the crests approach, a high-speed craft (with drogue small enough to allow acceleration but large enough to offer control) will naturally attempt to take off down the wave like a blueblooded runaway, sometimes spurting away from a peculiarly steep stinger, but usually running slower than the seaway. She will be much slower in the troughs and on the normal nonbreaking faces, but will jump out at nearly the same clip as a sliding spindrift, thereby robbing heavy water of its power. What a far safer position this is, compared to lying crosswise in the troughs, just waiting for the broadside cannonade.

A tropical cyclone is the sea's most ominous threat, so multihull sailors will wish to familiarize themselves with the concept of cyclone evasion. Coast Pilot volumes for hurricane areas include discussions of cyclone evasion, as do many other nautical texts. The subject is complicated by the fact that these storms often follow an undetermined path, wandering in loops and zigzags, which makes evasion an inexact science, but generally there is a textbook procedure that will take the sailor and his vessel away from the anticipated path. To state this procedure succinctly is also to cover the subject incompletely, but the following is included to illustrate the concept of cyclone evasion tactics at sea.

You are well out at sea in a multihull, and you suspect the passage of a cyclonic depression to be imminent.

1. Face into the wind.

2. In the northern hemisphere, the storm center is probably on your right.

3. Go left!

4. Sail or motorsail closehauled on the starboard tack (wind from starboard side) if your boat will safely take you on that heading.

5. If not, try a broad starboard reach with storm jib and bridle-drogue.

   Note: This starboard tack evasion tactic is valid unless you have reason to suspect that you are directly in the path of the eye. Storms usually follow a general course in a given area—see pilot charts. If your local wind does not change direction as it builds in velocity, this may indicate you are in the path of the storm. In this case, running dead downwind will take you toward the "navigable" side of the center. The next step suggests a remedy in case all of this analysis becomes too much:

6. If quartering seas are boarding dangerously, run dead downwind.

7. Avoid lying ahull until the storm has passed by and *seas* have moderated.

8. Directions and tacks are reversed in the southern hemisphere.

Great advantage can be taken of evasion tactics if the storm's position, and its anticipated path, are analyzed early enough, when prevailing conditions will still allow the boat to be worked to windward. Sailing into the wind, under much-reduced sail, and perhaps with the assistance of about half-throttle from the auxiliary engine, will probably take you away from the path of the storm center—if you sail on the correct tack. This will normally be with the wind coming from your starboard bow in the northern hemisphere, and from the port bow down south: "Starboard North, Port South." The earlier you start to evade the storm, the longer you can keep going to windward and the farther from the eye you will get.

The weathergoing power of some multihulls is difficult to understand. Their shallow draft and light weight tell us that multihulls simply should not go to windward, especially in heavy weather. But many multihulls are not shallow. Some are deeper than their keelboat counterparts (our 31-footer draws six-foot-six with the centerboard down). And weight, in itself, does not appear responsible for a given hull's ability to penetrate the crests; rather, it is *narrowness.* Narrow multiple hulls, joined with sufficient space between and ample clearance underneath the wing, can work their collective way to windward with surprising drive—if the craft is given plenty of lateral resistance. A big, deep centerboard will send the vessel climbing up the wind and waves with absolute minimum leeway. Combine narrowness with the stability to carry sail in heavy air, and you've got a seaboat that will claw uphill faster than the crew can stand it.

A good example of windward ability was provided by a new 38-foot trimaran I saw launched from an open beach. Hard aground at low tide, she waited for the water, which arrived in company with a stiff wind and a sizable surf. At the appropriate moment her sails were hoisted and she simply slammed her way seaward, grinding to a halt in every trough but lurching forward on each crest until the surf was left behind. I found it hard to believe it myself, but I saw it happen with my own eyes.

Traditional sailors are sometimes astonished by the upwind ability of a good cat or tri. Phil Weld told me (and my tape recorder) of sailing in a succession of Atlantic gales in his 60-foot tri *Gulf Streamer* in November 1975:

> Oh, we've been through some pretty good poundings. . . . We were coming down from England and I had aboard two top British yachtsmen—Donald Parr, Vice Commodore of the Royal Ocean Racing Club and one of the three Admiral's Cup team skippers, and Steve Allison, his sailing master. Both had been rather skeptical about multihulls. After the third gale off Gibraltar . . . well, we had just been pounding into a southeaster, absolutely closehauled every inch of the way. We weren't going very fast. And here I was, hoping to show off to my monohull friends, but we didn't get one little reach the whole trip. After about the fourth day of this, Donald said to me, "You know, I have to admit that we would have been heaved-to in a monohull long ago. I'm absolutely amazed that this boat can still go to windward in this stuff."

Gulf Streamer was a remarkable craft, but no more remarkable for her kind than the Admiral's Cup contenders. One good boat, racer or cruiser, monohull or multihull, will go against the wind about as well as another of similar size and emphasis, regardless of how many hulls she has.

Phil Weld must be ranked as remarkable, too. While most of us are grateful for our boat's ability to beat around the backside of a cyclone so we can avoid it, Phil is the sort of sailor who will *chase* the storm.

In *Gulf Streamer,* he purposely approached from behind the same storm that capsized the *Meridian* (because she sailed straight into the dangerous front quadrant). While tropical storm Amy was raising havoc off Cape Hatteras, Phil was in Bermuda with his beautiful Newick-designed boat, having recently finished first in the 1975 Multihull Bermuda Race. After a good rest he decided to sail out in pursuit of the tropical storm, just to get some heavy-weather practice:

> I don't want to make my little flirtation with Amy sound frivolous, because I realize that for those who were in trouble, like the *Meridian* people, it was very serious. But for me, that storm was an opportunity. I used it in a conscious effort to test myself in storm conditions.
>
> When I told the fellows in Bermuda that I was heading off to find Amy, they told me I ought to have my head examined. But I said no, it was quite the opposite. I told them that in just a year from now I will be competing in the OSTAR. I will have been at sea for 20 days, coming from England. I will very probably be racing to improve my position and I might find myself in this exact same circumstance— confronting a tropical storm—this very date. I wanted to know . . . I told them I wasn't worried about the boat . . . but I wanted to know if *I* could handle racing in a storm.
>
> My friends reminded me that the storm center was reported to be only 115 miles north of Bermuda . . . 115 miles, gee whiz! They said I'd be with Amy by midnight. And they were right.

Phil Weld in the hatchway of Gulf Streamer *describing his "flirtation" with tropical storm Amy. This is the overhead surface on which he later found himself standing, waist deep in Gulf Stream water.*

So about noon on June 29 (the day *Meridian* capsized), I left Bermuda, reaching down the channel from Hamilton under just the reefed main. There was a seagoing tug going out to rescue a monohull that had called in to say there was a woman aboard with a broken arm. *Gulf Streamer* sailed right past the tug.

By about three in the afternoon the old wind gauge was showing 40, so I tied in another reef. I'd gotten 50 miles of searoom from Bermuda—she was going that fast. I was receiving regular reports of the storm's northeasterly progress and felt that with 50 miles of searoom I could evade the center even if it were to loop and double back. I was reaching on the port tack. With the storm's counterclockwise rotation, this of course was taking me directly toward its center. I could come about at any time and head straight away from it. So I said, I'll just climb up on the backside of this thing and see what it's like.

It kept breezing up through the night so I dropped the main and continued under just the staysail. At about four in the morning I looked at the speedo and we were sprinting casually at 14 knots. The seas were building and I had to be alert. But I was getting sort of noddy, so I said to myself, "Look, you've been at this for 17 hours. It's time you hove-to and got some sleep."

But I hung on until dawn, thinking I was still pretty well out of the storm, and when dawn came I looked to the north and there it was—a great big mushroom cloud coming out of the ocean, huge black thunderheads. It really looked like the photographs of atomic mushroom clouds—very spectacular. I thought to myself, that just *has* to be what they mean by a storm center. I think I'll wait here.

Actually, I'm not a very good racer because I'm too conservative. But I've never regretted shortening sail. Now was my chance to try heaving-to in a real storm, and get some rest.

So I lashed the helm hard down to leeward and pulled the staysail clew around to windward. I raised the centerboard, leaving only about two feet exposed, and the boat just jogged along with about two knots of headway, with about two knots leeway as well, and she held her head roughly 30 degrees to the wind.

Every time I turned on the wind gauge it would whang right up to the peg at 60. Once in a while I'd see a really large wave coming, and if the rhythm was wrong the boat would sort of bobble on the crest. But most of the time she just sat there like a great gull . . . quite comfortable down below. But if I stuck my head outside, the wind would just take my breath away. I once emerged partway into the cockpit with a cup of coffee in one hand, and the wind siphoned it right out of the cup.

You know, I've got very big ears, and when the wind flattens them against my head, I can tell it's blowing pretty hard. But I've got to be very careful not to give the impression that I was experiencing anything like what the *Meridian* went through. I was on what is called the "navigable" side of the storm, the side away from its direction of travel, and so I avoided the worst. When it passed to the east, I continued for Gloucester in fair weather. But what the *Meridian* people went through I can only imagine.

Less than a year later Phil Weld did not have to imagine. He found himself inside *Gulf Streamer*'s inverted cabin, standing on the cabintop as the water rose to his waist. There was no cyclone this time, just the leftovers from an old-fashioned North Atlantic gale. Phil and one crewman, Bill Stevens, were on passage from Florida to England for the start of the OSTAR, for which Phil had so thoroughly prepared. The great-circle course had taken them along the north wall of the Gulf Stream and a satellite photo later revealed a dramatic eddy where they capsized.

The storm of the previous day, combined with the turbulent Stream, generated a true rogue wave. Stevens, who was in the cockpit at the time, later described the sea as "a 40-foot, double-crested mountain of water." Such waves are extremely rare—oceanographers say one in 200,000 can be four times normal height—but they can knock off even supertankers. This one gently set the "great gull" on her back. Weld later commented philosophically, "I feel almost as if I'd been struck by lightning."

Gulf Streamer's crew survived the capsize in relative comfort. They were well prepared, and were rescued after four days by a passing ship attracted by their rockets.

When tape-recording Phil's account of his flirtation with Amy, I had recently come from the interviews with Clint Spooner, and so was able to relate to Phil the object lessons learned aboard *Meridian* in the same storm. The conversation occurred one afternoon in Gloucester harbor aboard *Gulf Streamer* some time before she was capsized.

Phil was fascinated with what Spooner had learned. He asked searching questions about where and why they had cut *Meridian*'s access hatches; how far had the waterline risen; where should his Calamity Pack be stowed? Clearly, Phil intended to take advantage of what was learned by the *Meridian* tragedy in making his own careful capsize preparations. But neither one of us realized that afternoon in Gloucester that his new knowledge would be tested so soon.

Just a few months later, Phil Weld would return to say that capsize preparations definitely work. He would make several valuable suggestions of his own. And he would build another trimaran much like *Gulf Streamer*. (She had been picked up by a Russian vessel and taken to Odessa.) The new boat was also designed by Dick Newick, but unlike her fiberglass-and-foam predecessor, she was built of wood/epoxy by none other than the Gougeon Brothers, the originators of the Wood Epoxy Saturation Technique, known as the WEST System. And her name? *Rogue Wave*.

That yarn relates to the closewindedness of multihulls, and to storm evasion tactics, and leaves one thinking that surely, if one trimaran could sail into the storm on purpose, the other could have sailed away from it on purpose—if the crew had been able to analyze the danger in time.

Dr. Rodger Stewart, the man who lost his life aboard *Meridian*, was an atmospheric scientist for NASA, but not a meteorologist. His field was the detection of atmospheric pollution with sophisticated instrumentation. He remembered his undergraduate introduction to the revolving tropical storm as typified by the typhoon of the Southern Hemisphere, but Amy was in the Northern Hemisphere, where tropical depressions revolve counterclockwise. If he had known the "right rule" (Face the wind; the storm center is probably on your right), he might have avoided the storm. As it was, *Meridian* headed directly into it—west, with a south wind blowing. To make matters worse, because the storm was unseasonably early, it was not detected by the weather broadcasters until late.

There may have been another influence on her course, too: land ahead.

RIGHT: Rogue Wave. *(Photo by Jim Brown, Naked Eye)*

There is an almost irresistible temptation for the uninitiated skipper to head for land in a storm. This was probably the cause of the *Triton* capsize, and it may have contributed to several others. When circumstances become threatening, a soaked sailor longs for the harbor mouth, perhaps the worst place for him to head if he has to cross paths with a depression, or run off diagonally across huge seas to get there.

To second-guess a cyclone's path is no easy matter. Depending entirely on local observations is risky, but they help if compared with weather reports. If there's talk of a low pressure area, then it's time to keep an hourly log of wind force and direction. Watch for very high wisps of cloud, and for a very long swell. Is the swell coming from about the same direction as the suspected direction of the eye? What's the barometer doing? It may rise shortly before it starts to fall. Armed with this information, and other considerations that deserve to be studied in a book about marine weather, you may discover that things are adding up to indicate a revolving tropical storm. Don't wait too long. Take your evasive action early, even if it means sailing away from the harbor.

And of course you can always begin by staying away from cyclone areas in cyclone season. Nothing complicated about that.

A more technological approach is in the offing: it is called the weather facsimile receiver or Weatherfax, and it prints out a graphic weather map by radio signals. These benevolent black boxes cost something like $2,500, but their usefulness will inevitably increase demand and lower price. Phil Weld has one in his new *Rogue Wave,* and he feels strongly that for anyone who makes a lot of ocean passages, it's well worth the price. In *Rogue Wave* Phil has left out the bloopers and the pump toilets and the pressure water and the shag carpets and even the galley sink. That's the way he likes it, and it isn't just for racing: the Welds use their boat for ambitious voyages, and they know a very simple interior works best. But even for the racing, Phil believes the Weatherfax should not be left behind, as long as those who have the sets will share their weather information with other competitors. For offshore cruising or racing, no other black box imparts greater safety, because it assists the skipper in analyzing all kinds of weather phenomena, so that evasive action can be taken *early.*

In the meantime we have traditional ways of analyzing weather, which still work and deserve to be learned. Black boxes do have a way of breaking down.

Once an evasive course is decided on, by whatever method of weather analysis, it will likely require sailing into the wind—a prime argument for fine windward performance in a cruising boat. And I don't mean under power. Marine engines have a way of breaking down, too.

When your multihull can no longer slog to windward safely, you confront the central issue in this whole discussion of preventing capsize through seamanship: shall we lie ahull or run off?

You can always try the simplest thing first—just stop. It will probably work fine. Drop the sails, secure everything on deck and below to withstand the very worst, and allow the boat to drift. She will likely orient herself beam-on to the waves. If there is more than one wave system running, she will probably choose to lie beam-on to the smaller, shorter waves caused by the local wind. Very well, now, how's she doing? What does she have to say to you?

If the ocean isn't trying to climb aboard, that means the boat is saying, "I'm all right—leave this to me. You go to the chart and get a good position, and try to figure out what's going on around here. And you had also better get some food and some rest."

But let's say she doesn't like lying in the trough. Maybe she complains about what happens at the crests. It's hard for her to step sideways over the white stuff. When she hops (one leg at a time) from the face to the back of the larger waves, there's no spring in her step. She lurches and jerks from one hull to the other—sluggish going up, but hard and quick and noisy coming down—wham, bam, no thank you, ma'am. Who can eat and rest and navigate like that?

So, let's try to get her headed up a bit. Can we make her lie obliquely to the waves? A bit of sail perhaps, to give just a little steerageway, with the helm tied hard alee to steer her up against it nice and slow . . . ?

Maybe heaving-to at a diagonal attitude will work, but if things are really picking up out there, then sooner or later she's going to get caught broadside by a bad one. This time can be postponed, perhaps, by setting out a drogue from the windward bow to help hold her nose oblique-to-weather, until it gets even worse.

Maybe it never gets worse. Very well. Lying ahull is your answer. Some multihull skippers say they've ridden out some awful stuff this way, and I'm sure it's true. But was it awful enough for big, bad greenies to pounce aboard? To punch in windows and rip off hatches? And maybe even bash in topsides and break down superstructures? Apparently not, for them. But it has been that bad for others. We know it can get just that awful, for any boat. Is there *anything* you can do?

Let's admit that we're talking about very scary stuff now, the fear of which makes most of us stay home. But for those of us who go, or would like to, it would be nice to have some preplanned procedure, an ace-in-the-hole against the very rare but dreadful possibility of getting caught out in a real survival storm.

Every ocean sailor has his own opinion on this matter, and each of us is ready to give his—so here's mine:

First of all, I would not dangle any heavy object from the side of a multihull. If a sea anchor or parachute is attached to the weather hull, and is weighted, or allowed to sink beneath the boat, it reduces the vessel's ability to rise above the waves. Water ballast, if added to the upwind hull, has the same effect. It is just possible that adding water ballast to the central hull of a trimaran could help prevent capsize. Clint Spooner has suggested that this might have saved *Meridian.* My contention that ballasting tends to hold the vessel down, and thus invite structural damage from waves, is answered by Clint with a reminder that several multihulls have survived without damage for months at sea, through several storms, when inverted and half-filled with water. Therefore, I offer the point for discussion, while still suspecting that adding water ballast would invite being beaten into pieces. I'd rather be upside down.

Keelboats that attempt to deal with survival weather by simply "lying down to take it" are, in my opinion, asking for something worse than capsize. Structural damage, and the loss of watertight integrity, can happen to any boat, no matter how strongly built. I attribute the unexplained loss of many fine yachts to this tactic of lying ahull. If the sea bursts in, all at once, what chance does the crew have—the crew of a sinkable yacht—to get into a life raft? Turning and running downwind, especially if that exposes a great gaping cockpit perched out on the stern, doesn't offer much of an alternative.

I would choose a boat with a cockpit located forward of the transom—the bigger and deeper the cockpit, the farther forward and better defended it should be.

Second, I might try to lie ahull or lie hove-to in moderately heavy seas, but when the boat clearly tells me to cut it out, I'd run off with the bridle-drogue, and be damn glad that I was in a multihull. In survival conditions, multihulls may have the advantage over monohulls.

Please hear me out. Given good design and good handling, the multihull seems to have at least as great a chance of staying on her feet as the monohull has of staying on the surface, because neither likes to be left hove-to, and multihulls are much better suited to running off. They have the speed to accelerate away from heavy water; they have wide beam to make use of the bridle-drogue to prevent broaching; and they will bomb along downwind without tripping over the drag of their own underbodies or rolling their rails down.

And if the worst should happen, at least the multihull will leave you with a place to live.

So much for hypothesis. Actual experience by which one can measure the comparative wisdom of running off or lying ahull is rare. There is no such thing as a textbook storm, and deciding what to do in threatening conditions can be very confusing. Any discussion of these considerations is therefore open to a lot of theorizing.

But the foregoing postulations on how to prevent capsize in storms are not offered without actual experience. I've seen one ripsnorter myself, and accounts received from several sailing friends justify my position.

The first comes from Commander E. T. Sullivan, USN, Ret., of the yacht *Manta,* and it indicates the distinct possibility of structural damage from boarding seas. "Sully" has cruised the South Pacific with great thoroughness in his 38-foot Off Soundings-class trimaran. He and his Japanese crewman, Norio, are perhaps the most widely experienced multihull mariners among my clients. Here are excerpts from Sully's letter of December 26, 1975, from Tauranga, New Zealand:

Hey, Norio. When you have a minute, give me a hand, will you?

This is our fourth visit to New Zealand. Last summer we had our first refit in 45,000 miles and five years of sailing. In our travels we've had our fair share of all types of weather, including 132 knots of wind in the harbor at Truk Island, but our worst at sea was when we left Tauranga last June enroute to Fiji.

Friday the 13th about 150 miles east of North Cape (noted for bad weather), a NW storm hit us. We reduced finally to storm jib, but were still making 7 knots, which we thought too fast. It wasn't the wind so much as the towering confused seas.

We decided to get the storm jib in and lie ahull. This is our normal procedure and we find it quite safe and comfortable. But these were not normal seas and it was not comfortable. A rare sea would partly board us; this had not happened before.

After a few hours there was a sharp crack and a jolt like a truck had hit us and a wave came all the way aboard and over. Norio put on a lifeline to check topside. He reported the rudder broken, lifeline stanchions bent over, a vent gone, but everything else seemed okay. We did not know at that time that the port float had been holed and was flooding. Lost the wind vane then also.

More seas started to board us. There was no way of recognizing a list, at least not for us, in those seas. However, we had lost buoyancy because the port float was flooded. During the night one forward window was pushed in, frame and all. It was terrifying! Like someone turning twenty fire hoses on you. The water was immediately over the cabin sole. Everything soaked from overhead to bilge. Even the galley drawers were flooded through the hand pulls, it came with that much pressure.

I got on the pump. Norio, brave man, got out one of the storm covers and boarded up the window from the outside. By that time I had the water out. I had recently installed a big, new double-action pump.

A couple of hours later, *two* of the cabin side windows went *simultaneously port and starboard* when seas boarded from either side. Again the same results and the same drill. Thank God for carrying those prefab storm covers . . . .

The third day we were able to pump the float dry. The hole was above the waterline, about four inches long and one inch wide, pushed from the inside out. There was nothing in this float except sail bags. Later we found four frames broken, one of which punched through the hull . . . .

We jury rigged and sailed back into Tauranga, boat and crew very beaten up . . . .

The weather officer here told me we had experienced some 30 hours of 70-knot winds. And the New Zealand shipwrights were amazed. They said that if she'd been a traditional planked hull we would have lost her. Judging from the broken frames, they said the blow on the float would have sprung planks from end-to-end. Must admit we were two scared guys for awhile . . . .

The confused seas that damaged *Manta* may have made it impractical to tow a bridle-drogue, but nonetheless this case illustrates the potential for structural damage when the boat's side is presented to the storm.

Sea Spider is a 31-foot trimaran built by Jamie Spence. Jamie and Jacque cruised the Sea of Cortez and Central America for over three years, and then crossed the Pacific to the Marquesas in 1977.

On the next leg to Tahiti, they anticipated a two-day tradewind run to the Tuamotu Archipelago, where they had planned a stopover. But unsettled weather gave them a severe navigational challenge in getting through the reefs, and also prevented them from stopping.

Sea Spider was then set upon by a tropical anti-cyclone that blew her all around French Oceania. Tahiti was finally reached 20 days after their departure, and nine of those days were spent in very threatening circumstances. Here are excerpts from Jamie's story "GALE!" which first appeared in the May/June 1978 issue of *Multihulls* magazine:

Every time I try to describe the character of the seas, within an hour I find that everything has changed. Basically, there are large waves about like you would expect for this wind force, but running through them maybe five or six times in an hour is a set of incredible giants which come down like mountains in motion. Whitecaps are packed-in tight and growlers run all around us with white streaks blown over their faces. The wind picks up and lulls. The lulls are short and of about Force 7. The squall gusts are much harder for me to judge but they must sometimes exceed Force 8 and they blow for much longer duration than the lull. Occasionally, the air is full of water and spume, and the rain does not fall into the ocean but comes in sheets which are blown along about a foot above the surface. At these brief times, it's hard to tell where the ocean stops and atmosphere begins. The sky is packed solid with row after row of low black clouds lined up perpendicular to the wind direction . . . .

At 15:00 there seemed a chance to get a sun shot through clouds so I snapped in my harness and sat on the cabin top with the sextant. Jacque was steering and watching the chronometer. She had the top hatch board removed so she could see the clock and she crouched low in the cockpit. Her harness was not snapped in. The horizon would appear as a lumpy line in my sextant for one second, then the back of a wave would block it out for 6 to 8 seconds. Tough shooting. Suddenly with an awesome roar, the boat was hurled as if from a catapult and broken water smashed

Sea Spider *and wave.*

over the entire boat with great force and velocity. For a moment she was totally inundated by the breaker. At the same time, she was hurled down the face of the wave like an overflowing beer mug sliding down a steeply inclined bar. She was hit from an angle of 45 degrees abaft the beam and the port float bow buried in the white water. For an instant, I thought she was going to be hurled over but she fell back on her feet and the wave passed under us. Down below, stuff that had remained securely in place for years was strewn all over the boat and everything in all the lockers was packed up on the starboard side of the locker. Soup on the stove was thrown over the counter. About a bucket of seawater flew past Jacque into the forward cabin and nearly all of it landed on the bed. The rest went on the charts. Water squirted in around the sterncastle window and wet the other bed aft. Fortunately, we had fallen off to 290 degrees to ease the motion for my shot. I wouldn't want to catch a wave like that abeam. I set the tire on the bridle, and now we're running off . . . .

I call the drogue "de spare tire" and despair is what I feel. This is the third night of this roaring, rig-shaking gale and I forget how many nights of tension in the Tuamotus. Everybody has a limit to their capacity to handle stress. I'm at the end of my string and the string is stretched as tight as that drogue line . . . .

A couple of nights ago I took down the storm stays'l to slow the boat and it immediately went into the trough so I got the sail up quickly . . . . We still must run her dead downwind. The stormstays'l is on the headstay now and the centerboard is down a little bit more. It's raked back about 45 degrees to try to help us stop surfing sideways down the big ones. Ten degrees off dead down is mellow. Twenty is OK but we get some sideways surfing. Forty degrees off and all hell breaks loose. Waves smack us on the floats and climb right up over the cabin and we surf wildly sideways down the face. . . .

Last night it really blew. At 20:00 a big one struck us on the port side and threw everything out of the cabinets again. When Jacque came off watch at 24:00 she looked about finished and said she had a tense watch . . . .

This afternoon the wind has subsided. A beautiful tropic bird came and flew around our masthead. He seemed quite insistent that we follow him to weather, so now we are punching our way out of this with storm jib, staysail, and deep-reefed main . . . .

A rainbow has come to bridge our ocean path. I think it's over now . . . .

In Papeete, we learned that the gale was an anti-cyclone which developed in the Antarctic and strayed far north of the usual path of these storms. The wind force was reported at 50 knots, which is a whole gale of Force 10, with virtually unlimited fetch. Another vessel in the vicinity of the breaking waves reported 70-knot winds, which are hurricane force with a value of 12 on the Beaufort scale. The weather here remains unsettled and trading ships leaving Papeete have returned to shelter after encountering the large waves beyond the channel.

Far from diminishing our commitment to the sea, our ordeal has deepened it. Where once lurked fear of her unknown fury, now lives the reality of experience . . . .we're a hard team to beat down.

Sea Spider came through that trial undamaged, but the accomplishment belongs to Jamie and Jacque. Only with great vigilance on the helm—and for such a protracted period—was capsize averted. Jamie agrees that his drogue was too small (a tire from a Honda automobile), and there was no chain to hold it down. At least they had something ready to drag. And fortunately, they also had lots of cruising experience before getting caught in a major storm. We are fortunate to have this example of multihull seamanship, and the story speaks for itself.

The wisdom of running off can also be judged from the experience of Mark Hassall when he and his family were caught out in a South Pacific cyclone in his 37-foot trimaran. Coincidentally, this encounter occurred in the same water as did Sullivan's, while Mark and family were enroute from Fiji to New Zealand in 1972. This cyclone was the worst to strike North Island in 17 years, and belted the coast with sustained wind velocities of 70 knots.

The following description, taken from a book called *Love For Sail,* is a result of tape recordings made by Mark throughout his three-year world cruise. This was recorded during the cyclone:

> It's just turned daylight and the clouds are really movin' across the sky. Looks like they're doing 40 or 50 miles an hour. I've got the main reefed down to where even the sail number is rolled up. That's all that's up. We're logging 10 knots. The seas are big. They're breaking around us. (Loud clatter of utensils, hissing roar of wave) . . . .there went half the stuff in the kitchen. Excuse me. (Deep breath) The boat swings into 'em every now and then, although Tillie's really doing a pretty good job [Tillie is the self-steering device] . . . I have the tire drogue ready, and some warps. I may try using them here shortly. The barometer's dropped some more.
>
> (Speaks loudly, as if calling long distance. Voice trembling, interrupted by heavy breathing.) I just threw out a 200-foot warp. And I got it doubled over . . . from the transom of the main hull . . . around to the winch, so it's pulling double. I just saw 13 knots on the Sumlog . . . right after we got the warp out. And it's . . . almost no sail up. I'm glad the wind's blowing in the direction that we wish to go in. And we still got plenty of searoom before land. We got another 150 miles to go anyway . . . .

ah.... things are, ah, re-e-e-ally rockin around

(Returns with composure.) Things have gotten worse instead of better. Just had a rainstorm and the wind increased considerably. So we put out the tires and chain on the two bridle lines. And we also have the other warp out, so we're draggin' them both. I've still got the small bit of mainsail up, and we seem to keep heading in the right direction, and keep ahead of 'em. I don't like the idea of getting broadside to this stuff. If I take down that sail I don't think we'll move out as well . . . .

Occasional waves are breaking into the cockpit now [central cockpit located 14 feet from the transom]. The wind's picked up quite a bit of force. Things really rockin' around. Hope it breaks . . . .

(Sounds of water dripping inside cabin and roaring wind outside—Mark has jocular tone.) Well, you won't believe . . . the wind's still increasing. It's almost gettin' to be a joke. I chickened out—just took down the sail . . . we've pretty much ceased our forward motion by lying ahull. Maybe it's the safest position . . . don't know . . . .

(Short of breath.) Well, we're learning! We took down the sail and hove-to . . . but . . . for about five minutes. That's all we could take . . . we laid broadside to the big waves and they started crashing on deck. So we got out the little storm jib and I set it on the headstay. Now we're sorta on a broad reach with the storm jib pulling us along by the bow and the bridle holding us stern-to. Tillie's taken over again. Motion's a lot better . . . .

This evidence supports the bridle-drogue theory perhaps unfairly. Sullivan would later say that any drogue might have been ineffective in his storm because "the waves were coming from all directions." Similarly, Mark later lay ahull in that same hurricane because he was running out of searoom. The storm had reached a state of maturity characterized by longer wave length and less steepness at the crests:

We hove-to all night while the big ones came combing on by. But they weren't jumping on us like they did before, and we stayed right side up! Had my doubts for awhile. They were big waves, but it seemed she'd stay on her feet, so we lay in the trough. . . .

But Mark's experience in the height of the storm definitely supports running off.

Adlard Coles, author of *Heavy Weather Sailing*, holds the opinion that the best method for surviving great storms in small yachts is to run off at great speed, carrying as much sail as the craft will stand up to. Well, the multihull doesn't need much sail to run off at speed, and more than any other configuration, it will stand up. On downwind courses, a good cat or tri will really run off straight and stiff. If it gets too wild, the bridle-drogue will act like a downhill brake—the steeper the grade, the more pressure on the pedal. But a handkerchief-sized jib is always used, sheeted flat athwartships to the outboard hull, which prevents flogging.

In some storms, the largest waves and the local wind do not agree in their direction of travel. Therefore you may elect to trim the necessary sails for a beam wind, or even a head wind, in order to keep the largest waves approaching from dead astern. The engine and the drogue will help in this maneuver. It is the *waves* that are to be run from, not necessarily the wind.

There is recent evidence that "de spare tire" has served well in monohulls. Single-hullers cannot benefit from a wide bridle, but one report suggests that the drag of a tire was actually sufficient to "pull the boat stern-first out of the breakers."

Running off requires searoom, lots more searoom than lying ahull. Fortunately for Mark Hassall, and for Jamie and Sully, there *was* searoom. No small craft can be expected to go to windward in survival weather, so the ultimate predicament is to be in a great storm with no room to run. One recourse is to heave-to, and risk structural damage or capsize in order to reduce speed.

Another is to try a parachute sea anchor, such as the extremely rugged type sometimes available as surplus. Diameters greater than 10 feet give diminishing returns, and floats or trip-lines have been found to tangle: they are unnecessary for retrieving the parachute, anyway. The temptation would be to set the para-anchor from the bows, but experience tells us that this will not hold the vessel head-to-sea. Any amount of sternway—and there is some on the crests—causes the rudder to run backward and pull the boat around sideways, perhaps damaging the rudder also. The solution is to anchor stern-to with the parachute on a nylon bridle. Mark Hassall gives us an example from his trip around South Africa:

> We caught a downwind run out of Durban for the first 24 hours and then it turned on us and we had miserable weather. It was blowing right smack in our face, but we had the Agulhas Current behind us—just like a river. So I took down the sails and put out the sea anchor over the stern—the 10-foot parachute—and we continued all that night with the sea anchor out. The wind was howling and the waves were really charging at us. It's nasty with a strong wind against a strong current. But I experimented for a little while and found that by using two lines to the sea anchor, as a bridle leading up to the float sterns, I could get the stern of the boat to face directly into the wind. And the motion was suddenly quite comfortable. It was unbelievable—we were being towed against a wind directly toward our destination, which was East London. We were being towed down the coast of Africa, backwards, against the wind, by this terrific current.

178

USUAL SCOPE

STORM ANCHOR

This technique was not being used in the very worst of weather, but it is the only example at hand. One might expect repeated poopings in the stern-to position, but if the sterncastle window is securely covered, and the cockpit well protected and equipped with large self-bailers, this para-anchor tactic would be worth a good try if you were really backed into a corner. It might also serve for riding out any blow, and for holding position while waiting for daylight.

When anchoring to the bottom, or when mooring, multihulls will always benefit from using a bridle to the bows. And if you completely run out of searoom, it is just possible that the boat can be saved by long-line anchoring. Anchored multihulls can sustain a really vicious battering by wind and wave, especially if a bridle is used for at least part of the necessary scope. Two complete nylon rodes, all the way to a junction at the anchor chain, should

Anchor lines lead through snatchblocks on the outer bows and then inboard directly to cleats. This arrangement eliminates chafe because the lines have nothing over which to scrub.

179

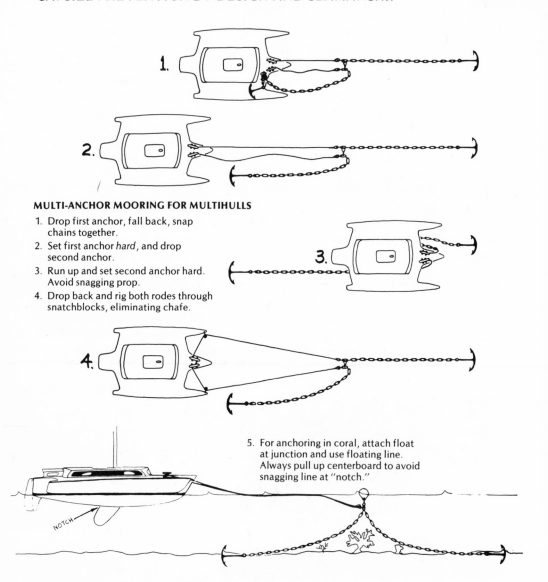

MULTI-ANCHOR MOORING FOR MULTIHULLS

1. Drop first anchor, fall back, snap chains together.
2. Set first anchor *hard*, and drop second anchor.
3. Run up and set second anchor hard. Avoid snagging prop.
4. Drop back and rig both rodes through snatchblocks, eliminating chafe.
5. For anchoring in coral, attach float at junction and use floating line. Always pull up centerboard to avoid snagging line at "notch."

NOTCH

be employed, not only because of the redundancy they provide, but because the bridle's "straightening" effect prohibits the boat from sawing left and right. This directional stability, combined with light weight and narrow hulls, allows the multihull's anchor to hang on to the bottom with significantly more tenacity than that of a heavy, swinging vessel that turns in the waves to expose its topsides to their power. The difference could mean everything in a no-searoom situation.

For the same reasons, bridle mooring would probably have prevented the few cases recorded of multihulls being capsized on their moorings by tornado-type winds. But mooring floats, if located at the bridle junction, become entangled in the lines. Two small floats should be used, and brought aboard with the bridle ends when making fast.

The same rigging is used for anchoring or mooring as when towing the drogue, except that the snatchblocks are attached to rugged strongpoints on the bows, instead of the sterns. The bridle lines are led through the blocks and inboard to mooring cleats to eliminate chafe. Chafed anchor lines have probably caused more shipwrecks than any other source. But in multihulls, snatchblocks on the outboard bows avoid the necessity for the lines to lead through anything on board that causes chafe, like chocks and hawseholes. Together with the redundancy of two rodes, this rigging offers great security when anchoring in a storm or mooring in the harbor.

The anchor bridle can be combined with two or more anchors beyond the junction to achieve multidirectional security in changing tide or wind, such as when anchoring in a tidal estuary. Once the two anchors are down, the crew can sleep, or leave the boat unattended, perhaps even when the anchorage is questionable. The addition of a buoy at the bridle junction, and floating line used for the bridle itself, provides security even when anchoring in coral.

Multihull seamanship goes well beyond preventing capsize, of course, but from the examples above, we see that these stable, nonballasted boats have a number of unique attributes. Whether they are climbing up to windward, lying in the troughs, running down the wavetrain or anchored in a cove, their peculiar combination of light weight, wide beam, shoal draft, great stability, and speed offers many new opportunities to pursue the art and craft of seamanship.

Can capsize be prevented? Yes, at least as well as sinking . . . if we use what we know. I think we know a lot, now, about preventing capsize, both by design and by seamanship.

So, let's *use* that knowledge!

8

Rescue and Self-Rescue

There is one key element in multihull design that remains largely unfulfilled at this time. If it were to be resolved, there would be no surviving basis on which to question the safety of the modern multihull. This element is self-rescue, the ability to recover from capsize without outside assistance.

At the 1976 World Multihull Symposium, a young man named Jim Ruiz wowed 500 participants with his fiery presentation of the "Ruiz System of Somersault Self-Rescue." Dismayed by the symposium's lack of emphasis on safety, Ruiz seized the microphone and, choking with emotion, he implored, "Here we've got the best multihull minds in the world all assembled in one room, and we've spent the last two and a half days talking about wing sails and hydrofoils and paints . . . all of this at a time when the only real problem restraining multihull development is capsize!"

An Olympic dinghy racer by background, Ruiz told the audience, "I remember when a dinghy capsize meant the end of the day; it was wait for the crashboat, tow ashore, bail out, and go home. Now when we go dinghy sailing we sometimes *practice* capsize. The new self-rescuing, double-bottomed dinghies of today can be dumped and righted in seconds, and we sometimes go out and see how many times we can capsize in an hour—just for fun.

"Now certainly there must be a way to arrange for self-rescue in an offshore multihull. If we could lick this one last drawback, our boats could be practically invincible! . . . far safer than any boats yet known to man."

After regaining his composure, Jim Ruiz was invited to explain his proposal. The audience and the panel members were literally shocked into their senses by the realization that maybe, just maybe, this guy was onto something. Using his beautiful catamaran model as a prop, he explained how the craft had been designed with features to encourage somersault after capsize. Flooding the bows, to a point amidships where flotation is installed,

182

TOP LEFT: Capsized catamaran model is rigged with spinnaker-pole A-frame. Bows are flooded and lifting of the waterbag commences. BOTTOM LEFT: The waterbag's weight overcomes the longitudinal stability of the flooded catamaran. A winch in the cockpit is used to haul on the pole lift. ABOVE: Somersault progresses until buoyant bows bail themselves nearly dry. (Photos courtesy of Multihulls *magazine.)*

produces a bows-down floating attitude when the model is capsized. Two spinnaker poles are then stepped on the underwing to form an "A" frame and a large water bag is suspended from the apex of the "A." The crew now hauls on the pole-lift with a cockpit winch. Instead of lifting the heavy water bag, the strain rotates the boat end-over-end in a somersault. Foam flotation in the bilges causes the craft to drain herself enough to make final pumpout a reasonable task.

At this point in the symposium it was time for lunch, but nobody ate. Everyone moved outside Toronto's Harbour Castle Hotel to watch Ruiz demonstrate his model in a rather choppy Lake Ontario. It performed the somersault several times, with and without the mast, and the crowd loved it.

During the after-lunch programming, each panel member commented, with fine constructive criticism, on the Ruiz proposal. Interestingly, several designers had independently concluded that a longitudinal recovery had great promise, but they had not proceeded with testing. So it was Carlos Jim

On these two pages, Rob Wright demonstrates a modified "Ruiz system" self-rescue of his 21-foot Tremolino trimaran. (Photos by Jim Morse)

Ruiz, a dinghy racer from El Salvador, who stole the show. He pointed the way toward a high-performance, comfortable cruising craft that is very forgiving when accidentally driven ashore, that will not sink at sea, and that can even recover from capsize with the assistance of the crew.

At this time, however, the Ruiz system is untried in a real seagoing

multihull. But the day is coming. Somersault self-rescue has already been accomplished with more than models.

Robert Wright, a *Tremolino* sailor from Michigan, has used a modified version of the Ruiz system to successfully recover his 23-foot trimaran three times; one test was conducted singlehandedly, "just to be sure that I could do everything myself."

LAND HO!

With these achievements to show the way, the "invincible" offshore multihull is sure to follow. Yet there are certain obstacles that will probably prevent rapid adoption of self-rescue features in many multihulls. As with the 5-mph bumper and the collision air bag for automobiles, self-rescue features will make multihulls a bit more costly and complex.

Here again, the racing contingent can spearhead the development of self-rescuing multihulls. Right now a bit of experimentation and research would make it real.

Or a bit of inducement from those who write the racing rules. How about a rule that says: "Any multihull that includes proven self-rescue features will receive a whopping advantage in its rating." *That's* what rating rules are good for!

With today's harsh criteria for competition, such as transoceanic single-handing, it seems that the criteria for safety should be equally stringent. I propose that capsize habitation be included in the safety regulations, and self-rescue in the rating rule. *Then* we could start talking about state-of-the-art multihulls. The spinoff could be far-reaching, extending even to the development of *monohulls* that cannot sink.

Beyond self-rescue is the matter of salvage. Almost all capsized multihulls are eventually recovered. Even after shipwrecks, fires, and collisions, something is usually left worthy of salvage. However, recovery attempts often cause damage that, in light of experience, now appears needless.

Because these boats are lightweight and will "stand up" when grounded (instead of lying on their sides), a unique opportunity presents itself to the salvager of a stranded multihull. Whether the craft is stuck on a beach or reef, and the object is to move her into deeper water, or to pull her ashore for major repairs, or even if she is intentionally grounded for the purpose of hauling out to perform a simple bottom job, the multihull usually can be

186

dragged along on her own bottom. The nature of the surface must be considered, and some form of skid can be built if necessary.

Dragging the boat is sometimes complicated by certain design features, such as deep fixed keels, fixed rudders that run deeper than the hulls, or lightly constructed bottoms on which the entire weight of the craft cannot be rested safely. Nor do these features contribute to the cruising nature of the craft. By contrast, a retractable rudder, or one that is well protected by a fixed skeg and does not run deeper than the hull, presents less liability. Some form of shallow "shoe" or "minikeel" on the hull is very helpful. It will allow the entire weight of the loaded boat to come to rest abruptly on a "hard spot," and it offers great forgiveness when the boat is grounded accidentally or beached purposely.

The essential rules for dragging the boat are simple enough. First, the pulling force should be applied as low as possible. If one attempts to drag a stranded boat from a point on deck (such as from the mast or a samson post), the resultant downward vector may tend to cause the hull to plow and thus damage the underbody. Second, the pulling force should be applied in such a way as to cause the craft to come along straight. A trimaran resting on its central hull and one ama might tend to "crab" sideways when dragged. A catamaran dragged by one hull will do the same. This crabbing effect can be canceled by the use of a bridled towline for dragging the boat.

Because most deck cleats are not strong enough to withstand the force required to drag the boat, special strongpoints can be installed, or a harness can be rigged around the hull(s) so that pulling from behind is accomplished. A very strong mooring eye built into the stem and the transom, just above the load waterline, might someday be extremely useful in recovering the stranded craft. If the vessel's design includes a shallow keel, a notch in the trailing edge or an eye in the leading edge of this keel could be used to great advantage for dragging (but the notch should be shallow and rounded so as not to foul on anchor lines). With the dragging force thus applied to the shallow keel, the strains are confined to a portion of the hull that is admirably suited to such abuse, and the hull sits on top for the ride.

These simple rules, plus built-in strongpoints and careful rigging practice, can give the cruising multihull enormous versatility. The boat can be hauled

Rollers make it easy. A long plank is attached to this minikeel via a block bolted to the plank. The block fits up into the centerboard slot. Lines from the block lead up through the trunk to the cockpit winches to secure the plank in place. Now, pipe rollers can be used with more planks to transport the boat practically any distance.

Beach maintenance is best accomplished in two tides. By beaching the craft sideways to the grade, with a halyard leading inland to a tree or an anchor to ensure heeling uphill, easy access is gained to the downhill half of the craft's bottom. On the second tide, sides are reversed. This trimaran's minikeel holds the rest of the bottom high enough for access.

LEFT: The 31-foot Comet *was badly wrecked on rock ledges in heavy surf. Owners Ken Bloom and Mary Funk waded ashore. Even when partly filled with sand, the remains were towed out to sea through the surf for salvage. (Photo by Ken Bloom) CENTER: With one outrigger destroyed and both remaining hulls holed,* Comet *floated at this attitude and was towed 20 miles at six knots to the nearest harbor. (Photo by Mary Funk) BOTTOM: With a new starboard ama and other repairs, the original owner-builders soon relaunched* Comet *and have since crossed the Pacific. (Photo by Mary Funk)*

TOP: Brent Whipple's Tattoo was washed ashore on a sandy beach when the anchor dragged. (Photo by Don Raupp) CENTER: Volunteers rig a towing harness around the stern for "dragging the boat." (Photo by Don Raupp) BOTTOM: A harbor tug from nearby is solicited to drag Tattoo afloat, but the timing isn't right. A set of Pacific swells disorients the tug and batters the trimaran. Notice that the wave has curled to the left but is still building on the right. The tug tried to pull Tattoo straight through this eight-foot vertical breaking wave, but the boat jumped over instead, and there is only spindrift on the deck! Of course she will do the same thing out at sea. Tattoo survived undamaged and has since doubled the Pacific. (Photo by Don Raupp)

out on a suitable sand beach or mudflat for routine maintenance or seasonal storage with just a powerful come-along or tackles, or with the assistance of a wrecking truck or tractor. Hauled up beneath the palms or the pines, a cruising boat becomes a comfortable, if temporary, waterfront retreat.

Some multihulls have strongpoints built in to facilitate hoisting by crane. Because they are light, these boats can be picked up by a bridle rigged to the chainplates, or to special tangs installed for the purpose. The bridle is made of nylon, rigged for equal strain on all four parts, and stowed aboard in readiness for routine launching and haulout, or for emergency right-side-up rescue. No slings or spreader bars are necessary, just the big hook on the crane.

The same procedures can be used to hoist or drag the boat to safety in the face of an oncoming great storm. How preferable this is to trusting one's mooring or dock to guard the vessel through something like a typhoon!

If the day (or night) should ever come when you and your multihull find yourselves washed up by the surf on some lonely beach, or stacked up on some jagged reef, then a little preparation might be responsible for your extrication. If strongpoints have been installed or if you have a dragging harness well in mind, local aid can be applied most effectively. Even when you're stuck off by yourself with no assistance, if you've got a good hard dinghy that will really row—even while burdened with anchor and chain—then you've got a good chance of kedging off (or kedging on) to safety with a multihull.

The multihull can also be dragged over the sea. Several instances are known of attempts by merchant vessels to salvage capsized multihulls with cargo cranes. The method employed was to lift up one side of the multihull and thereby hope to flip it back on its feet. These attempts are not usually successful, and they often result in substantial damage to the multihull. Because of the enormous weight of water held inside the stricken boat, cable slings tend to cut into or slip off the hull being lifted.

Alternatively, recent experiments with multihull models indicate that there is a very much more effective means by which the rescuing vessel can right a capsized multihull at sea. This method does not involve cranes, as no lifting is needed.

Instead, a towing hawser is attached to the multihull at a point, or points, that will encourage rotation, and the salvaging vessel only needs to pull.

Depending on the size and type of the capsized multihull, and the power of the towboat, and the sea conditions at the time, the towing hawser may be attached in either of two ways.

Case 1: For trimarans with centerboards or daggerboards in the central hull, a hawser may be rigged through the centerboard trunk and secured inside. The trunk provides a ready stongpoint from which towing strain is applied at the highest above-water position. Model tests indicate that if the multihull is relatively small in relation to the power of the towboat, rotation can be achieved by towing in any direction: from the side or end of the

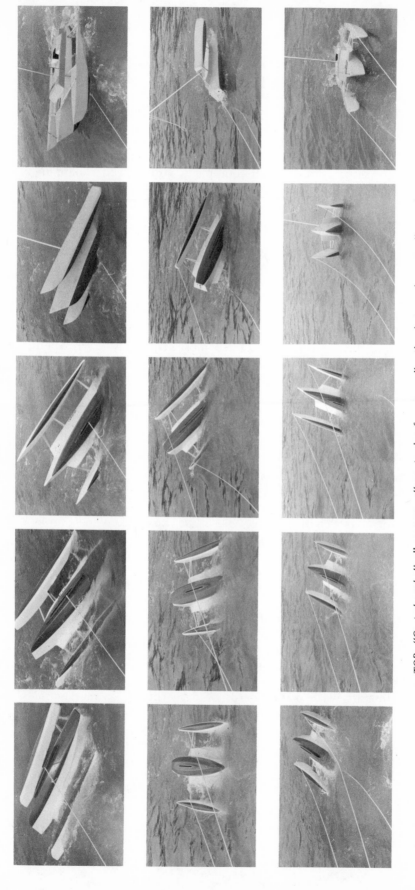

TOP: "Centerboard sling" recovery allows towing from any direction but requires a towline strain about equal to the multihull's displacement weight. (Photos by Tom Crabb)

CENTER: This bows-down somersault shows that even poor towline alignment succeeds, indicating that tow-over should work in difficult conditions. (Photos by Tom Crabb)

BOTTOM: Bows-up recovery begins with towing on a single sternline. This is to align the multihull with the bridle for a directionally stable rotation. Towline strain equals about one-fourth the multihull's displacement when the ama bows are flooded. Completed recovery leaves the tow-over bridle ready for towing the re-righted craft at sea. (Photos by Tom Crabb)

multihull. This procedure has obvious advantages in rough sea conditions, or in any situation where the towboat would experience difficulty in maneuvering to pull from a specific direction relative to the axis of the drifting multihull. The castaways could have the "centerboard sling" ready rigged, and the salvager could simply pass a line to them for attachment to the sling, and pull.

Case 2: If the multihull is very large or the power of the towboat is proportionately small, a tow-over bridle may be attached to the multihull at positions to encourage a somersault, as in the Ruiz Self-Rescue System described earlier in this chapter. The bridle would appear to require the towboat to maneuver for pulling from a specific direction. But the need to maneuver can be easily overcome by rigging a third, separate towline to orient the multihull correctly to its bridle. A longitudinal rotation, bow-over-stern, seems to be the easiest, so the multihull is oriented with its sterns pointing toward the towboat. With slow initial towing on a single hawser attached to the centerline of the multihull's stern, the capsized boat would be pulled in line behind the towboat so that the two parts of the tow-over bridle can be adjusted to equal length and made fast to the towboat. Then, the stern line is cast off, and the towing strain comes onto the tow-over bridle attached to the multihull's bows. A longitudinally stable somersault can be achieved.

Judging from tests, this method of recovery is extremely effective. Resistance on the submerged mast causes rotation to begin at once; however, the sterns will also begin to dive easily even with the mast removed (such as when there is a dismasting caused by capsize). Flooding of the hulls greatly encourages rotation and might allow a small towboat to rotate a rather large multihull.

Furthermore, flooding of the hulls—whether on purpose or by accident—contributes to followthrough once the somersault has begun. Water inside begins to flow toward the downward end and generates the so-called "free surface effect." When the vertical is reached, the momentum of the moving water inside the hulls helps break out the mast and complete the somersault.

Because of this water's momentum, it is not certain what effect the larger scale of real boats will have with regard to stability in a capsized position. Judging from the tests, a capsized multihull with a maximum of airlock and a minimum of flooding would require a towline strain about equal to the boat's normal right-side-up displacement. This is a lot of towing!

However, varying degrees of flooding produce substantial reductions in the towline strain required to somersault. Allowed to flood at will, with all airlock violated, the Searunner model tested required a towline strain equal to only about one-fourth the boat's normal displacement weight to accomplish righting.

The disadvantage in flooding, of course, is that after the somersault is performed, the water somehow must be removed. Small amounts of foam flotation in the bilges would lift the craft partway to its normal waterline, allowing much of the water to run out by itself. Suitable plumbing is required to allow this partial draining, and then efficient pumping would complete the salvage. Therefore, the physical condition of the crew and the degree of preparation for draining and pumpout remain challenging obstacles to accomplishing the complete recovery of a capsized multihull. Without at least partial pumpout, towing home could be a slow process.

The tow-over tactic has its best chance for success if the multihull is rotated bows-over-sterns. If the sails are still set on the mast underwater, this rotation will allow them to "luff" through the water so that they do not impede the somersault. And once the craft is righted, the tow-over bridle forms a ready-made harness for towing the recovered multihull.

Multihull towing is best accomplished with a bridle, which will cause the craft to come along home most obediently, even if towed at high speed in rough water, assuming that most of the water is pumped out. Towing downwind might require the use of a bridle-drogue attached to the sterns of the multihull, a wise precaution before any deep-sea towing is begun.

During the somersault operation, it is important that the two parts of the bridle be of equal length and stretch to give lateral stability. A short, stout bridle with its junction at the towboat's bitt gives best stability. With the multihull positioned close astern of the towboat, the towboat's prop blast aids in the somersault, making it possible to right the multihull without either of the vessels making much if any headway through the water; speed is not necessary. The prop blast effect would perhaps make it possible for a small towboat to recover a rather large multihull. In the case of a large commercial vessel coming to the aid of a capsized multihull, clearly it would be the prop blast alone that could accomplish most of the righting. A separate towline is used for initial towing to align the multihull with its bridle; a short bridle is employed to make maximum use of prop blast; and the elevation provided by the ship's high stern will further encourage rotation.

Once the vessel is on its feet, the prize is nearly won. By patching and pumping, or draining and bailing with a bucket—or even with none of the above—the craft probably can be recovered. By contrast, towing an upside-down catamaran or trimaran, or lifting it up while its hulls are half-filled with water, is folly.

At this writing there is no full-size experience with multihull tow-over, but the purpose of the model tests, and of these descriptions, is to encourage the salvager (and the skipper of the capsized multihull) to try these tactics.

The crew of castaways could make salvage preparations while they are awaiting rescue. The centerboard sling or tow-over bridle can be rigged, probably the nonstretching lines for the storm drogue bridle could be used. A separate towline should be made ready for the purpose of aligning the multihull with its bridle.

If an access hatch has been cut in the hull, some form of patch must be prepared before somersault, to allow pumping out and towing. A fancy epoxy adhesive would need to be mixed. Salvage and damage control will be greatly facilitated by keeping a can of plastic roof cement in the Calamity

Pack. A type surprisingly effective in bedding underwater patches is the kind designed for use on wet roofs—it sticks in the rain.

With the hatch patch planned and ready, ship's valuables can be secured against loss to complete preparations for the anticipated somersault. When rescue arrives, all that is needed is a heaving line thrown from the rescue vessel to run the towlines aboard. Probably the multihull skipper will want to explain the tow-over tactic to the rescue crew, and conduct the operation himself from on board the towboat.

If conditions are calm, the righted multihull can perhaps be hoisted aboard the rescue vessel, especially if crane-lift strongpoints are installed and a tested crane-lift bridle is already stowed aboard. In this case the capsize hatchway need not be patched; it will form a huge scupper to drain the craft as it is being hoisted.

It was the somersault self-rescue concept from which the idea of multihull tow-over was deduced. If a spinnaker pole and a water bag can generate the necessary force to rotate the craft, then how easy it would be to accomplish the same stunt by towing! The tow-over procedure may be more immediately significant because it will doubtless be a while before most offshore multihulls are designed and built with the necessary features to achieve self-rescue. Practically all existing multihulls can be recovered by means of tow-over at the present time.

Somersaulting may not qualify the multihull as invincible, but it surely makes salvage a different story from raising a boat that's on the bottom!

As we learn how to prevent capsize, how to prepare for it, and even how to recover from it, much of the fear goes away. At least this has been my own experience. In the early days of trimarans, the late Fifties, we openly spoke of "the obvious danger of capsize." With successful experience at sea in the early Sixties, the phrase changed to "the apparent danger of capsize," and ever since, we have simply lived with that apparent danger.

After three years of cruising with my family in the early Seventies, I was fairly well convinced—in spite of the nagging threat—that our boat with our crew could be fairly called "noncapsizing." But then, at the conclusion of our travels, we had the shattering experience of interviewing the survivors of the *Meridian* . . . and I knew that it might have happened to us.

We had just sailed ten thousand miles, and our clients had sailed tens of thousands, without a single capsize. But from the *Meridian* accounts I was forced to admit that we had been sailing in a pathetically unprepared condition. Searunners had always included special life-raft compartments, and we had always paid lip service to emergency preparedness, but our real capsize preparations were chillingly naive. We had had no direct experience on which to build.

About a year after the *Meridian* incident, I was preparing *Scrimshaw* for a passage from the Virginia Capes to Maine, and the memory of *Meridian* made capsize preparation imperative. I knew that to take my family offshore without it would make the passage insufferable; my conscience would really

The Ruiz system of somersault self-rescue was also applied to the Searunner model, with success. Partial flooding of the amas resulted in a very stable vertical attitude.

After the somersault testing, Roger Hatfield, the builder of the model, and the author decided to try some high-speed tests. (Photo by Tom Crabb)

Both researchers own life-size versions of the model and were interested to see how much abuse she would stand. (Photo by Tom Crabb)

TOP: At skiing speed the model was turned back and forth across the wake of the towboat in attempts to make it capsize. These dynamics do not represent the real world of boat and sea, but the challenge to crash the model was irresistible to almost everyone. (Photo by Tom Crabb) BOTTOM: Everyone failed, but we came close . . . close enough to be amazed at the model's surefootedness. (Photo by Tom Crabb)

beat me down. So I faced the ugly problem by spending three days on preparations.

We sailed to Maine and back, and—to my very great personal relief—that nagging threat of capsize-caused catastrophe has never since sailed in our little ship. I know for sure that we could still get dumped, but it is less likely now than ever before. The peace of mind that comes from preparedness is, in itself, a mighty preventive. And even if it should happen, I'm not afraid of it as before. We have alternatives established. I heartily recommend capsize preparation to all multimariners. Not that it makes the boat invincible, but it certainly makes a trip more pleasurable. The Calamity Pack may consume a bit of money and storage space, but it more than pays its way by making room for confidence.

The statistical chance for capsize will always exist, like the statistical chance for sinking, but it is no longer simply accepted and endured. We can now design multihull vessels that have an accumulation of features to prevent capsize. We can sail those vessels using tactics of seamanship that prevent capsize. We can prepare our boats to contend with capsize should it come.

Even all of that doesn't utilize the multihull's full potential for safety. The emphasis placed on the capsize hazard is truly disproportionate because disasters like fire and stranding are much more common. More than one multihull sailor has found himself with a charred and soggy mess in one hull but a dry bunk in the other. Experienced cruising keelboaters will appreciate the multihull's potential to survive shipwreck with somewhat reduced consequences. And the opportunity to replace the titanic threat of sinking with something as tractable as capsize . . . well, that begins to approach the invincible.

9

Capsules of Change

Well, John, in that you are reading this, I'll assume you've been with me all the way. This hasn't been a simple answer to your point-blank question about the multihull concept. But one issue still remains; in order to justify any cruising boat, I suppose we'd better ask ourselves just what the thing is for. Surely it is not for years of aimless wandering only.

The real application of a seagoing sailboat seems to lie not upon the water or the wind, but in the sailor's mind, and the results are measured in such terms as growth, awareness, lifestyle, catharsis, and overview.

The basic stuff of cruising, in my estimation, is change. Mariners who move about the earth by windpower are the most inoffensive of all free agents. They are neither plaintiffs nor defendants, but instead eyewitnesses to the world's accelerating rate of change.

When a multitude of destinations are separated one from another by adventure at sea, the experience is like stepping off onto another planet, and coming back occasionally for a fresh view of earth. Contrasts in societies, and economies, and environments, become very sharp, the effect being strongest when one returns to his own homeland. Sea travelers may perceive history in every port, and when making overland excursions from those ports; yet they must always navigate in the here and now. Given these coordinates of past and present, and having become uncommonly cognizant of the exponential workings of time, they can then draw their own projections for the future. Some sailors thus become aware of patterned movements within the biosphere. Everything from politics to lunar cycles to ethnology to seasons seems to make integrated sense. If need be, sea people can respond to these movements with great mobility.

To function as a sailor, an envoy, a crew, a student, and even as a family under such formative conditions is quite a valid and challenging undertaking. The boat becomes far more than a recreational plaything; it is a capsule of change.

Jack and Charlotte Clementson with J.B. aboard Eleuthera.

Gerard and Marjorie Arseneau, with crewman Tom McEachern of Honeywind.

If this is what the boat is for—these subjective applications—then it seems strange that one type of boat could be considered better than another, as long as both types work. And I can tell you, John, after having sailed in each, that monohulls and multihulls can both set a course for change and get there. Opinions vary as widely as do cruising craft themselves, and the ocean seems to permit us our preferences.

There is one thing, though, about contemporary boating that really sticks in my craw. In order for a seagoing sailboat to justify its—the hell with its concept—to justify its very existence today, in terms of the money, energy, and premium materials consumed, then it had better be good for something besides just zipping around! And if it is any good at all for living aboard and sailing offshore—for transporting its owners to the edge of change—then it deserves to be used for those purposes, and not to spend its life in some flooded parking lot as a testament to wasted wealth.

That's one thing I like about the multihullers, John. They really use their boats. Most of the ones I know are on the great cruising circuit. We see them stopping off and moving on, and a lot of them are getting good. They've gained enough experience to be worthy of the term "cruising sailors." Oh, yes, some multihullers are the kind who can't sail, and some skip out on their marina fees. Some smuggle dope and some swipe coconuts from the

200

Patrick Lockett and Donna Flemming aboard Lotus.

Roger and Cynthia Hatfield aboard Mandala.

poor. But that faction exists all across the boating board today—you know that. They're a bit more conspicuous in multihulls, I'll admit, but why blame that on the boat?

I see a growing number of experienced voyagers who share a genuine preference for multihulls, and they are not naive or fanatical. These are men and women who have been out there—out beyond the yachting centers, beyond the lakes, bays, and rivers, beyond the Coast Guard, beyond their own language and their old lifestyle and their native landmass, out beyond the horizon day and night. They have switched oceans and mixed cultures and have come to know the heady thrill of getting on their boats at home and getting off in another world as other selves.

That old antithesis between land creature and marine environment is, for some of us at least, pleasantly resolved by these buoyant, sprawling multi-boats. Each of the several hulls has its own purpose, but they are developed for each other. Their forms combine in operation to produce something more than a one-piece implement. They are cruising machines. They meet cruising requirements because they invite harmony between the sailor and the sea.

A stiff initiation to the water world, aboard any boat, will quickly teach the neophyte that a preponderance of "cruising requirements" must be met by the sailor himself. That's the hard part, and no blooming boat design will ever take over his responsibility. Man's conflict with the sea, and with himself, is put before him to resolve—continually. In this ongoing resolution there is need for absolute collaboration between the instinct and the intellect. Some of us have found that the multihull stimulates that collaboration.

That's why I love my boat, John. Not to say that you don't love yours. I've known monohull boat-love too. There are lots of wonderful things about a "real" sailboat that I have lost in my conversion to multihulls. The swing and sway, the lee rail under, the "groove," and the "bone in her teeth" that only a heavy jaw can chew.

Especially the older boats, the big ones. They were something to be loved. I never could get too excited about small cruising monohulls. It seems that nothing really starts to happen until over 50 feet—better yet, 150 feet. Give me something big enough to carry her boats in davits. Deep enough to make the leadsman scream when he hits three fathoms. And high enough to give a spar climber that old folk-song view of "people on the earth they look like a pig." I worked in some of those big, old beauties. They could drive along at multihull speeds, without cheating. They had enormous power, which was always having it out with the sea. We miss that sensation with multihulls. The resistance is almost gone. And with it goes part of human dominion over nature and part of boat-love too.

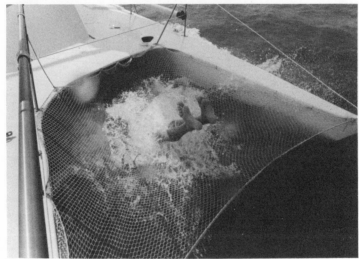

(Photos by Tom Crabb)

But another part fills in. Of all of man's floating contrivances, multihulls must surely be his most boisterous creatures of the interface. Besides all of the practical advantages of good speed in cruising, a fast boat adds a welcome new dimension to the old-time plodding pace of traveling by wind. This is the kind of race where the only win is related to the start: "Hey! We made it. We're finally underway." And the boat imparts a buoyant spirit to the sailors. In the right conditions, they can really rip across the water together. It's a blast, and anyone who sails can't help but thrive on it.

Take downwind running, for instance. For hours I have gazed astern, with my chin resting on the sill of our aft-facing sterncastle window, and contemplated our perfectly parallel wakes:

203

CAPSULES OF CHANGE

At night they carve
Incessant
Phosphorescent
Esses
Up the faces of the waves.

And the waves,
With illuminated graces
Strung along their tops,
Each one appears to overtake us
But it comes up close—and stops.

Or is it that we start?
Yes!

So now we run along together,
Almost standing still together,
Elevating up and down apart.

Falling behind,
Syncopating left and right,
Spurting ahead,
Synchronizing on and off.

Never rolling,
Always carving,
Smoothly soaring
Onward through the water
And the time.

Parallel wakes.

Ah! John, there is no greater feeling of belonging with the sea than when running off in a multihull, at the same speed as the seaway. If the wavetrain really builds up big, running off can also be the most terrifying thrill on this planet. But even then—especially then—there is no human domination over nature. The vessel and the crests willfully avoid encounters. Both the sea and the craft submit to one another. It is the most copacetic sailing I have ever known.

Going against the wind is something else again. The whole scene is profoundly shifted when heading up:

> Not dead weight down beneath
> (Like a light bulb or a schmoo)
> Rather,
> Live buoyancy out beside!

> Great stiffness, disproportionate to size
> Big rig strains,
> Ship-like power,
> Sails that stand up in the wind
> And really *pull.*

> Strong winds on the nose,
> Steep seas up ahead,
> Jerks, bucks, slams, bumps.
> Weathergoing sometimes better,
> Chop-punching sometimes worse.

> Sharp crests fail
> To slap back
> Narrow hulls
> With fine bows
> And deep foils.

> We change down to staysail
> And reef deep the main.
> We crank the sheets in "one more click."
> We dig the leeward ama deep
> And fly the other free
> Of each colliding comber in the gale.
> And climb!
> I tell you we can *climb.*

> Man's rightful place at sea,
> It has been said,
> Is when he never really goes against the wind.
> But, free of lead
> (And even when he goes contrary,
> Toward the place from where it comes),
> Works *with* the wind instead.

Uphill sailing isn't exactly "copacetic" in any boat, but that's the time when I love my boat the best. The apparent wind phenomenon—generating your own power with your own forward motion—is really wild stuff in a fast, stiff, narrow-hulled machine. It's the time when one can best feel the sense that outrigger stability makes. Neither the ocean nor the boat submits, yet they are locked in the tightest of embraces.

Permit me one last comparison of boat-love. In this I think there are no differences between us. If you could speak here, I suspect that you would tell me why you love your boat, perhaps in terms of what the thing has meant to you in life. What else are we speaking of, unless it's how we want to spend our lives? And when you look around your boat, you surely see a lot of things that I can't, reminders of what she has meant to you in life already.

You might point out to me those gouges in your topsides, and tell me of the Indian in that big dugout canoe. He came pulling up beside and banged into you, hard. Then, grinning, he offered you a nice, fresh fish. That's why he'd come, and he didn't know that your boat was not carved out of a solid log like his.

You might call my attention to that piece of dried banana peel, after many months still twisted in midflight around your backstay, since the time you sailed all night in a blow, in a swimsuit, and ate them green.

All those little holes in your cockpit seat? Yes, they would be from that harbormaster who had hobnails in his boots, but who later returned barefoot, with his whole family, for a memorable meal on board and the reciprocal ashore. The hack marks in the foredeck? Must have been the time that your kids were learning to decapitate a coconut, with a dull machete, in the rain.

You could show me that computer card from the Panama Canal, with instructions thereon to keep it posted in your radio room. What radio? What room? We'd get a good laugh from your Rhinoceros Beetle Inspection Certificate and your De-Ratification Stamp. I would marvel at the hokey ad-art in your collection of rum bottle labels, and admire the mallet that you made for pounding conch at Glover's Reef.

But none of that stuff would mean as much to me as it does to you, like those lovely goblets that you drank from with your wife to celebrate her first celestial landfall. She must have been proud to be a navigatrix.

You would have some other first-time stories, like the first time your youngster asked if he could borrow the boat for a little spin, by himself. Or the first time that your older youngster asked if he could leave the boat and travel overland, with a friend. It wasn't easy to say yes, was it, John?

Adjusting to the ocean, readjusting to the land, foreign culture block, homeland culture shock, and political clash, the energy crunch. Your new understanding of time, of speed, and of distance. The highball that was mixed with heavy shots of strong, clear distillate. Family life on board . . . "Shall we just sail away forever?" It wasn't easy to say no, was it, John?

And there's your boat. Right there on the mooring, ready. She has taken

La Una.

CAPSULES OF CHANGE

The people you'll meet . . .
Guatemalan highlanders

San Blas Cuna Indian

Belizean black Carib.

And there's your boat . . . snuggled in the sand.

you on quite a trip already. She has shown you that you can build, destroy, sail, live, love, hate, cry, laugh—you might even die—all on a boat. No matter what the type. In her you have been borne upon the deep oceans, and together you have snuggled in the sand. She has taken you to places, and people (incredible *people*) unapproachable from a 50-footer or a 150-footer, at a price you can afford. She is small, but she is yours—your own cruising capsule, for the conquering of ocean space. And the destination is a constant: change.

Cruising may not change the world, you say, but it has changed the vision with which you look out upon the world. John, I understand.

Did you say that you built the boat yourself? Imagine that! You *designed* her, too? Wow, talk about fulfillment. Hot stuff, these little boats of ours. That's love-of-boat, I tell you. If your kind of boat has done all those things for you, I'm sure you must love her very much. I respect you for your choice. My kind of boat will do the same, and so I'm hoping that you may extend respect to me.

"Yachting history has shown too often that progressiveness is acceptable only if it does not include too much progress."—Howard Chapelle.

THE END ?

Index